ECOLIBERATION

OUTSPOKEN

SERIES EDITORS: ADRIAN PARR AND SANTIAGO ZABALA

Pointed, engaging, and unafraid of controversy, books in this series articulate the intellectual stakes of pressing cultural, social, environmental, economic, and political issues that unsettle today's world. Outspoken books are disruptive: they shake things up, change how we think, and make a difference. The Outspoken series seeks above all originality of perspective, approach, and thought. It encourages the identification of novel and unexpected topics or new and transformative approaches to inescapable questions, whether written from within established disciplines or from viewpoints beyond disciplinary boundaries. Each book brings theoretical inquiry into a reciprocally revealing encounter with material realities and lived experience. This series tackles the complex challenges faced by societies the world over, rethinking politics, justice, and social change in the twenty-first century.

Ecoliberation

Reimagining Resistance and the Green Scare

JENNIFER D. GRUBBS

McGill-Queen's University Press
Montreal & Kingston • London • Chicago

© McGill-Queen's University Press 2021

ISBN 978-0-2280-0681-7 (cloth)
ISBN 978-0-2280-0682-4 (paper)
ISBN 978-0-2280-0737-1 (ePDF)
ISBN 978-0-2280-0738-8 (ePUB)

Legal deposit second quarter 2021
Bibliothèque nationale du Québec

Printed in Canada on acid-free paper that is 100% ancient forest free
(100% post-consumer recycled), processed chlorine free

Library and Archives Canada Cataloguing in Publication

Title: Ecoliberation : reimagining resistance and the green scare / Jennifer D. Grubbs.
Names: Grubbs, Jennifer D., 1985– author.
Series: Outspoken (McGill-Queen's University Press)
Description: Series statement: Outspoken | Includes bibliographical references
    and index.
Identifiers: Canadiana (print) 20210128844 | Canadiana (ebook) 20210129158
    | ISBN 9780228006817 (cloth) | ISBN 9780228006824 (paper) | ISBN
    9780228007371 (ePDF) | ISBN 9780228007388 (ePUB)
Subjects: LCSH: Green movement. | LCSH: Direct action. | LCSH: Social change.
Classification: LCC GE195 .G78 2021 | DDC 320.58—dc23

This book was typeset in 10.5/13 Sabon.

To my resilient and relentless Mama
And to my rebellious children,
Emory, Simon, Tevye, and Durruti

Contents

Acknowledgments

The other night I was lying in bed, wedged between three of my four sleeping children, pecking away at the glowing laptop that was precariously resting on a pillow, finishing this manuscript. I imagined how many people raising children before me have stolen sleep from themselves to work on something they feel passionate about. As I kissed my babies next to me, I couldn't help but imagine the structural challenges that continue to marginalize women in academia.

I finished this manuscript in the height of a global health pandemic, amidst a state-mandated lockdown, with three children in virtual school and a breastfeeding toddler, and without childcare. The physical and emotional labour that mothers do is not only devalued, particularly in the US, it is expected. Dani, Laura, Ariel, Adrian, Lindsey, Marianne, Samantha, Jacie, Vallie, and all the folks juggling the visible and invisible work that our world demands of us, we deserve better. We are tired, we are buried, and we are sick of being valourized. I don't want recognition for my exploitation; *I want to not be exploited.*

As I reflected back on the work that it took to transform almost a decade of research and activism into a manuscript, I was reminded of the kind and generous people who made that possible. Not simply the village of people that taught, encouraged, and challenged me to do better. Not just those who cooked a meal or borrowed one of my children for the day so I could work longer. But also, those I have never met – those that struggled and demanded that our world look radically different than its current iteration.

We are charged to do this work because our world is being crushed inward by climate change, speciesism, racism, transphobia, xenophobia, and fascism. We cannot afford *not* to. We cannot afford *not* to dismantle these distinct violent structures. We cannot afford to ignore the interconnected, intersectional relationships between oppressive ideologies. *We cannot afford not to be outspoken.*

My gratitude extends to the activists who have lost sleep while meticulously planning how to enter the laboratory and safely remove beautiful creatures from torturous cages. The individuals who blockaded, chanted, sabotaged, who staged "die-ins," who faxed those inked-out pages; *your political imaginary is beautiful.*

Despite the beauty of your political imaginary, the upside-down state of morality has created a legal system in which the torture and murder of some is not only profitable, it is legally protected. My heart extends to every political prisoner who is or has been incarcerated, and to those who love someone who is or has been incarcerated. I realize that I am inspired by the very actions that cost them, Marius, Jalil, Daniel, Leonard, Ronnie, Judi, Julia, Jeremy, Red Fawn, Samar, to name a handful, so much more. May we all continue to fight so that there comes a day where all are free, *where all cages are empty.*

I feel quite insignificant within a vast history of anarchists, feminists, anti-racist organizers, and other radical revolutionaries. I'm humbled and honoured to contribute to a global social movement discourse that engages within and beyond the classroom. I am indebted to William Leap for seeing something beautiful in that messy paper I wrote in his Linguistic Anthropology class many, many moons ago. I became a better scholar under his guidance and support. He provided an intellectual space where I could process that very first home demonstration I had ever attended. For that, and for so much more, I am eternally grateful.

I am continually encouraged and challenged by a slew of brilliant scholar-mentors. The time and energy you all spend providing your students and colleagues with compassion and empathy does not go unnoticed. I am honoured to have worked with each of you: Daniel O. Sayers, Rachel Watkins, Matthew Thomann, Carol Adams, Marti Kheel, Greta Gaard, Nikki Lane, Mary Ann Davis, Joowan Park, Jason Del Gandio, Debarati Sen, Delores Koenig, David Vine, Adrienne Pine, Stephen Depoe, Amy Lind, Carol Glasser, Lisa Hogeland, Deb Meen, Ashanté Reese, Michelle Gibson, James Crocker-Lakness, and many others. My colleagues in the Social Sciences Division at Antioch College, Dean Snyder and Téofilo Espada-Brignoni, thank you for your intellectual and collegial support throughout this process. You each have influenced my scholarship and this book. *In a world full of "bucket dippers," I'm thankful to have some "bucket fillers" in my life.*

My heartfelt thanks to the team at McGill-Queen's University Press, especially Khadija Coxon. I am deeply grateful to everyone who helped shape this book. I am humbled to publish alongside scholars in a series dedicated to outspoken voices in the academy. Thank you to Adrian Parr and Santiago Zabala for including me in this challenging and engaging series.

Lastly, I express my gratitude to my family for their patience and understanding while I was absent or preoccupied and working on this manuscript. My research team consisted of my four (mostly) feral children, a partner who never ceases to put wind in my sails, and a sister who was always up for an adventure. Samantha, you are woven into these stories, and this work literally would not have been possible without your camaraderie along the way. My siblings, David (Marianne), Samantha (Aaron), and Ariel (Jonah), are the definition of #squadgoals, and my parents, Mark and Elana, continue to sacrifice and give of themselves every single day. My parents will always be my rock. I am blessed enough to have my grandmother Helen, my Mama, still present in mind, body, and spirit. I am grateful for her, and yet also carry the emptiness from the losses of my other grandparents and those no longer physically here. Without them, my ancestors, there would be no me. *Without them, there would be no us.*

My partner, my co-conspirator, I would choose you again and again. When you find a stranger who you're willing to hop in a car with and drive to Canada for an anarchist convergence, keep that special person in your life forever. Michael, a decade of building a life and revolution with you has been energizing, thought-provoking, exhausting, and soul-fulfilling. Cheers to a lifetime of writing together, supporting one another, and resisting both oppression and repression creatively. *I hope we leave our children with a radically reimagined world.*

My beautiful, feral babies, Emory Sheindal, Simon Bella, Tevye Yosef, and Durruti Robert: let my sleepless nights and persistence remind you that your worth is your own. You each bring something to this world that no one else does. You carry privilege and you are tasked to use it to disrupt the systems that deny that very same privilege to others. In the ways that you are denied privilege, you must resist as your ancestors have done. Let the revolutionaries described in these pages remind you that *if there is oppression, there must be resistance.*

ECOLIBERATION

Introduction

Baby, what's that confused look in your eyes? What I'm trying to say is
that I burn down buildings while you sit on a shelf inside of them. You
call the cops on the looters and pie throwers. They call it class war, I call it
co-conspirators. 'Cause baby, I'm an anarchist ... You watched in awe at the
red, white, and blue on the fourth of July. While those fireworks were explod-
ing, I was burning that fucker and stringing my black flag high ... You have
faith in the elephant and jackass, and to you, solidarity's a four-letter word ...
'Cause baby, I'm an anarchist, you're a spineless liberal. We marched together
for the eight-hour day and held hands in the streets of Seattle, but when it came
time to throw bricks through that Starbucks window, you left me all alone.

(Against Me! 2002)

I was holding a large sign that had a picture of a maimed beagle and
the words "This is not my kind of 'science,'" chanting along with other
activists. We were outside the private residence of an employee of a company that does animal testing. After ten minutes, a neighbour came outside and began to scream at us. He explained that the person we were
targeting had a young baby who was probably trying to sleep, and, more
importantly, that we were targeting a "good person." The neighbour's
reaction reflected a certain social script, in which we were bad activists,
needlessly attacking an innocent good person and his family.

One of the activists, designated in advance as our public relations representative, stepped aside and began to engage the neighbour in a conversation. Our PR rep lowered her voice and changed her tone. She slowly
explained the details of an experiment that involved injecting a beagle
with chemicals that this good person had facilitated. The neighbour's initial expression of anger turned to disgust. His brow softened. His clenched
mouth relaxed. His crossed arms released and fell by his side.

A home demonstration, like the one described above, takes place at the
private residence of an employee or business associate of a target of an

activist campaign. It is an example of one of the direct action tactics used in the North American animal and earth liberation movements (AELM). I became active in these movements in 2011, while living in Washington, DC (WDC). For many years before, I had been involved in mainstream animal and earth advocacy – I was a good activist. Mainstream advocacy can be broadly divided into two camps: 1) welfare and conservation, 2) and rights and sustainability. The animal welfare and ecological conservation groups are focused on protectionism and harm reduction, mainly through fundraising and raising public awareness. The animal rights and ecological sustainability campaigns are somewhat more attuned to issues of systemic inequality and injustice, and they are mainly focused on policy reform. Over time, I had grown frustrated with the individualism of these movements, and their entanglement with green capitalism. There was also a common, often unarticulated assumption that good activism was synonymous with indirect action – appealing to authorities, particularly those with corporate and state power. The budding vegetarian me at seventeen had relied on People for the Ethical Treatment of Animals (PETA) for dietary suggestions. Over the next two years, I would shift from a vegetarian diet to an intersectional vegan politic. I found myself distancing from groups like PETA and Farm Sanctuary. Disenchanted, I was no longer compelled by these campaigns that advocate for welfare and rights within the existing systems. I was inspired by those who refuse to work within the system and wanted to work alongside those who demand a holistic reimagination of society. I found myself in the thick of a movement predicated on total liberation, by any means necessary (Pellow 2014).

The following book examines the ways in which eco-activists in the AELM, as an example of leftist social movements, queer [rearticulate and reimagine] traditional forms of protest through their oppositional articulations and resistance to constructed social and ecological hierarchy.[1] The book further interrogates the mechanisms of repression deployed by the state-corporate-industrial complex to silence eco-activists through the construction of the ecoterrorist.[2] Eco-activists advocate an intersectional analysis of the exploitation and commodification of beings and ecologies within capitalism, the state, and paradigms of power, and speciesism.[3] Animal industries are structurally positioned with corporate sovereignty through vanguard legislation that overtly represses activists through surveillance, harassment, arrest and prosecution, and incarceration. Following a decade of prominent actions by animal and earth liberation activists, the early 2000s marked a distinct period of political repression known as the Green Scare. Although some argue the Green

Scare began in 2004 with the FBI's Operation Backfire, others argue it began two years prior, in 2002, at a US Senate hearing on ecoterrorism in 2002 (Pellow 2014, 177). The details of the coordinated, multi-agency investigation, Operation Backfire, are unpacked in chapter 4, and expose the sovereign powers of animal industries and attempts to fragment activists through fear (Potter 2011, 178). However, eco-activist Daniel McGowan, one of the people convicted as a result of Operation Backfire, was articulating the concept in a different setting in 2002. In a zine entitled *Welcome to the Green Scare!* published by Spirit of Freedom, or North American Earth Liberation Prisoner Support Network, he names this specific political moment:

> Just what is this *Green Scare*, you say? Well, when we use that term, we are referring to tactics that the US government and all their tentacles (FBI, IRS, BATF, Joint Terrorism Task Forces, local police, the court system) are using to attack the ELF/ALF and specifically those who publicly support them. Similar to Senator Joe McCarthy's campaign and the House of Un-American Affairs (HUAC) of the 1950s, legislators, property rights advocates and industry spokespeople are using threats and propaganda to crush any public support of underground resistance … Their strategy – a combination of introducing legislation to make punishments for direct action worse and to take out the support structures of the underground ecological movement. (Spirit of Freedom 2002, 1)

The zine includes an overview of the congressional hearing, including a summary of questions that were asked. Craig Rosebraugh, the ELF spokesperson from 1997 to 2001 and the co-founder of the NAELFPO with Leslie James Pickering, was at the hearing and faced formal questioning.[4] Representatives berated Rosebraugh, reminding him that good protestors don't break the law and that mink only exist to be murdered and skinned for coats. Within a capitalist system that is predicated on the privilege of species (speciesism), the animal body can be brutally dismembered through the processes of commodification, while the pervasive lack of industry regulations naturalizes and celebrates it. Speciesism permits a naturalized sovereign power over animal bodies and creates a discourse of justice around penalizing animal liberators.

Over the years, I have engaged in multifaceted ethnographies of the decentralized, clandestine AELM, and studied up the state-corporate-industrial complex.[5] Through an emphasis on individual standpoints and performativity, I engage in participant-observation during demonstrations, convergences, general assemblies, and legal proceedings. The book utilizes ethnography as an anthropological method to connect local modes of knowing with larger structural and ideological issues of power.

One of the most unique and distinguishing features of the AELM is their characteristic use of direct action. The movement is not constituted by formalized groups of people, though many of the same activists travel from campaign to campaign, and from collective to collective. There is no stable ideology, though many of the activists involved are against speciesism and hierarchy in general. The majority identify as anarchist, and at the very least are anti-authoritarian and anti-capitalist. Most are committed to intersectional politics, seeing speciesism and animal liberation not as a single issue, but rather as part of a matrix of intersecting forms of domination that oppress humans, non-humans, and the earth.[6] The AELM are a series of loosely overlapping campaigns and collectives that use direct action to confront exploiters and dominators. This involves identifying targets, such as animal enterprises and resource extraction enterprises, and planning and executing campaigns to directly stop or interfere with the targets. The cases most familiar to the general public involve physically liberating animals from places like farms and labs, or direct blockades to physically prevent clear cuts and pipelines. But the AELM also often act to inflict financial harm on targets, as a way of stopping them long-term. This might involve illegally acquiring and exposing video footage of a target's brutal practices, or it might involve using confrontational pressure tactics, such as home demonstrations, to push secondary or tertiary targets to cut ties with the main target.

The AELM's uses of direct action are complicated by the fact that the neoliberal state is deeply invested in protecting the interests of animal agriculture, the use of vivisection in academic and commercial research, and natural resource extraction.[7] In North America, governments at various levels have played a major role in repressing activism that poses a serious threat to the financial interests of these industries. Most notably, in 2006, the US government reframed the 1992 Animal Enterprise Protection Act, a state law, as the Animal Enterprise Terrorism Act (AETA), now a federal law.[8] This move not only increased the state's authority to target activists, increasing existing penalties and allowing enterprises to seek restitution; it also defined direct action against these enterprises as terrorism. This use of the term "terrorism" was a rhetorical move, designed to exploit anxieties connected with terrorism discourse around 9/11, and to construct a cultural divide between good, legitimate, legal advocacy and protest, on the one hand, and bad, radical, anarchist, and terrorist activism, on the other hand.

· This book offers a window into the worlds of the AELM and their largely misunderstood uses of direct action from the vantage point of an anarchist, vegan, Jewish mother and student-turned-scholar. From 2011 to 2017, my involvement in these worlds was dual – I approached the campaigns not only as a committed activist, but also as an ethnographer engaged in academic research. That period involved difficult, tumultuous times, and the political often became personal. I was, at various times and in various ways, pushed hard to question myself as an activist. And, at times, it felt too difficult to resist the state's deliberate repression of my voice and power. Since 2017, and, more notably, since the presidential election of Donald Trump, my activism has pivoted. I have not changed my position on animal and earth liberation, nor has it changed as a core value. But the suffocating climate of neo-fascism, white nationalism, anti-Semitism, and toxic masculinity has shifted my attention. My earlier activism with the AELM very much informs my contemporary engagement with the Movement for Black Lives (M4BL), Antifa, and intersectional feminist organizing. In 2018, a month before giving birth, I travelled to the US/Mexico border to provide mutual aid to displaced and detained families awaiting asylum hearings. While attending an asylum hearing, I listened as children shared the gruelling details of their lives prior to leaving their country. They had been separated from their parents and made the physically difficult journey with cousins and friends. They were detained by US border agents and imprisoned at Tornillo Migrant Detention Center. I was reminded how humans are animalized through language, and how that language is used to justify subjecting them to egregious forms of violence.[9] I was also reminded that the logic to oppress is flexible and enduring.

One of things I learned from my experiences with the AELM, and one of the main messages of this book, is that activists use a range of tactics, including political theatre, to dramatize and queer narratives and norms of good versus bad activism that can be applied to interconnected social movements. In the scene described at the beginning of this chapter, a neighbour reveals that he identifies, maybe unconsciously, with the ideology of bad activism. One of the activists, the PR representative, switches registers, and adopts the neoliberal script of a good protester. All the while, the rest of us activists continue chanting aggressively and confrontationally in the background, holding up grotesque images of animal cruelty. A central argument of this book is that there is a playful volley between these two sets of actions, which generates what queer theorists call performativity. The activists playfully perform both good and bad activism at once.[10] This disarms the neighbour of his preconceptions and enables the images and information about violence to animals to have an impact. The entire scene is a performance or political play, staged on the sidewalk. Following the work of Stephen Duncombe, I suggest that this is an example of how our society's overwhelming orientation to emotionally stimulating images, media, and performance – as opposed to rational argument – can be exploited in queer ways by activists for the good.

The fluidity and temporality of direct action campaigns within the AELM is both a rearticulation of resistance and a response to political repression. The fascistic shift in US politics under the Trump administration illustrates the importance of flexibility, imagination, and tenacity within specifically anarchist activist circles. Over the years, I have engaged with countless campaigns and collectives that emerged, rose to prominence, retreated or dissolved, only to reappear anew with the same actors under a different name.

AELM CAMPAIGNS AND COLLECTIVES

They are mainly defined by their strategies of resistance, particularly direct action – although many are also explicitly or implicitly anarchist. I describe here the main campaigns and collectives relevant to this book. While this is not a thorough history, I emphasize that the strategies that define each campaign or collective, evolve in relation to other campaigns, and in relation to new tactics of repression. In solidarity with the activists, I use pseudonyms for many of the campaigns and collectives in the book. Over the years, many of the campaigns and collectives have dissolved and activists have reconfigured themselves into other ones. Despite the temporal nature of some of these campaigns, I have used present tense to describe them. Although their actual names are not used here, I would like to think this linguistic choice to give them present-tense-permanence honours the important work done in a particular time and place. I use the term "eco-activist" throughout the book, and unless otherwise stated, I am referring to anarchist anti-speciesist activists.[11]

1 *Animal Liberation Front (ALF) and Earth Liberation Front (ELF)*

The ALF and ELF must be distinguished from other campaigns discussed in this book because they are monikers that autonomous, clandestine activists invoke when they engage in an act of nonviolent direct action. In other words, activists work anonymously and underground, either in small groups or individually. The history of these collectives is inspiring and deserving of attention and detail, but outside the scope of my focus here.[12] Although the ALF and ELF are distinct from one another, they are both labels tagged with acts in defence of other-than-human animals and ecologies with an agreed-upon set of principles. Many above-ground activists find themselves in affinity with both the ALF and ELF. Although the ethnographic research discussed in this manuscript does not focus exclusively on ALF or ELF activities, the activists I worked with, and the activities that they engage in beyond what I include here may very well be done in the name of either moniker.

Activists rely on a secure way to publish their communiqué, a detailed account of what occurred, the motivation and significance of the act, followed by a claim that invoked pseudonyms and/or a moniker like ALF or ELF. The North American Animal Liberation Press Office (NAALPO) and the North American Earth Liberation Front Press Office (NAELFPO) are legal, above-ground entities that serve as a clearinghouse for things like communiqués. Communiqués serve as an important tool to both contextualize the action and articulate the aims of the action (Loadenthal 2017). Although the NAELFPO has essentially been defunct since 2001, their principles align closely with the ALF. The ALF principles state:

a To liberate animals from places of abuse, i.e., laboratories, factory farms, fur farms, etc., and place them in good homes where they may live out their natural lives, free from suffering.
b To inflict economic damage to those who profit from the misery and exploitation of animals.
c To reveal the horror and atrocities committed against animals behind locked doors, by performing direct actions and liberations.
d To take all necessary precautions against harming any animal, human and non-human. (North American Animal Liberation Press Office "FAQs" n.d.)

One cannot become a member of the ALF/ELF because there is no centralized membership or leader. The only thing that unites individuals under the auspices of these monikers is the use or advocacy of direct action to directly disrupt violence against animals and ecologies. This includes (but is not limited to) direct rescue, property destruction, undercover investigation, and blockades that target individuals and corporations that participate in animal and ecological abuse. For example, many of the acts committed by activists identifying themselves as the ALF do so with the short-term aim of liberating animals from captivity, laboratories, slaughterhouses, and other sites of exploitation. The long-term aim, or cumulative goal, is to force animal industries into capitulation. These guidelines claim that the destruction of property is not violence, adhering to the anarchist principles that all property is theft and that capitalism itself is a form of violence (Proudhon 1840; Bakunin 1970; Graeber 2004b; Amster et al., 2009; Bonanno 1999). The ALF and ELF guidelines strictly state that activists must take all precautions not to harm any living being during their act of liberation.

In defending their choice to adopt nonviolent direct action, the NAALPO cites other liberation movements that violated laws that were themselves unjust, such as war resisters, Underground Railroad "conductors," and "Righteous Gentiles" during the Holocaust. Similar to the argument regarding moral madness by scholar and Holocaust survivor Elie Wiesel, the NAALPO emphasizes the inverse morality that legalizes animal exploitation and death. The concept of moral madness refers to an upside-down morality where acts of violence are deemed both moral and legal, and acts that resist said violence both immoral and illegal. Wiesel argues that to justify systemic violence is to be implicated in the violence, regardless of the state of legality or temporal morality (Cargas 1981; Wiesel 1982). It is within this vein that the term *freedom fighter* is invoked to describe non-Jews who resisted the Nazi regime and offered refuge or assisted Jews toward liberation. Despite the potential legal and social sanctions, there were those who enacted strategies and tactics to immediately alleviate destruction. In a sense, resisters create an alternative state within the states of exception. The suspension of morality when destroying the remaining old-growth trees in a forest or removing the last native Bengal tiger from its habitat requires a unique moral madness. Thus, freedom fighters resist this moral madness by destroying a computer that houses data gathered from torturing chimpanzees in captivity or creating an oceanic blockade to prevent a fishing ship to pass. In Marshall Curry's 2011 film, *If a Tree Falls: A Story of the Earth Liberation Front*, McGowan reflects on the overwhelming sense of environmental loss in Oregon, "Sometimes when you see things you love being destroyed, you just want to destroy those things." The ALF is distinct within the umbrella "animal advocacy" movement, with a public commitment to liberation by any means necessary in that it is invoked when activists challenge capitalism through illegal direct action, oftentimes destroying the material property used to exploit animal bodies, while simultaneously adhering to a strict nonviolent policy and alignment with civil disobedience.[13]

2 Earth First!

During the same years that the ELF and ALF actions were appearing in the US, Earth First! (EF!) arose out of the Pacific Northwest with a similar commitment to ecological justice. Borrowing directly from the *Earth First! Journal*:

"Earth First! formed in 1979, in response to an increasingly corporate, compromising and ineffective environmental community. It is not an organization, but a movement. There are no 'members' of EF!, only Earth First!ers. We believe in using all of the tools in the toolbox, from grassroots and legal organizing to civil disobedience and monkeywrenching. When the law won't fix the problem, we put our bodies on the line to stop the destruction. Earth First!'s direct action approach draws attention to the crises facing the natural world, and it saves lives." Guided by a philosophy of deep ecology, Earth First! does not accept a human-centred worldview of "nature for people's sake." Instead, we believe that life exists for its own sake, that industrial civilization and its philosophy are anti-Earth, anti-woman, and anti-liberty. Our structure is non-hierarchical, and we reject highly paid "professional staff" and formal leadership ("About Earth First!" n.d.).

Unlike the ALF and ELF, EF! hosts summits for above-ground activists to gather, skillshare, and form meaningful relationships with likeminded folks. As an activist, EF! provided me with meaningful spaces where I could interrogate my own complicity in the exploitation of the earth. While working on this manuscript, I attended several annual gatherings, and reaffirmed a deep admiration for the kind and generous folks that occupy and spike trees, glue locks, drop banners, and engage in all of the other physically dangerous, precariously (il)legal acts to protect and defend ecologies. The history of EF! has been captured in many of the same texts that historicize the ELF and ALF, but also by activists who proudly call themselves an EF!ers (Foreman 1993; 2003; Scarce 2017; Bari 1994; Davis 1991; Manes 1991).

3 Stop Huntingdon Animal Cruelty (SHAC)

SHAC was formed in 1999 by three British activists in response to an undercover investigation by PETA that captured hours of violent vivisection conducted inside Huntingdon Life Sciences. SHAC, as both a

campaign and collective, emphasized secondary and tertiary targeting, the complementary relationship between public and underground
organizing, a diversity of tactics, and the importance of establishing
concrete targets with concrete motivations.[14] The SHAC model, a direct
action campaign, utilizes a method of naming, shaming, and blaming
individuals who hold top positions with secondary and tertiary corporations connected to the international vivisection and breeding lab,
Huntingdon Life Sciences (HLS). The strategy is used to target HLS
through pressuring clients, shareholders, connected financial institutions, and associated corporations to sever their ties with HLS. The
tactics used span a continuum of legality, and range from street protests, leafleting, home demonstrations, to aggressive forms of sabotage
including arson.

4 Animal Liberation Always (ALA)

The ALA collective is a small WDC-based direct action collective that
has unofficial ties to the international SHAC campaign. ALA adopts
the SHAC approach of targeting secondary and tertiary actors associated with HLS. It maintains a website with little information about
the history of the organization or its constituents. Instead, the website
primarily serves as a community resource with an "ALA board" open
to user posts, a detailed repository of WDC protest laws and National
Lawyers Guild (NLG) contacts, upcoming events, and resources including local groups, prisoner support networks, and leftist news outlets.
The campy phrasing throughout the site retains a sense of play, tagging
slogans on each of the resource tabs. Some of these include "There is
no JUSTICE! Just US!"; "We will never back down, never compromise
and WE WILL ALWAYS WIN!"; and the phrase "Taking Aim at Animal Exploitation" written across a picture of a billiards board in the
"ALA board" section (Animal Liberation Always 2011). The collective
is decentralized, non-hierarchical, and thus does not have central leadership figures. The website reflects this lateral structure by not identifying key individuals with the collective to contact. It is only through
attending several demonstrations and participating in several other
protests in the WDC area – not affiliated with the animal liberation
movement – that I became familiar with those individuals. Because of
increased government repression of SHAC, ALA maintains they have no
official affiliation with the international campaign (Animal Liberation
Always 2011). This is widely disputed amongst activists and was discussed several times during the demonstrations I attended.

5 Britches Brigade

Britches Brigade is an international anti-vivisection campaign based on the SHAC model of inflicting economic damage on vivisection companies by pressuring secondary and tertiary targets.[15] For example, Britches Brigade has used pressure tactics on major airlines to end transportation of primates, dogs, and other animals to laboratories. The founders of Britches Brigade used crowd-sourcing fundraising to organize a US tour of cities with specific airline offices, in order to mobilize pressure tactics at a local level. I attended demonstrations with the collective outside of the Greater Cincinnati/Kentucky Airport as well as outside the corporate office in Wilmington, Ohio.

Britches Brigade is explicitly intersectional, and the website states, "Animal liberation means liberation from any form of oppression" (Britches Brigade n.d.). Other campaigns, such as ALA, tend to have a culture of intersectionality in practice, in virtue of the commitments of the activists involved – people who are visible in anarchist circles and explicitly intersectional campaigns and collectives.[16] Bridges Brigade, however, integrates a critique of other forms of oppression as interconnected to speciesism.

6 The Pathway to Liberation Campaign

The US Pathway to Liberation Tour, a campaign of Bridges Brigade, does not tolerate any kind of "fascist, racist, sexist, homophobic, transphobic attitude or behavior and stands in solidarity with all those individuals and collectives who fight for a more just and equal world." (Pathway to Liberation n.d.). The multi-issue focus was put into practice further with the collaboration of several eco-activist collectives on the "Liberation in Flight" and focuses on mobilizing a local collective to then continue the pressure tactics after the travelling activists left. The activists provide signs, chant sheets, and megaphones. The tour collaboration was articulated through a declaration issued on their website:

> This summer, Bridges Brigade, Gathering for Total Liberation, and the Earth First! Journal present the Liberation in Flight, a collaborative nationwide tour with three distinct objectives:
>
> a to intensify Bridges Brigade's campaign against Delta Air Lines and the broader Pathway to Liberation campaign to end the transport of animals to labs,

b to share skills and build connections within the grassroots animal
   and ecological activist movements, and
c to promote coalition building and solidarity with a diversity of
   movements and communities. (Pathway to Liberation n.d.)

The campaign relies on social media to increase awareness and visibility, as well as to recruit activists. The third tour, titled "Rooted in
Rebellion: Animal Liberation from the Ground Up," was a collaboration between an activist in Britches Brigade and an activist from
Total Liberation Conference. While in Portland, Oregon, in 2014, I
attended the Gathering for Total Liberation convergence before heading to the Earth First! Rendezvous. The gathering served as a meet up
for activists (as well as folks who also identify as academics) to engage
in dialogue that built and reinforced coalitions. These coalitions were
enriched with skill-set sharing of both tactical and strategical knowledge. The partnership between Britches Brigade and the Gathering
for Total Liberation convergence maintains the paramount focus on
intersectionality.

7 Gathering for Total Liberation

Gathering for Total Liberation focuses on supporting grassroots movements, creating and strengthening networks, engaging in direct action
campaigns, and publishing critical analyses on the Gathering for Total
Liberation website. Although the collective engages in direct action and
partners with campaigns, Gathering for Total Liberation is more focused
on facilitating critical thought and dialogue to maximize movement
effectiveness. The focus is explicitly intersectional. The collective states
their rationale behind the structure and content:

> We aspire to create a forum to unite animal liberationists, land
> defenders, and organizers to share skill sets and resources, to report
> and recruit, to coordinate campaigns, and to promote solidarity, coa-
> lition organizing and mass movement building against the structures
> that underpin animal use and ecological destruction on the continent
> – Euro-settler colonialism, white supremacy, patriarchy, capitalism,
> neoliberalism, and border imperialism. We want to progress beyond
> the conventional one-dimensional analysis and structure of mobiliza-
> tion and advocacy that has long been our calling card. (Gathering for
> Total Liberation n.d.)

Through the movement magazine, annual national conference, and facilitation of networks and tours, Gathering for Total Liberation serves as an analytic tool and organizing vehicle to unite the oftentimes-severed connections between animal liberationists and land defenders that share a fundamental anarchist and anti-speciesist politic.

8 End Captivity Now

The End Captivity Now campaign focuses on an animal-use amusement park in North America. This grassroots campaign solely focuses on the closing of one specific amusement park but draws from activists engaged in animal liberation more broadly. The park has historically been the site of controversy and attention from the anti-captivity movement long before this specific campaign. For the last two decades, the region had seen a proliferation of animal liberation campaigns and collectives. These grassroots animal liberation campaigns are centred around building community and increasing sustained pressure against animal-and-ecology use industries. The collectives I worked with in the region are all familiar with and active in this particular campaign, which emerged in the early 2010s. Within the first year of the campaign, it had grown in size and momentum, with demonstrations that grew from the tens to the hundreds of activists.

Films like *Forks Over Knives*, *Blackfish*, and *An Apology to Elephants* had popularized the longstanding message of the AELM: animals are sentient, ecologically interconnected to humans, and do not belong in cages for human entertainment (Cowperthwaite 2013; Fulkerson 2011; Schatz 2013). As the campaign in grew in size, so too did the magnitude of political repression the activists faced. I supported the campaign from afar and travelled throughout North America to join the demonstrations and interview activists. The activists were public about the harassment they experienced but found themselves censored by legal processes that limited their ability to speak freely. The campaign continued to put pressure on the park, and the park continued to put pressure on the campaign. Rather than refer to the actual entity the campaign is targeting, I have given the target a pseudonym, "Caged Entertainment."

ACTIVIST RESEARCH AS METHOD

Distinct from the anthropological discussions on social movements that tackle neoliberalism, capitalism, political theatre, sovereignty, and ecological concerns from a single-movement perspective, this book addresses these concepts through an engaged activist-ethnography of the AELM.[17] Although these areas are each significant anthropological discourses, they are often fractured literatures and they discuss social movements as individual entities rather than as part in parcel to larger, coalitional networks that ebb and flow without institutional and ideological borders. There remains a gap wherein this book interjects, and it provides an interconnected theory that illustrates how activists and tactics travel between movements to critique human, animal, and ecological exploitation through an intersectional lens. The expansive theoretical framework in this book fills a growing gap wherein these anthropological concepts exist disparately.[18] Further, these tactics and ideological critiques of speciesism are neglected within traditional anthropological texts focused on dissent. Confrontational direct action, when included in the literature, has been portrayed as reckless property destruction, misguided protest, non-unified and scattered demands, and as advocating delusional visions of utopic revolutionary change. Anthropologists have further distanced themselves from anarchist direct-action activists, as well as the theories that undergird their strategies and tactics, through the valuation of single-issue activism. This book inserts an applied theoretical framework in the literature by providing an anthropology of confrontational direct action that challenges neoliberal capitalism, speciesism, and state authority simultaneously.

Feminist Ethnography

Within activist anthropology, there is great emphasis on research design and being explicit with your commitment to reflexivity and measuring the potential impact of your work on the communities in which you are immersed. Lila Abu-Lughod and Nancy Naples interrogate ethnographic methods within the growing discourse of feminist anthropology, which have been adopted and expanded by many contemporary anthropologists. Abu-Lughod insists anthropologists utilize local modes of knowledge and expression, such as song and prose (Abu-Lughod 2008; 2013). Activist ethnography incorporates flexibility and reflexivity into the research design. Deductive ethnographic methods make space for alternative modes of expression rather than demarcate which modes are not visible.[19] Naples provides a transparent manuscript detailing her experience with ethnography in various social justice movements. Feminist anthropological research has attempted to subvert traditional ways of knowing that perpetuate patriarchal assumptions about "truth" and "objectivity" (Naples 2003, 15). These anthropologists provided a useful framework to examine the ways in which activists make sense of both resistance and repression. Rik Scarce, sociologist, describes how his commitment to research ethics was challenged by political repression:

> [Research ethics] is particularly important to me because, in 1993, I was jailed for more than five months on a contempt of court citation after I refused to fully cooperate with a federal grand jury. The grand jury was investigating an Animal Liberation Front break-in at the university where I was studying for my PhD. My research was on radical environmentalists, including the ALF. I argued that, as a scholar, the First Amendment shielded me from forced testimony and that the American Sociological Association's "Code of Ethics" directed that I not violate promises of confidentiality that I made to research participants. I never answered the grand jury's questions, and after 159 days imprisoned in the Spokane County (Washington) Jail, a judge released me. ("Rik Scarce" n.d.)

Activist ethnography, a method within anthropology, facilitates a critical engagement with repression. Rather than adopt a top-down approach, feminist anthropologists such as Melissa Wright and Iris Marion Young implement a praxis approach to social justice research. Marion Young re-examines the hegemonic construction of social justice as redistributive (Marion Young 1990). The interrogation of the distributive model facilitates the subsequent discussion of radical social restructuring. Eco-activist confrontational direct action asserts that oppressive structures cannot be reformed into equitable structures. Young's conceptualization of "rights" further complements the AELM's critiques of environmental and animal "rights" activism. "Rights are relationships, not things, they are institutionally defined rules specifying what people can do in relation to one another" (Marion Young 1990, 25). Young's framework was useful to analyze the ways in which activists politically position themselves with non-confrontational and confrontational modes of activism. Throughout the book, I incorporate informal conversations with people that illustrate how respondents articulate their use of either confrontational or non-confrontational protest, and their understanding of the political constraints through repressive government measures. I use anecdotal references to illuminate periods of intensive engagement with various collectives in the AELM and with collectives with tertiary connection to the movement. By integrating these narratives into the contemporary literature, it collates and creates a historical context of both political activism and political repression of an underrepresented movement in academic literature.

Linguistic Anthropology

The book is not only a repository of my own ethnographic notes as an activist, but rather, it is a collection of activist stories and experiences told through a particular linguistic lens. The activists I have worked closely with have co-constructed a vernacular that is continuously negotiated. Similar to how William Labov, a linguistic anthropologist, examined the ways in which African Americans utilize a well-formed set of rules that constitute African American Vernacular English (AAVE), I am interested in the distinct ways individuals co-create linguistic systems that ought to be included in larger discourses surrounding language. In Labov's politically important 1972 piece, he both validated and institutionalized what had previously been dismissed as slang (Labov 1972). Eco-activists, in a different way, negotiate shared linguistic systems that come through in chants, proclamations, and communiqués. Expanding on this localized ethnographic method I invoked the engaged approach provided by Charlotte Linde to examine how life stories are formed and told to co-construct our sense of self, and Stephen Levinson's useful, pragmatic approach to the study of language in his insistence that the analyses of speech acts and the presentation of technical linguistic tools such as deixis and presupposition should be approachable (Linde 1993; Levinson 1983). The analysis focused on units of discourse that go beyond the unit of a sentence (Levinson 1983, 18). The interviews and field notes represent a diverse range of life stories from activists, capturing the external social exchanges and the internal narratives (Linde 1993, 51). Further, there were times I relied on overhearing, a challenging form of listening that relies on inference and interpretation (Bubel 2008; Leap 2020).

I utilize Susan Hunston and Geoff Thompson's evaluative framework to look for evaluative clauses that provide insight into how activists understand their activism in relation to the state (Hunston and Thompson 2001, 2–25; Hunston 2002). Evaluation is found throughout the ordered structural parts of the text and provides insight into how respondents perceive their activism in relation to eco-activist movements. In an effort to preserve local modes of knowledge and expression, and the subjectivities of the respondents, the data analysis focused on evaluation (Hunston and Thompson 2001, 6). As the book illustrates, demonstrations themselves follow an ordered structure with optional abstract statements that summarize the purpose of the demonstration, can offer evaluation, or serve an interactive function (Linde 1993, 69). The demonstration proclamations and chants also include orientation, narrative clauses, and the coda to conclude the spectacle. There are

distinctions made between the carefully scripted and rehearsed proclamations and those spontaneously delivered without prior scripting. The
focus on narrative and evaluation within the corpus facilitates a rich
anthropological discourse on social movements, subjectivities, and perceptions of state repression.

Queer Linguistics

Similar to how Motschenbacher investigated normative discourses of gender and sexuality found in French and English translations in the Euro-
vision Song Competition (ESC), this analysis utilizes a queer linguistic
approach to examine how eco-activists engage in direct action as disidentification despite the repressive state acts of interpellation (Motschenbacher
2010, 96–9; Leap 2015, 665). The ethnographic description of events
not only provide textured detail, but these lend particular value when
analyzed through queer inquiry because they illuminate "the conditions
that lead the song-writers or performers to retain or suspend (or attempt
to do both) normative authority of national linguistic tradition in such
instances" (Leap 2015, 665). Though the book does not focus on linguistic discrepancies between translations, nor does this analysis focus specifically on how eco-activists use language to challenge normative discourses
about sexuality or gender, the analysis falls within the linguistic trajectory of both queer linguistics and critical discourse analysis because of the
focus on activists' voices and "how language enables (at times disguises)
the intersections of sexuality, gender, race, class, and other forms of social
inequality" (Leap 2015, 661). I am particularly interested in eco-activism because of the interrogation of interrelated paradigms of power that
address species. The analysis of social issues that follows was guided by the
written, spoken, and performed texts of eco-activist insofar as this inquiry
"must be discourse centered, and that that the analysis of discourse must
take the form of a critical inquiry; that is, it must engage, not obscure
the conditions of the speakers' experience as located within structures of
power" (Leap 2015, 661). Further, the book is anti-normative in its aim
to disrupt subject formation and interpellation through disidentification,
and fulfills the themes of queer linguistics if we can extend these themes
to address normative discourses of dissent: "(1) the normative authority
associated with sexual discourses, (2) the performative and metaphoric
expressions of normative authority in discursive practice, (3) normative
authority and institutional practices; and (4) the tensions between global
vs local voices expressing normative authority in everyday life" (Leap
2015, 676).

This methodological approach facilitates a queer inquiry, or queer(ey) ing of the use of direct action by eco-activists to produce and reproduce disidentification in the face of state repression, as well as the state's retaliatory interpellation of that disidentification through the construction of the ecoterrorist.

Throughout the book, I am cognizant of the polysemy of the messages shared in person and in digital spaces (Fauconnier and Turner 2003, 112). Stuart Hall points to the issues of disconnect with message encoding and decoding in television, and argues that messages are always already interpretive (Hall 1980, 173). This research interrogates the intentionality in the encoding process, but also the ways in which each audience plays a role in the decoding process. The messages from the speech event are negotiated through performance and audience reception, "Importantly, repetition and subversion are not properties 'of' text but reflect the engagements of speakers and audiences with text production and reception" (Leap 2011, 562). The sidewalk is the activist stage and can become a site of disidentification that can elicit disidentificatory thoughts from the audience (Muñoz 2009, 1–15). I capture the tensions between intentionality and audience reception by connecting the performative functions of protest with the inconsistencies, tensions, consistencies, and cohesiveness in the text before, during, and after public events (Hill 1995; 2005, 159). Previous research with the WDC-based animal liberation collective indicates several key words used in demonstrations: "you," "us," "animal," and "they." I am particularly interested in the collations with these terms as a way to examine how activists articulate their politics and positionality in relation to the targeted individual/corporation (Baker 2008, 76). Through critical discourse analysis of the participant-observation ethnographic data and digital media, this book addresses the ways in which activists attempt to capitulate structures of power through direct action.

NEGOTIATING ACTIVISM AND ACADEMIA

The late David Graeber was an inspiring example of how our politics guide our scholarship, and, organically, our scholarship guides our politics. The selection of research subject, participants, methodological tools, theoretical framework, and analysis consistently place the principal investigator in an active role. This book is a symbiotic extension of a larger political agenda to strengthen a praxis approach between the academic anthropological endeavour and activism. Specifically, the book developed out of personal activism within the AELM as a self-identified eco-activist.

The intimate relationship between the researcher and research partici-pants provided rich ethnographic data, but it also required transparency and reflexivity. Rather than solely be held to academic standards of rigour, the following book is held to the rigour of my peers. As such, I embrace my subjectivities as both honest and theoretically valuable, falling within a history of activist anthropologists that maintain personal and political commitments to the spaces in which they dually occupy as researcher and participant (Abu-Lughod 2008; Chomsky et al. 1967; Chomsky 2012; Leap 1996; Graeber 2004a; 2009a; W.L. Leap and Boellstorff 2003; Scheper-Hughes 1995; Wright 2006). Throughout the book, I place myself within the larger context of the demonstration, the convergence, or the exchange within digital media. In this sense, my role is interwoven into the narratives included in the study, however it is not the central focus.

As many scholars have pointed out, the journey into "the field" is not a monolithic experience across anthropology as a discipline. When began the work, I negotiated a series of assumptions while utilizing a methodology that conceptualized the "field" as a fluid, fragmented, oftentimes digital space without geographical borders. I was met with resistance from folks who demarcated "the field" from other spaces by the presence of physical luggage being transported across constructed borders that are geographically distinct and isolated from my own com-munity. David Naguib Pellow, an inspiring scholar-activist in the AELM, has taken us inside the complicated, messy ways in which activist ethnog-raphy functions (Pellow 2014). There was an assumption, by some, that I would physically enter a space that was not my own, or at the very least, that I would maintain the dual position of both researcher and member of the respective community. The reliance on geopolitical borders and a sense of otherness in this logic highlights the lingering effects of colonialism within anthropology. My response to this critique challenges these gener-alizations about the anthropological exercise of ethnography:

> According to Michel de Certeau, "What the map cuts up, the story cuts across." This pithy phrase evokes a postcolonial world criss-crossed by transnational narratives, Diaspora affiliations, and, especially, the movement and multiple migrations of people, some-times voluntary, but oftentimes economically propelled and politi-cally coerced. In order to keep up with such a world, we now think of "place" as a heavily trafficked intersection, a port of call and exchange, instead of a circumscribed territory. A boundary is more like a membrane than a wall ... "location" is imagined as an itiner-ary instead of a fixed point ... "local context" expands to encompass

the historical, dynamic, often traumatic, movements of people, ideas, images, commodities, and capital. (Conquergood 2002, 145)

In some cases, I did pack a bag and physically cross geopolitical borders. When possible, I spent days, or months, living out of a suitcase and immersing myself in a strangely familiar site (Miner 1956). Other times, I found myself archiving various digital media platforms, or simply grabbed a jacket to take with me to a demonstration just a few miles from my home. The spaces which I occupied to participate with and collect data throughout this ethnographic study are linked together through intermovement political affiliations, social networks of activism, nepotistic interpersonal connections, and happenstance. This provided a series of rich sites that embody the fluid and flexible functionality of direct action activism and the ideological leanings of eco-activists. As a participant in these communities, my voice is woven consistently throughout the texts. Rather than constantly manoeuvre the dual role of researcher and activist, I came to define myself as an activist that also does research. Thus, the role of researcher oftentimes became suspended to prioritize my identity and commitments as an activist. Perhaps not surprisingly, my role as a mother was more in tension with the roles of activist and researcher than those were with one another. The role of mother became a perpetual structural barrier to entering and manoeuvring spaces, thus limiting my ability to gather a wide range of data throughout the research.

Embodied Resistance and Reproductivities

This book emerges from rich history of anthropologists that grappled with the tension between the personal and political boundaries between themselves and their research subjects. The struggle, however, yields a destabilization of sorts that is capable of providing emotionally rich narratives that exist within the invisible borderlands between our academic and political selves (Anzaldúa and Moraga 1983, Cantú, and Hurtado 2012). The convergences, demonstrations, courtrooms, and classrooms are but merely stages in which we perform versions of ourselves. They are the physicality of an embodied location that does not require luggage, travel, or transgressing geopolitical borders. The role of an activist is to transcend the geographical limits that often isolate us from one another. Simultaneously, the role of the anthropologist is to immerse oneself, to live amongst, and to become deeply embedded in a particular culture. As a mother of four children, and companion to a Great Dane rescue, who also works a full-time academic job, and engages in political activism in a range of social movements, I manoeuvre both structural and symbolic barriers. For example, throughout the data collection and writing of this manuscript, I carried four pregnancies to term and breastfed on demand. There was no more than two consecutive months that I was not sustaining another life either through pregnancy or breastfeeding. Each time a demonstration was called, a court hearing was held, and a national convergence was organized, I weighed my ability to attend with my ability to travel with children. This ongoing, gendered negotiation, the domestic duality of "mother" and "activist academic," that I wrestle with continues to inform if and how I engage in both direct action activism and research.

When I attended my first home demonstration in WDC, I was five months pregnant with my first child. In jest, one of the activists referred to me as the "vegan breeder." This was not in the vein of eugenics, but rather, it was a condemnation on human reproduction as a hypocritical act that runs counter to vegan politics, and environmentalism more broadly. The activist also told me that he had been electively sterilized and published his critique of human reproduction in a zine, if I wanted to check it out. Anti-natalist conversations permeate the AELM, particularly amongst white male vegans. An activist recently shared that they had a vasectomy on social media, and quickly received hundreds of "likes" and dozens of comments.[20] Several notable comments include: "Why oh why oh why bring life into this world. It seems ill-conceived to me," "Congrats on the surgery. It was the right thing to do," "Got spayed thirty-two years ago. No regrets," "Bravo!!" "All men should be like you," "Thank you for being responsible," "I'd love to treat you to dinner on behalf of all women for doing this," "I'm childfree by choice," "Congrats. Appreciate that shit," "Even if I had to update it yearly, it would still be worth it," "Thank you for not bringing more humans into this overpopulated world," "Good on you," "Appreciation," "Aw, I remember when vegan dudes made group outings out of their V's back in the day," "Always good to see others who are not interested in procreation." The comments were both congratulatory and appreciative, thanking this person for undergoing elective sterilization. Many of them shared that they themselves had a similar procedure, and six went as so far as to "welcome" him to the "club." The anti-natalist arguments contain many sound critiques of human reproduction, but some of the arguments echo colonial, racist rhetoric that has been used to justify the forced sterilization of Black and Brown bodies throughout history. Reproductive choice is and should be just that, a choice. Everyone should have free access to accurate healthcare information, exams and diagnostics, barrier methods and contraception, elective sterilization, medical procedures, medication, abortions, and so much else. But, in the US, where healthcare is a luxury of the rich, many of the decisions around health care (specifically sexual and reproductive health care) are constrained by a multitude of oppressive systems (homonormativity, classism, sexism, racism, religion, to name a handful). After a decade in the movement, I am still unsettled by how often human reproduction functions as an exclusionary identity politic.

I learned early in my own activism that although I have access to a multitude of privileges in dominant culture as a cisgender woman with a cisgender male partner who is the biological father of our four children, these privileges often do not translate within eco-activist circles. These decisions, specifically the decision to birth children, have even been at the centre of public debate between activists. In 2013, I was invited to weigh in on a keynote discussion for the Institute for Critical Animal Studies North America Conference. While backpacking in Peru, I was contacted by someone I did not know who wanted quotes to use in their "pro-natalist" position speech. He heard that I was one of the few women in the AELM who had recently given birth.[21] This indicated that people had utilized word-of-mouth and social media to clearly mark me because of my reproductive choices. We exchanged emails, and I kept bringing the conversation back to agency and autonomy. He had never shared with whom he was debating, or any communication about how he intended to incorporate my words. The remarks were shared during the debate, and then posted online for discussion. I later found out that the person with whom he was debating was actually a friend of mine. Come to find out, the debate centred around two cisgender women in a male-dominated movement justifying and defending their reproductive choices. Neither one of us clung to the pro/anti-natalist dichotomy, and instead focused on our own decisions. The public conversation, however, was polarized and reductionist. We both used our public forums, our personal blogs, to nuance the conversation more directly after this public discussion. In a movement so clearly guilty of valourizing men as leaders of the leaderless resistance, it was fascinating to see this gendered "morality Olympics" about reproduction and respectability politics play out.

Years later, my friend and I reconnected and reminisced about this "debate." As we shared how our lives have changed and engagement with activist communities evolved, I began speculating about how differently my own trajectory would look today if I had not been pregnant in 2011. I wondered if my relationships with activists would have been stronger, or if I would have met different resistance when I became pregnant at a later date. As life would have it, I swapped out the label good protestor for bad protestor when I was already pregnant with my first child. Because pregnancy is a physical embodiment, particularly on a 5'3" petite frame, it was difficult to closet my pregnancies, though I wouldn't have done so regardless. Thus, I have not attended an AELM demonstration without a child, either physically with me or in utero, since July 2011. It is not uncommon to find me at a demonstration with a baby in a sling and a sign in my hands. In one large march in WDC, I kept to the end of the cluster of demonstrators and used the stroller as a physical barrier to keep the police back. Outside of the Freddy Mac office building with several hundred protesters, I stood at the front, face to face with Department of Homeland Security officers that were aggressively holding canisters of pepper spray, and repeatedly chanted, "I am eight months pregnant." The use of the body as strategic capital for the movement is not a new topic for debate amongst feminists (Collins 2006; Nicholson 1997; Williams and Chrisman 1994). However, it is worth noting the dialectical tension between the ways these sexual and reproductive choices are seen as privilege for dominant culture and grounds for exclusion and being discredited by eco-activists in the AELM.[22]

I negotiate the dialectical relationship between researcher and activist and provide an honest and reflective dialogue about actualizing radical social change in spite of state repression. Through a multi-year participant observation ethnography based on anarchist anti-species activism in North America, problematized by my own subjectivities, and interspersed with a transdisciplinary methodology, this book contributes to an intersectional discourse on social movement theory. Further, this research provides an important praxis in the ever-expanding gap between direct action and academia. The stories told are anonymous, unless the activist has done so publicly. Many of the actions discussed are illegal, and, at best, taboo within a good/bad protestor framework. The morality is not debated, though I believe these movements, strategies, and tactics are powerfully necessary. The data derived, and theories professed are an important part of crucial debates in the fields on anthropology and communication. I engage this research with the perspective that I am always already in a boundless field of study. As an eco-activist who both ideologically and politically identifies with the intersectional direct action used by many of the eco-activists in this study, the site of research lies in my lived reality. Whether it is showing up to work and concealing my politics or carefully crafting a public presence in the realm of social media, I am always already negotiating the ways in which I penetrate "the field."

Throughout the research and writing of this book, my role within the movement also shifted in personal ways. I began the research as a PhD student living in WDC with a well-established record in both ecofeminist and anarchist circles.[23] During the preliminary data collection, I met my partner and, less than a year later, gave birth to our daughter, Emory. I became pregnant again in the middle of the data collection period for the study, and gave birth to our second daughter, Simon, just two months before attending a large demonstration with the End Captivity Now campaign. My family relocated from WDC to Cincinnati, a politically and socially isolating move that has dramatically impacted my access to the collectives I was deeply invested in. In the concluding months of data collection, I started to experience the isolation of raising children in radical leftist circles. I began a full-time job in 2013, while also teaching a 2 x 2 course load as an adjunct instructor. The text became personalized in a new way in 2016, shortly after the birth of our third child, when my partner was arrested during the anti-inaugural protest referred to as J20. The manuscript evolved as the case unfolded, and I found myself living the theories I discussed years prior about disciplinary punishment. The embodied repression reached a point of crisis when I found out I was expecting our fourth child as my partner awaited trial for the J20 arrest. The physical constraints on my body from pregnancy and child-rearing oftentimes restricted my ability to travel for demonstrations and convergences.

The economic constraints of maintaining employment while paying for both childcare and companion-animal care have placed additional barriers on my capacity to publicly engage in direct action, because of the public nature of my job as well as the lack of access to paid time off of work. These experiences shaped my structural analysis in the book through personal narratives that otherwise remain outside of academic discourses. It became an important political exercise to make space for these challenges that disproportionately marginalize women and mothers in the academy. Simultaneously, I recognize the ways in which my experiences are shaped by my privilege: co-parenting, cisgender performance, white skin and (presumed) class mobility, graduate education, physical ability, and documented citizenship. These are listed in no particular order or priority, nor is the list exhaustive.

Privilege is insidious and it goes without saying that I am both conscious and unconscious of the depth of these structures. With full acknowledgement of the privileged spaces I occupy, it is also worth exploring the structural privileges I am denied as a "female," as a mother, as a minority [God-questioning anarchist] within a minority religion [Judaism], and as a non-tenure line, assistant professor within a commodified academic climate of precarious employment. These nuanced identities are embodied and performed, negotiated and transgressed, and inform the ways in which I think about, engage with, and contribute to activist and academic discourses. The book is a constant negotiation of this duality, the worlds of activism and academics through the lens of standpoint theory. I intentionally localize and utilize the structural privilege of institutionalized knowledge to produce scholarship that advances radical social change. In this vein, the book relies on the dialectic of political commitment and academic scrutiny.

The following vignettes are windows into the much larger collection of stories, and they illustrate the ways in which eco-activists engage in and articulate direct action and how activists resist state repression. The early demonstrations in 2011 shaped the subsequent interactions, as well as the structure of the book itself. It was while attending my first demonstration with ALA that I saw how gender and reproductive choices reinscribed patriarchal divisions that oftentimes place men at the forefront of social movement organizing. Because of practical spatial issues (such as attending evening punk shows, standing next to or holding a bullhorn to chant, or travelling ad hoc to demonstrations with others) I struggled with the tension between wanting to access these spaces and wanting to care for my child(ren). Breastfeeding was one overtly visible physical barrier that placed time constraints on my absence, and also informed my risk-assessment when engaging in direct action. A simple detainment in police custody could mean hours away from my child who I breastfed every few hours. As I travelled throughout North America, I took notes. The notes were scribbled on napkins, scrap paper, and the back of receipts. I took voice memos in the car while my children slept, and I would rapidly type notes on my cell phone if I was able to sit in the passenger seat. I awoke before my children to write the random thoughts that kept me awake at night, and in some cases I snuck out of bed only to fall asleep at the computer. These are the stories recollected in the stolen moments of my overlapping domestic roles during this transformative journey into direct action activism.

The stories included here are merely parts to a larger whole, and in many ways, parts to a larger "whole" that is fragmented between the documented and the forgotten. There are stories told in this book, stories I have told in other publications, stories I have saved to tell another day, and stories that will never make their way onto paper because I am protecting the activists who shared them. Because of the influx nature of non-hierarchical direct action campaigns, this book captures a particular time and space within the AELM. The collectives and campaigns are fluid in that the activists travel between them, their titles change, and they disband and reorganize in the face of victories and defeats. The activists I work with face ongoing repression that impacts their ability to speak freely about their involvement. I am intentionally vague in places to protect those individuals whom I respect, and whom I have made a commitment to protect in this work. The degree to which their fluidity is public and transparent varies, and thus it is not always annotated in the text here. As I move through the AELM, I am keenly aware that the roadmap I use today may not be the roadmap for tomorrow. It is in this vein that my ethnography is distinct, leaving no breadcrumbs behind for others to follow.

THE SPECTACULAR RELATIONSHIP BETWEEN REPRESSION AND RESISTANCE

The book is divided into three segments: constructing the "ecoterrorist," direct action and performativity, and political repression. The book concludes with a discussion about the ways in which these segments weave together, with a call to action for activist academics.

Constructing the Ecoterrorist

Chapter 1 provides a framework to understand the ways in which ecoterrorism is constructed during the George W. Bush presidency. Specifically, this chapter outlines the structural overlay between neoliberalism and capitalism to create a distinct type of sovereignty: corporate sovereignty. The public tragedy of 9/11 provided a strategic moment for corporate-government ties to proliferate terrorism rhetoric. In this chapter, I disassemble the temporal space in which ecoterrorist assemblages were made visible.[24] By conflating citizenship with conspicuous animal consumption, the violent commodification of other species is erased from public discourse. In its place, the rhetoric of the ecoterrorist assumes a terroristic nature to ecological and animal liberation. The relationship between tragedy and opportunity was clearly articulated by Naomi Klein in her 2007 publication, *The Shock Doctrine*. In order to understand the creative potential of direct action, and the mechanisms of repression activists face, this era of terrorist-mongering and vanguard legislation must be unpacked. As the chapter alludes, this particular construction of the ecoterrorist was at its height throughout the first decade of the 2000s. The rhetoric built on previous fear-mon-gering promulgated by conservatives such as Ron Arnold, who in 1983 coined the term "ecoterrorism," describing it as a "crime committed to save nature" (Sorenson 2016). The effective journalist coverage of Green Scare cases, combined with the mainstreaming of anti-factory farm sentiment in the US, took some of the wind out of the sails of "eco-terrorism" by the time Barack Obama took office in 2008. WDC-based journalist Will Potter founded Green is the New Red to centralize and publicize Green Scare cases. Additionally, the us/them rhetoric that so neatly aligned with ecoterrorist/good protestor under George W. Bush was abandoned. The chapter concludes with the ways in which this terrorist assemblage was resumed, and rearticulated, by Donald Trump during his presidency.

Into the Field

The work of chapter 2 is to incorporate the ethnographic fieldwork with the theoretical framework laid out. The chapter begins with a detailed discussion of what direct action is, and how the AELM incorporates it. I participated in the End Captivity Now campaign for several years, until the collective announced they were dissolving the campaign due to legal pressure. Despite having dynamic, amazing activists engaged in the campaign, the campaign itself was utterly non-distinct from many of the campaigns I have worked with. The campaign made visible just how prescribed direct action protests in North America are. The chap-ter walks through the ethnographic complexities of travelling to and between, acclimating within, and understanding distinct activist com-munities within the AELM. Specifically, I nuance each of these social pro-cesses through a particular lens, identity, and experience.

In chapter 3, I build on the work of performance theorist Erving Goffman and social theorist Guy Debord. Their work is paramount to conceptualizing the ways we [dis]engage with performativity and spec-tacle. Using Duncombe's eloquent application of Debord, I am partic-ularly interesting in examining the rhetorical functions of direct action as spectacle. After spending years engaging in various forms of political theatre, and suddenly feeling conflicted by the contradictory nature of critiquing yet performing neoliberalism, I used Duncombe – a scholar who had expanded the notion of the spectacle – to look differently at these protests. I revisit these demonstrations to ask, "How can spectacle be used for good?" If the spectacle is meant to alienate ourselves from everyday life, and the presentations of ourselves become a fragmentation of who we are, then how can spectacular direct action be something to celebrate? I turn to queer performance theorists to address this question through the concept of play. The complexities of political theatre are teased out through a queer analysis of playfulness. With the help of rich ethnographic notes, the tension between mourning, joy, confrontation, respectability politics, and so on are made visible. The revolutionary potential of direct action as a playful spectacle is made possible, in some ways, through the obvious repression the AELM faces.

Chapter 4 examines the ways in which the state represses eco-activists in the forms of both monarchical and disciplinary punishment. Through a contemporary (re)reading of Michel Foucault's concept of power and punishment, revisiting Louis Althusser's concept of inter-pellation, I look back through Green Scare tactics. Specifically, I looked to federal investigations and surveillance, public trials and sentencing, as well as legislation that targets leftist activism. Although the AETA represents a particularly obvious type of punishment, surveillance pro-duces docile bodies in a different way. The prevalence of infiltrators and informants in the AELM has fostered a palpable need for security culture. Additionally, the strategy, a legacy from COINTELPRO, engages in "bad jacketing," which has reinforced a toxic environment for a movement to address existing sexual assault from within. In this chapter, I closely examine the ways in which the state disciplines the eco-activist.

Chapter 5, in conversation with chapter 4, takes a dialectical approach to political repression. Whereas the previous chapter illustrates how the state uses coercive, violent tactics to disrupt and dismantle the AELM, this chapter points to the powerful ways that activists talk back. Not only is the direct action itself a form of punishment, but the sophisti-cated ways in which anarchists foster security culture is further refusal to subject to the interpellation as the ecoterrorist.

Each chapter advances a critical engagement with eco-activist direct action, state repression, and the performative ways in which activ-ists resist. The book establishes a necessary praxis between anthro-pological discourses of power, activism, and the use of digital media to reimagine the potentiality for revolution in our physical realities. Anthropological literature on social movements emphasizes political positionality within normative party categories such as: republican, democrat, libertarian, moderate, conservative, and liberal (Hodges 2011). This book adopted a queer understanding of direct action and activist identity that takes into account how activists negotiate tactics, strategies, and political positionality.[25] Queer, as both a concept and framework, provides a productive epistemology to examine the ways in which activists both destabilize and rearticulate the state's repressive paradigm of good versus bad through performance. Specifically:

> Eve Sedgwick's recent reflection on queer performativity ask us not only to consider how a certain theory of speech acts applies to queer practices, but how it is that "queering" persists as a defining moment of performativity ... The performative is thus one domain in which power acts as a discourse ... The term "queer" emerges as an inter-pellation that raises the question of the status of force and oppo-sition, of stability and variability, *within* performativity. The term "queer" has operated as one linguistic practice whose purpose has been the shaming of the subject it names or, rather, the producing of a subject *through* that shaming interpellation. (Butler 1993, 571)

The deployment of queer as a liberal binary of assimilation and trans-gression, however, has also called into question the contradictions and complicities that warrant reflection (Puar 2007, 24). The potentiality of a queer inquiry is expanded through reflexivity and the creative reartic-ulation of what constitutes "assimilation" and "transgression."

Queering the Activist

Queer theory emerged through political activism, and was in response to the constant conflation and naturalization of sexuality and gender when discussed by feminists (Voss 2000, 184). Sexuality studies, as a separate dis-cipline, was emerging by the 1990s, with the foundational texts including Eve Sedgwick's *Epistemology of the Closet* (1990), Judith Butler's *Gender Trouble* (1990) and *Bodies that Matter* (1993), Teresa de Lauretis, and later, the many works of Jack Halberstam.[26] Despite the contentious evolu-tion of both the activist and academic deployment of queer in the academy, the term powerfully connotes questioning, challenging, and disrupting nor-mative discursive practices. Anthropologist Sara Ahmed situates "the per-verse" as a useful starting point for queer theorists, "for thinking about the 'disorientations' of queer, and how it can contest not only heteronorma-tive assumptions, but also social conventions and orthodoxies in general" (Ahmed 2006, 78). This destabilization of normative categories that queer-ing has been utilized to accomplish by postmodern and poststructuralist theorists challenges normativity that lies in "creating an always-contested and re-negotiated group identity based on difference from the norm – in other words, a postmodern version of identity politics" (Voss 2000, 184).

Queer theorists posit that because of the destabilization of normativity that is not exclusive to sexuality or gender, the theory is accessible across disciplines and global spaces. Specifically, there has been an emergence of activists and scholars that are engaged in various projects of destabilization in the AELM. There has been a dramatic increase in the number of available conferences, activist convergences, academic publications, zines and leaflets, and other-than-human animal sanctuaries that in one way or another connect themselves to the political project of queering the boundaries of species.[27] I served as a guest editor for the *Journal for Critical Animal Studies* and published their first journal issue dedicated to queer theory and activism. The introductory essay provides a snapshot of contemporary attempts to queer, rearticulate, and reimagine through acts that destabilize the boundaries of species:

> It is inherently queer to disrupt the normative tropes of hierarchy that naturalize speciesism. Or is it? How queer is critical animal studies? If speciesism is the normative ideology, then anti-speciesist thought functions as a queer act within academia. Although a great deal has been written on queer thought and critical animal studies, these discussions primarily exist in isolation from one another. Thus, we, as critical animal studies scholars, should ask ourselves how critical thought itself is intercepted, co-opted, re-appropriated, and constrained to fit within a single-politic agenda. Further, we must interrogate the ways in which we are alienated from our colleagues and insurrectionary comrades who contribute to queer thought. (Grubbs 2012a, 4)

Throughout the book, I reassert the premise that not only is it inherently queer to challenge the species boundary of human and animal, it is also a queer project for eco-activists to engage in confrontational direct action as a disidentification from the state's acts of interpellation.

Queering Direct Action through Political Theatre

This book contextualizes the use of political theatre and play within history of subversion through exaggeration in drag performance as a queer mode of disidentification (Conquergood 2002; Goffman 1959; Muñoz 2009; Taylor 2003). Activists engage in confrontational direct action, such as home demonstrations and vigils, to queer the paradigm of good versus bad protestor and to create disidentificatory thoughts through the protest as a spectacle.[28] Guy Debord of the Situationist International famously critiques "the spectacle," arguing that authentic social life has been replaced by mediated representation (Debord 1967). We no longer relate as humans, but as commodities that are filtered, or mediated, through the confluence of capitalism, advanced technologies, and mass media. As Debord states, "the tangible world is replaced by a selection of images which exist above it, and which simultaneously impose themselves as the tangible par excellence"; the spectacle "is not a collection of images, but a social relationship among people, mediated by images" (Debord 1967, 36, 74). Today, the proliferation of digital activism (sharing an article or sending a formal complaint through email) is one example where the mediated representation can impede physical, confrontational direct action. Although Debord's critique of spectacle predated the ways in which technology would permeate our everyday lives, they can certainly be applied. Thus, one would ask, if spectacle functions as a way to alienate ourselves from ourselves, how can this be celebrated as something that can be used for good? This tension is not resolved in the book, but is rather teased out and rearticulated through more contemporary readings of Debord.

The performative nature of direct action creates a spectacle that in turn produces what Kenneth Burke refers to as terministic screens within Irving Goffman's metaphor of theatre. Relying on the metaphor of a photograph to illustrate his concept of terministic screens, Burke explains: "When I speak of 'terministic screens,' I have particularly in mind some photographs I once saw. They were different photographs of the same objects, the difference being that they were made with different color filters. Here something so 'factual' as a photograph revealed notable distinctions in texture, and even in form, depending upon which color filter was used for the documentary description of the event being recorded" (1966, 45). Terministic screens are comprised of a set of symbols that create a screen or framework through which the world makes sense. Burke adds: "Not only does the nature of our terms affect the nature of our observations, in the sense that the terms direct the attention to one field rather than another. Also, many of the "observations" are built on implications of the particular terminology in terms of which the observations are made ... much that we take as observations about "reality" may be but the spinning out of possibilities implicit in our particular choice of terms" (Burke 1969, 49).

Speciesism itself, for example, is naturalized through ISA's and represented as spectacle through metaphor. The presentation of the human-over-animal hierarchy is depicted in movies, songs, commercials, billboards, political metaphors, and everyday sayings and practices. These representations (or screens) maintain and perpetuate both the idea and practice of exploiting animals for human use. In this sense, then, many humans relate to nonhuman animals as commodities, as mere representations of actual sentient creatures that have lives and existences of their own.

However, despite Debord's persuasive critique of mediated society, the spectacle can be appropriated for positive and profound social change. According to Duncombe, media technologies are here to stay. Rather than shunning such technologies, activists must learn to critically appropriate those technologies in the service of progressive causes and liberatory practices. Media technologies not only are imprinted in daily existence, they also contain powerful tools for subversion. Duncombe agrees that the overarching, dehumanizing spectacle described by Debord must be critiqued and overturned. However, Duncombe also argues that there are liberatory elements within the spectacle. Learning to tease out those elements can enable activists to disidentify, to create an alternative spectacle – one that teaches people to be reflective, ethical, conscientious, and active creators rather than passive consumers. For example, despite a primitivist resistance to technologies in the AELM by anarcho-syndicalists, activists, more broadly, have critically appropriated those technologies in the service of progressive causes and liberatory practices. Potter launched a Kickstarter campaign in response to repressive legislation in six states that made it illegal to take photographs or video footage inside agri-vivisection industries (Potter 2014). Potter proposed purchasing drones to capture aerial footage of these industries as a way to reappropriate the technology primarily used within a context of state violence. It is within Duncombe's framework that eco-activists employ spectacular direct action strategies.

The book addresses the growing gap between anthropological discourses regarding political theatre, theoretical critiques of neoliberalism and capitalism as they connect to speciesism, and the specific use of direct action in the AELM. Although there are significant contributions within the field of anthropology to these areas separately, no discourse weaves these areas together cohesively. Animal and earth liberation activists are actively engaging with anthropological theories power and resistance, yet they remain underrepresented in the literature. Additionally, under the Trump administration, the US has seen a dramatic increase in the prevalence of anti-anarchist, anti-Antifa rhetoric that marginalize eco-activist activists within broader the broader animal and advocacy movements. Thus, it is within the interest of producing relevant, contemporary critical scholarship that we examine the ways in which terrorism rhetoric is deployed to repress dissent, and how those who are dissenting fight back in creating ways.

My partner and I were sitting on the couch, about to dive into an old episode of *The Office*, when I asked him something about his pending court date. He was one of the 234 people arrested on 20 January 2017, after being kettled in a crowded intersection during an anti-inaugural demonstration.[29] After I asked my question, Michael, my partner, looked at me with concern. He signalled for us to go in the other room to speak and pointed to our cell phones. We turned our phones off and went in the kitchen. Our lives had become a series of choppy, tense conversations that typically ended with more confusion than clarity. We spoke in code around our children, relying on creative analogies and word substitutions to keep them in the dark about the impending trial. We made up stories about why he needed to go out of town for court proceedings, and why he needed to get a new phone after his was seized when taken into custody. Here we were, sitting by ourselves in the family room, and I struggled to formulate my question in a way that solicited a minimalist answer. In the intimate spaces of our home, surveillance felt omnipresent, along with the looming threat of a grand jury. I have so many questions, so many emotions, that have still to manifest in the right words to vocalize. And yet, I had no trouble articulating political repression, disciplinary punishment, and direct action when I began working on this manuscript several years ago. This book is an amalgamation of the perplexing ways that the political becomes the personal, and the personal becomes the political under the suffocating mechanisms of repression. In turn, the book is infused with the beautiful, creative ways that these mechanisms are undermined and structurally dismantled.

Neoliberal Capitalism and the Construction of Ecoterrorism

Fencing was ripped down and nearly 2,000 mink were released allowing them to clamor toward freedom. Both farms sat near the edges of mostly undeveloped public lands, allowing plenty of habitat for the newly freed native predators. Cage after cage, row after row, shed after shed, latches were opened and nesting boxes removed allowing the mink to escape to their rightful home. They spaced out the releases in order to disperse the noise from disturbed mink away from a singular location. The surreal and beautiful moment where the mink explored in the moonlight will be carried in the hearts of those that gazed upon them for a lifetime. The approving chorus from coyotes in the nearby hills still echo in their ears. Days later, these activists found themselves before another sprawling fur farm complex. Watching for nearly an hour to be sure there was no movement from within the compound, they sat patiently, preparing to penetrate the property and rip down another fence... Beneath a bright moon, nearly full and neon pink behind the haze from the massive nearby wildfires, they proceeded to the perimeter. Cutting vertically though the chain link from top to bottom in two places 20' apart, they prepared the fence to be felled by just a few quick snips along the top when the time came... Caging the wild is a heinous offense against life – against freedom. Every cage is worth emptying, and to begin this work is not difficult... These activists lamented at one point that this activity wasn't better training for assailing human prisons, too, but know any action can sharpen skills useful for confronting every industry.

(Anonymous K 2020)

What about animals slaughtered for our consumption? Who among us would be able to continue eating pork chops after visiting a factory farm in which pigs are half-blind and cannot even properly walk, but are just fattened to be killed? And what about, say, torture and suffering of millions we know about, but choose to ignore? Imagine the effect of having to watch a snuff movie portraying what goes on thousands of times a day around the world: brutal acts of torture, the picking out of eyes, the crushing of testicles – the list cannot bear recounting. Would the watcher be able to continue going on as usual? Yes, but only if he or she were able somehow to forget – in an act which suspended symbolic efficiency – what had been witnessed. This forgetting entails a gesture of what is called fetishist disavowal: "I know it, but I don't want to know that I know, so I don't know." I know it, but I refuse to fully assume the conse-quences of this knowledge, so that I can continue acting as if I don't know it.

(Žižek 2012, 3)

The political economy of animal-and-ecology use industries has been the subject of eco-activist critiques over the last century. The chapter addresses the question of what the political economy of animal-and-ecol-ogy use industries is, and how is leftist resistance interpellated within the ideological, social, and economic [super-]structures of the state.[1] In particular, the fusing of international corporations and geopolitical enti-ties through globalization has created a moving, intangible target. Yet, in the wake of massive globalization that veils individual accountabil-ity, the neoliberal rhetoric of individual [citizen] social reasonability is pervasive within the rhetoric of the good protestor that identifies with participatory democracy as the primary means of dissent.[2] The contra-dictory logic fits into the larger theoretical aim of this book to examine the performativity of power that enables the state to appear rational and fair, while simultaneously constructing eco-activists as irrational, unfair eco-terrorists. The increased occurrence of AELM direct action from the late 1990s throughout the early 2000s sparked a rhetorical shift in how eco-activists were constructed.[3] This era of repression, referred to as the Green Scare, "includes surveillance, infiltration, intimidation, and imprisonment" (Pellow 2014, 167). Although I take up the tactics of political repression during the Green Scare in subsequent chapters, it is of note that the construction of the ecoterrorist was a necessary pre-cursor for those disciplinary measures to become naturalized. Eco-critic Lawrence Buell historicized the overlapping definition of ecoterrorism and terrorism. According to Buell, 9/11 was not the watershed moment for ecoterrorism. Nevertheless, Buell does contend:

To be sure, 9/11 did raise the public, eco-paranoia level, all across the political spectrum- most immediately, or obvious reasons in the United States. It increased the likelihood of cases like the harass-ment under the swiftly enacted Patriot Act by the US government's domestic surveillance organization, the FBI … In the history of ecoterror rhetoric and anxiety, then, 9/11 marked an intensification but not a major turning point, much less an inception point. That, in turn, should prompt one to ask: What is the deeper cultural logic at work here? … It made for swaggering on the national scene by such right-wing politicians as Oklahoma Senator James Inhofe, who as chair of the Committee on Environment and Public Works before the transfer of power to the Democratic party after the election of 2006, pressed for tightened FBI oversight over earth and animal liberation-ists, whom he went so far as to call "the number 1 domestic terror concern, [more so than] white supremacists, militias, or anti-abortion groups" (18 May 2005 statement). That was an extraordinary statement indeed for a politician from the state whose capital city had been, not long before, the site of by far the most horrific act of (far-right) terrorism ever carried out by an American citizen.[4]

The term ecoterrorism was not widely used or promulgated by the US government prior to 9/11, and the FBI adapted their loose definition of terrorism (more broadly) and ecoterrorism (specifically) to encompass "the use or threatened use of violence of a criminal nature against inno-cent victims or property by an environmentally-oriented sub-national group for environmental-political reasons" (Buell 2009, 153). The con-cept of moral madness again becomes relevant here. What was and was not constructed as terroristic speaks to, as Buell points out, the cultural context that legitimizes specific types of violence on specific bodies.[5]

TERRORISM AS A RHETORICAL DEVICE AND MATERIAL REALITY

The narratives used to describe, define, and reappropriate the events of 9/11 have shaped anthropological discourses. Scholars have interrogated the construction of terrorism, Islamophobia, and the repression of dis-sent in the United States. The "Global War on Terror" narrative crafted and promulgated by President George W. Bush reshaped vulnerability into aggression as the US went from "*victim* of terrorists" to "*hunter* of terrorists" (Hodges 2011, 88). This narrative naturalized a shift in sovereignty that led to the establishment of counterterrorism agencies. As the hunter of terrorists in the "War on Terror," the US government expanded the power and protection of counterterrorism agencies. By utilizing and manipulating 9/11 as disaster capitalism, the state effec-tively conflated civil duty with the suspension of constitutional freedoms such as free speech (Klein 2007). This shift was particularly relevant to the AELM because the government simultaneously constructed them as a terrorist threat. According to this logic, activists, not geopolitics or technology, were responsible for the crisis of capitalism.[6] Graeber historicizes contemporary political repression within a context of violence against the anti-globalization movement in 1999 (Graeber 2009b). Scholar David Price foreshadows this history, focusing on the use of surveillance that targeted and marginalized anthropologists sympathetic to Marxism, communism, and socialism. Price argues that the government played off of post-war vulnerabilities, such as a struggling economy and health epidemics, to naturalize the invasive forms of surveillance during McCarthyism that targeted academics (Price 2004).

Anthropologist Adrienne Pine elaborates on how restrictive laws redefine terrorist as "somebody who opposes the state ... paving the way to criminalize dissent, to criminalize resistance, to criminalize the right to freedom of speech and freedom of assembly in Honduras" (Fernandez 2011). Scheper-Hughes and Bourgois examine the global use of state-sanctioned violence through institutionalized torture abroad to manufacture consent (Scheper-Hughes and Bourgois 2003). Domestically, the US has relied on the carceral system to disproportionately punish political prisoners with tactics like solitary confinement. Although political repression had been a widely researched topic in anthropology prior to 9/11, in 2001 the rhetoric rapidly changed to centre around the construction of terrorism. Over the last twenty years, the rhetoric of terrorism has seeped into popular culture, domestic legislation, and international relations.

Construction of "Terrorism"

Prior to the events of 9/11, "terrorism" was less commonly used in government propaganda nor included in academic discourses (Jackson et al. 2011, 1–5). The events ushered in media and government narratives that crafted the binary of *victim/terrorist* (Gershkoff and Kushner 2005, 525). The binary further established an "us" [white] and "them" [non-white] dichotomy (Ahmed 2003, 37). The public was bombarded with hyperbolic language defending the future US engagement in an offensive war against the omnipresent "terrorists" (Gershkoff and Kushner 2005, 527). Within the media, the term terrorism was intentionally vague and was undefined within the parameters of its use after 9/11(Hodges 2011, 39). Bruce Hoffman, terrorism studies scholar, insists that government agencies define and deploy the term "terrorism" in convenient but inconsistent ways (Hoffman 2006, 32). The television programming produced by the US media consistently used the word "terrorist" while displaying

images of Arabs and Muslims in the subsequent days (Ahmed 2003, 24).
Although international political bodies invoke the term terrorism, there
lacks a widely accepted definition that demarcates what it is, and it is
not. The rhetoric of terrorism relies on this ambiguity and has been
manipulated by the agendas of statecraft (Chomsky 2002, 155). The
rallying cries for war that echoed after 9/11 demanded increased milita-
rism. This construction of terrorism, however, is intentionally malleable
enough to be applied to any persons challenging the state.

The government passed the 2001 Patriot Act, which conflated civic
duty with the sacrifice of civil liberties (Potter 2011; Esposito and Kalin
2011, 30). Despite widespread support at that time, the Patriot Act legally
stripped citizens of their right to privacy. Similar to Carlos Decena's discussion of the hegemonic confessions from the good sexual citizen, the
public was given instructions as to how to respond to 9/11 in the US
(2008, 407). The good US citizen was to perform patriotism through their
complicity. The propaganda from the government and media insisted that
the sacrifice of civil liberties would restore safety from "terrorists." The
good US citizen would comply with increased travel restrictions, racial
and ethnic profiling, and increased surveillance. In addition, patriotism
was conflated with consumerism, as demonstrated by President George
W. Bush's speech that encouraged citizens to support capitalist enterprises
(Skocpol 2002, 539). The American public was encouraged to engage in
air travel, and there was an increase in the purchasing and flying of the
US flag (Ahmed 2003, 32). The federal government continued the offensive campaign in 2003 by creating the Department of Homeland Security
(DHS), an entity specifically designed to "prevent terrorist attacks; prevent
the unauthorized acquisition, importation, movement, or use of chemical,
biological, radiological, and nuclear materials and capabilities within the
United States; and reduce the vulnerability of critical infrastructure and
key resources, essential leadership, and major events to terrorist attacks
and other hazards" (Department of Homeland Security 2012).

The language used to define the agenda of the DHS, however, relies
on the vague-yet-powerful rhetoric of terrorism. The media bombarded
viewers with images of Al-Qaeda operatives and questioned whether
Islam was a "terrorist religion" (Esposito and Kalin 2011, xxxi). The
construction of the "terrorist" relied on racist and xenophobic views
toward Muslims. It remained unclear who the "terrorists" were, and
what appropriate responses should be taken to deal with "them." The
DHS was established to monitor the privacies that had been hegemonically chiselled away by the Patriot Act. Again, through disaster capitalism, the US government was able naturalize increased security, state

violence, and a repressive agenda by promulgating the idea that there was an ever-looming *terrorist* (Klein 2000, 238). The construction of *terrorism* utilized xenophobic language that established an us/them binary targeting Muslims and those of Arab-descent (Hodges 2011, 47). The blatant discrimination played off of sensationalist media and government narratives about "safety" and "security." The changing political climate increased restrictions on free speech and dissent.

The political climate in the US has continued to evolve over the last two decades. As the "Global War on Terror" continued into the Barack Obama administration, President Obama expanded the scope of the "Global War on Terror" largely through use of "unmanned aerial vehicles" (UAV). In typical democratic way, President Obama continued the same logic to fight Jihadi terrorism, but with less bombastic bigotry and xenophobia. The war was expanded through a drone campaign in East Africa, but without the sabre-rattling that President Bush had leaned on. President Obama, most notably during this time, insisted that counterterrorism efforts focus on homegrown violent extremists. Under President Obama, the notion of an ominous threat (us/them) became secondary to a domestic agenda focused on expanding health care and responding to climate change. Although President Obama was not sympathetic to animal or earth liberation, he bolstered the importance of the "good protestor." The arc between President Obama's term and President Trump's term can be best illustrated in the handling of the Standing Rock Sioux encampment.[7]

The 2016 presidential campaign of Donald Trump was predicated on governmental policies that would bolster corporate interests. Then-candidate Trump celebrated his inexperience in politics and claimed he would "drain the swamp" and combat the "Deep State." He had a career based on exploiting communities, gentrifying-then-abandoning areas with failing casinos and hotels and mocking any compassion or concern with the environment. Once elected, President Trump rolled back environmental protections, defunded departments within the Environmental Protection Agency, and continued to advocate the return to coal mining. President Trump has positioned himself as the anti-politician-politician. He has simultaneously advocated for less governmental regulation of business, a defunding of federal government agencies, *and*, ironically, a fascistic centralization of federal powers under the president. He signals to both fascists and white nationalists, while trying to hang on to the support of "Don't tread on my rights" Republicans. He is unapologetically misogynist, racist, and xenophobic. The us/them rhetoric he promotes is explicitly tied to white/non-white, American/non-American nationalism.

The fascist creep under Trump has become a prominent platform for left-leaning social movements. In response to the increased anti-racist and anti-fascist organizing in the US prompted by the murder of George Floyd by the Minneapolis Police in May 2020, President Trump's rhetoric has had a sharp shift focused on the broadly used application and bombastic targeting of "Antifa."

The Trump administration has focused almost exclusively on expanding the rhetoric of terrorism to subsume the "radical left" and "anarchists." A quick read of President Trump's Twitter, @realdonaldtrump, shows how he recurringly used "ANARCHIST & THUGS" and "LAW & ORDER," oftentimes in contrast to one another in the same tweet. Although President Trump's rhetoric did not prioritize the AELM like previous administrations had done, his conflation of "anarchist" with "terrorist" illustrates the ideological evolution of vilifying anarchist direct action. The anarchistic politic of many activists within the AELM means that in addition to resisting systems of domination like fascism, capitalism and hierarchy, they also denounce speciesism. The flexibility of terrorism rhetoric from presidents Bush to Obama to Trump highlights the temporal nature of Puar's concept of terrorist assemblages.

Neoliberalism

The contemporary moment is defined by key characteristics that have been exacerbated by globalized capitalism. These characteristics facilitate a corporate environment that separates neoliberalism with from the political ideology of liberalism articulated by Thomas Hobbes and John Locke. Further, globalization has distanced the current economic and political reality from the liberalism promulgated in the years following the First World War by President Franklin D. Roosevelt. Neoliberal capitalism facilitates the reconceptualization of sovereignty to include corporations as a global power with state protection.

As discussed in chapter 1, the US government maintains a [neoliberal] performance of democracy, while still allowing corporations to operate as the exception through "corporate sovereignty" (Ong 2006, 7). Corporate sovereignty facilitates the exceptional status of capitalist entities, specifically animal-and-ecology use industries, by governmental deregulations while simultaneously hyper-regulating those who challenge said capitalist entities (Lovitz 2010, 38). This hyper-regulation is exercised through the surveillance, harassment, arrest, and subsequent prosecution of activists engaging in direct action against such industries. Speciesist capitalism (or capitalism that relies on the exploitation of animal bodies) not only permits violence against other-than-human animals, it also permits violence against human animals that are resolved to recapitulate animal-and-ecology use industries. The investigations, prosecution, and sentencing of eco-activists like Eric McDavid, Marius Mason, Daniel McGowan, Walter Bond, and other eco-activists, relied on rhetoric that conflated activism and terrorism and affirmed the sovereignty of animal-and-ecology use.

There is growing literature on the neoliberal reshaping of global capitalism and the nepotistic overlap between government and corporate entities.[8] The decentralization of corporations negates accountability by creating an elusive web of interconnected international entities. With the increasing prevalence of lobby groups and front organizations, as well as multinational conglomerates, the task of corporate-mapping and identifying a singular target has become increasingly difficult (Graeber 2009b, xii). The challenge, then, is identifying a central site, or government, that can be held accountable for monitoring "the market."[9] Globalization has increased that terrain through the global borders that place further restrictions of *what* laws can apply to *whom* in a global marketplace. The challenge for those hoping to dismantle this oppressive reality relies on deconstructing the illusive web of corporate-state alliances that decentralize the deregulated industries. The identified elements highlight the exploitative nature of neoliberalism and how it is hegemonically reinscribed in social relations.

Neoliberalism is loosely defined within a tangible framework of ten characteristics: the decentralization of state accountability, state/private sector alliances, ambiguity and uncertainty of policing bodies, citizenship defined through a consumerism/client model, David Harvey's concept of accumulation by dispossession, Jürgen Habermas's concept of civil society, transnational forms of governance, overlap of sovereignty, deregulation of industries, and the operating model of "best practices" that insists reality is quantifiable (Adamson 1983; Harvey 2007; Habermas 1984). The decentralized and deregulated state is driven by the global market, which is controlled by elite powerholders (Leap 2011). Habermas theorized that a necessary distinction must be made between the private sector plus government, on the one hand, and corporate spheres, on the other, in order to facilitate public engagement and protections of speech. As neoliberalism erodes the divisions between corporate/private sector and government, the public engagement of civil society becomes undermined. The ways in which government is intertwined with corporate/private sector are veiled by an amorphous web of authority. It is difficult to identify a central site of government that can be held accountable for

monitoring "the market," let alone a singular regulatory body responsible for a single function within the market (Graeber 2009b, 81). The
abundance of regulatory groups and committees has meant the obfuscation of actual regulation and accountability.

The economic wealth gap between the owning class [read: bourgeois]
is exacerbated from the labor class [read: proletariat] through processes
of privatization, financialization, manufacturing of crisis, and redistri-
bution through statecraft. This gap is made visible by dispossession of
resources, including geographical, industrial, and ecological (Harvey
2004; 2005; 2007). Harvey provides a contemporary application and
expansion of Karl Marx's theory of capital accumulation, specifically
the notion of "original" or "primitive accumulation" that fractures the
contradictions and disillusions of capitalism and predatory credit structures. Neoliberalism itself, however, cannot sufficiently describe the ways
in which agricultural industries operate within such significant spaces of
exceptionality within regulatory rhetoric (Agamben 1998; 2005). In other
words, how can we unravel the ways in which global capitalism protects
agricultural industries? Globalization is one of the processes in the manipulation of crisis to address the spatio-temporal "fix," as Harvey explains:

> capital necessarily creates a physical landscape in its own image at
> one point in time only to have to destroy it at some later point in
> time as it pursues geographical expansions and temporal displace-
> ments as solutions to the crises of overaccumulation to which it is
> regularly prone. Thus, is the history of creative destruction (with
> all manner of deleterious social and environmental consequences)
> written into the evolution of the physical and social landscape of
> capitalism ... Another series of contradictions arises within the
> dynamics of spatio-temporal transformations more generally. If the
> surpluses of capital and labour power exist within a given territory
> (such as a nation state) and cannot be absorbed internally (either by
> geographical adjustments or social expenditures) then they must be
> sent elsewhere to find a fresh terrain for their profitable realization if
> they are not to be devalued. (Harvey 2004, 66)

One example is how the animal-and-ecology use industries in the
United States negate environmental regulations and labour protections
under the FARM Bill. In 2018, the Environmental Protection Agency
(EPA) proposed legislation that would challenge how the FARM Bill
had facilitated farms moving Centralized Animal Feeding Operations
(CAFO) to avoid air emissions regulations (US EPA 2017; "USDA ERS

– Agriculture Improvement Act of 2018: Highlights and Implications" n.d.; Wheeler n.d.). Animal-based farms, seed patenting and genetically modified crops, animal breeding, and the animal-skin trade have all shifted operations within a globalized marketplace, and this has had irreparable impacts on populations (Shiva 2005). In order to naturalize ecological destruction and hunger, despite excess in the global West, agricultural industries have relied on the manipulation of crisis. Within the context of neoliberal scholars interrogating the contemporary manifestations of capitalism, Harvey relies on Luxemburg's apt foreshadowing of the credit crisis:

> Credit, though shareholding, combines in one magnitude of capital a large number of individual capitals. It makes available to each capitalist the use of other capitalists' money – in the form of industrial credit ... Credit not only aggravates the crisis in its capacity as a dissembled means of exchange, it also helps to bring and extend the crisis by transforming all exchange into an extremely complex and artificial mechanism ... We see that credit, instead of being an instrument for the suppression or the attenuation of crises, is on the contrary a particularly mighty instrument for the formation of crises ... In short, credit reproduces all the fundamental antagonisms of the capitalist world. It accentuates that. It precipitates their development and thus pushes the capitalist world forward to its own destruction. (Luxemburg 1900, 12)

The credit crisis exacerbates the notion of corporate economic hardship, when in fact, federal bailouts are almost exclusively provided to corporations. Individual consumers were presented with the manipulation of the crisis that relied on predatory debt through credit (credit cards, loans, payday advance, and so on). In a similar vein, agricultural industries have co-constructed a crisis that relies on lack of regulation and oversight. The Trump presidential campaign in 2016 relied on a promise to bring back antiquated agricultural and mining industries. His revivalist slogan, "Make America Great Again," romanticizes a return to these industries. Trump assured communities that were once reliant on small farming operations and coal mining that he would that lift environmental regulations. The implication in his rhetoric was that it was protestors and regulations, not advanced technologies and globalization, that had created their obsolescence. The crisis relies on vilification of an "other," and in this case, interpellating the activists' disidentification as ecoterrorism.

Neoliberal Capitalism

Anthropologists have engaged state sovereignty as it pertains to various layers of governmentality (Dean 2009; Gupta 2012; Hansen and Stepputat 2001; Nugent 1997). In a series of books together, Michael Hardt and Antonio Negri theorize how imperialism functions within a modern context. One of the many brilliant, complicated points they raise is how the project of empire expansion has shifted from nation-states seizing land to the seizing of capital and flow (Hardt and Negri 2001). This neo-Marxist approach posits that power is concentrated and multiplied through the expansion of capitalism into oligarchies and international governing bodies such as the International Monetary Fund (IMF). The layers of governmentality can be understood through Althusser's ideological state apparatus, Gramsci's concept of hegemony, as well as through anthropological articulations of sovereignty. Neoliberal capitalism relies on hegemonic citizenship, specifically through consumers perpetuating corporate power through consumption. Althusser expanded on the work of Marx, but with an emphasis on Gramsci's concept, hegemony, through his Ideological State Apparatus (ISA) model that provides a structural processing in which ideology [read: power] is a negotiation that is reproduced within hegemonic social apparatuses (Althusser 1970). For Althusser, ideology is not epiphenomenal. It is a process; both reinforced and reified "upward" and "downward." It is the reproduction of the conditions and means of productions that Althusser focused on. Eco-activist Jeffrey Luers articulated the banality of consumption, "When I think about the people who are out there sitting in their SUVs and sitting in front of their TVs and just consuming, consuming, consuming, it seems to me that most of them aren't doing it because they are evil and trying to consciously destroy the earth. It's just that they're not thinking about how they're living" (Dicum 2006). The state enforces its sovereign power through different forms of the repressive state apparatus (consent is gained coercively upon threat of violence) whereas the ideological state apparatus is a more neutralized site of power.[10] Capitalist entities such as corporations are constructed through a rhetoric of personhood that not only facilitates hegemonic consumption; it also facilitates vanguard legislation that protects corporations from regulation.

Marx articulated the ways in which commodities are fetishized, and how the act of consumption itself is viscerally tied to how individuals understand themselves in relation to society. However, this commodity fetishism is taken further when the corporations themselves, regardless of economic, environmental, and structural violence they perpetuate, become the fetishized entity. When doctors, teachers, and religious leaders praise companies like Johnson & Johnson, Delta Airlines, and AstraZeneca for representing the American ideal, it implies that criticism of these companies is thus an attack on the American ideal. Thus, corporations become anthropomorphized, and vanguard legislation mirrors the language and logic of hate crime legislation (Lovitz 2010, 93). In doing so, corporations, particularly agricultural industries, are granted a type of sovereignty and de facto sovereignty that is reinforced through public participation in neoliberal and capitalist structures.

Sovereign power is the central, often unrecognized, underside of modern/liberal forms of codified/regulated government (Hansen and Stepputat 2006, 297). Broadly defined, sovereignty refers to the ruling power a group or government can possess over a geographical location or group. A type of legal dominion per se. Sovereign power is oftentimes performed on and through the body, most visibly during states of war, marginality, extreme conditions, and fragmentations (Dean 2009, 22). De facto sovereignty is the ability to kill, punish, and discipline with impunity. Agamben's idea of the dual body of the citizen – the body with rights as a participant in the greater political community, and simultaneously, the biological body, a life that can be stripped of symbolization and humanity and reduced to "bare life" by a sovereign power – makes clear that we need to theorize the relationship between power and one's bare life (Agamben 1998, 6). This point contributes to the de facto sovereignty to place certain activists under surveillance, in interrogation cells, and in solitary confinement within federal prisons.

Aiwa Ong, anthropologist, articulates how citizenship has changed within neoliberal capitalism from an emphasis on a person's geographical membership to a value of their skills in the market. Although the US government still maintains a neoliberal performance of democracy, corporations operate as the exception through "corporate sovereignty" (Ong 2006). The term corporate sovereignty refers to the exceptional status of capitalist entities awarded through the deregulation of industry and hyper-regulation of public scrutiny (Barkan 2013; Lovitz 2010, 38). Dara Lovitz, legal scholar, examines the absence of effective federal animal protection laws due to the animal-and-ecology use industries' lobby presence (Lovitz 2010, 38). The Animal Welfare Act (AWA) and Endangered Species Act create a continuum of exceptionality for animal-and-ecology use industries (McCoy 2007, 55). The laws utilize the neoliberal rhetoric of animal welfare and environmental stewardship while creating exceptions for highly profitable industries. For example, mice are excluded from the

AWA, despite the estimates that over 85 per cent of animals used in research are mice. This means that there are no welfare guidelines or codes of ethics when using mice in research. Research labs and factory farms exist within states of exceptionality. The global climate crisis is a clear indication that we need to rethink our relationship with ecologies and species. But, under the logic of corporate sovereignty, it would be terroristic to undermine or challenge these romanticized capitalist entities.

CONSTRUCTING THE ECOTERRORIST

Eco-activists do not identify with the blatant disregard animal-and-ecology use industries display for "safety" and "security" as they pertain to sustainability through deforestation, global patenting of seeds, and genetic manipulation of species used in farming and vivisection. Through direct action, the activists disidentify with the speciesism naturalized through neoliberal capitalism. This disidentification is a necessary move for environmentalists to engage with a more transformative politic (Parr 2014; 2017). In response, the federal government interpellated the activists' disidentification as ecoterrorism, claiming that agitators posed a threat to safety and security in similar ways to the terrorists of 9/11 (Potter 2011). The state did so by manipulating the vulnerable public post-9/11 to support a broad security agenda that included heightened surveillance of non-state actors and the introduction of repressive legislation targeting eco-activist activists. The contradiction of the rhetorical project of constructing the ecoterrorist is analyzed by data scientists with the Prosecution Project: "In 2004, John Lewis, the Deputy Assistant Director to the FBI, noted that the 'ALF and ELF have become the most active criminal extremist elements in the United States.' However ... from 1999 to 2004, animal liberation extremists make up less than 12 per cent of the total prosecutions of all socio-politically motivated crimes" (Chapekis and Moore 2021, 25). Although the ecoterrorist is a rhetorical fabrication, the label tapped into a cultural context of speciesism within neoliberal capitalism. The blatant (and veiled) use of surveillance and targeted legislation would not have been possible without the proliferation of terrorism rhetoric that conflated activism with a national security threat. Despite the state's retaliatory interpellation, eco-activists did not modify their philosophy or strategy to fit this framework of good versus bad protest(or), but rather they queered the dichotomous nature. When interpellated within these mechanisms of repression, activists chose not to identify as the good subject (Pêcheux 1982, 158). Activism that challenged the state and further challenged systems of privilege that statecraft depends upon (capitalism, globalization, and sovereignty) was transformed to distinguish the good protestor (or the patriotic consumer in this case) from the bad protestor, which is most evident in the construction of the ecoterrorist.

The establishment of the DHS institutionalized the rhetoric of terrorism and used broad strokes to define its purpose. The propaganda used to define the good US citizen was held to demarcate the beliefs and behaviours of the good protestor (Lovitz 2010, 114). The binary construction of the good protestor/bad protestor permeated during the reconfiguration of dissent in the US after 9/11 (Dunmire 2011, 40). The good protestor would financially contribute to mainstream advocacy charities such as the American Society for the Prevention of Cruelty to Animals (ASPCA) and Save the Rainforest. The good protestor would participate in green capitalism by purchasing items such as hybrid vehicles (Parr 2009, 20). The good protestor would willingly uphold capitalism and unquestionably support the surveillance measures by the government. The good protestor would certainly not challenge economic entities or disrupt commerce of any kind.

The bad protestor, however, called into question the reappropriation of terrorism rhetoric to describe dissent (Jackson et al. 2011, 2). The bad protestor continued to challenge capitalism and the ideologies that uphold it. The bad protestor would engage in direct actions that included property destruction rather than leafleting ballot issues. As the months passed following 9/11, it was clear that the line between the terrorist and the bad protestor was blurred to provide a retaliatory interpellation direct action through disidentification (Leader and Probst 2003; Hoffman 2006, 32). The deputy assistant director and top official in charge of domestic terrorism with the FBI, John Lewis, testified before the Senate Judiciary Committee in 2004 regarding the threats from domestic terrorists. In the address, Lewis described the AELM as the number one domestic terrorist threat facing the US (Lewis 2004). The philosophy of liberation and the strategies of direct action pose an effective challenge to the hegemony of speciesism and capitalism. The challenges are so threatening that eco-activists, the bad protestors, are interpellated by the state as ecoterrorists (Liddick 2006, 141). The US government reified the conflation of eco-activism with terrorist into law with the passage of the 2006 Animal Enterprise Terrorism Act.

Animal Enterprise Terrorism Act

The Animal Enterprise Terrorism Act (AETA) is a federal legislation that amended the Animal Enterprise Protection Act of 1992 (AEPA) to broaden its application and increase penalties. A much wider array of nonviolent forms of dissent could now be considered as both federal crime and terrorism. The act was authored with broad and general language that does not definitively explain the nature of "animal enterprise" or what "interfering with" such an enterprise means; everything from a sit-in to bombing a vivisection laboratory after removing the animals (and harming no humans) might be considered "interference" and thus terrorism. Such loose language specifically enhances the government's power through interpellation and greatly denies the civil exercise of the first amendment. The act redefined already state-recognized crimes as federal offenses and redefined them within the realm of "domestic terrorism." The AETA became the vehicle for the US Department of Justice to protect corporate sovereignty in response to the high-profile cases Operation Backfire and SHAC-7 (Potter 2008, 677–9). The AEPA already protected many animal industries and instituted a restitution provision that required activists to pay a targeted vivisector to cover costs associated with repeating an animal study that was interrupted or invalidated, or a farmer the cost of loss of food production.[11]

Lovitz interrogates the overlap between politicians that sponsored the act and agricultural industries.

> Consider the business ties of Representative Stenholm, who tirelessly pushed for the Farm Animals and Research Facilities Protection Act and then its amended version, the AEPA. Throughout his congressional career, the United States agricultural industries gave Stenholm more than $2.5 million in donations ... Stenholm's top two contributors were the American Farm Bureau and the National Cattleman's Beef Association. The Dairy Farmers of America and the United Egg Association also were among Stenholm's top ten contributors. Stenholm's third largest contributor was the American Medical Association (AMA). Other Sponsors of the AEPA had financial ties with animal exploitative industries. (Lovitz 2010, 51)

Lovitz provides a detailed account of the contributions as well as personal investments of politicians that leveraged their positions to pass the act. Unhappy with the number of prosecutions and applicability of the act, an amended version was introduced into Congress in November 2005. From 1992 to 2005, agricultural industries had experienced millions of dollars' worth of damage. The AEPA had the promise of reducing the number of attacks but did not deliver. Following on the rhetorical curtails of 9/11, the AETA relied on the hysteria surrounding terrorism.

One of the most notable distinctions between the AEPA and the AETA is the replacement of the word "protection" with "terrorism," that explicitly rearticulated animal and ecological activism as terrorism. Through the lens of terrorism, the AETA granted de facto sovereignty over a much wider range of nonviolent forms of dissent. The act broadened the definition of "animal enterprise" to include not only commercial, but also academic enterprises that use or sell animals or animal products. It also increased the existing penalties, including fines that are based on the amount of financial damage caused in addition to monetary restitution. Similar to the AEPA, the AETA was introduced and cosponsored by politicians with a blurred connection to agricultural industries. Senator Dianne Feinstein (D-CA) and Senator James Inhofe (R-OK) each had financial investments in the industries benefitting from the act, and in the House, Representatives Thomas Petri (R-WI) and Robert Scott (D-VA) cosponsored the AETA.

The insidious relationship between government, lobby groups and front organizations, and industry were glaring:

Feinstein's spouse, Richard Blum, is the chairman of the board of the CB Richard Ellis Group (CBRE), a large firm that deals in commercial real estate and caters to enterprises that conduct vivisection on nonhuman animals. CBRE proclaims that it is "dedicated to providing the life sciences industry with the highest level of real estate services," as the company, "enhance[s] profitability" of the biotechnology, medical-device, pharmaceutical, and related industries. CBRE represents hundreds of such clients who engage in vivisection including American Pharmaceutical Partners, AstraZeneca, Bayer Pharmaceuticals, Chiron, DuPont, Eli Lilly and Company, Johnson and Johnson, Merck, Novartis, Pfizer, Schering Ploud, and Wyeth. Inhofe, who has called global warming "the greatest hoax perpetrated on the American people," owns approximately $250,000 in energy-related businesses, including oil and gas companies. The oil and gas industry have contributed over $1,223,723 to his campaign ... The Nuclear Energy Institute has contributed over $65,000 to Inhofe, seeking his support for a nuclear waste dump at Yucca Mountain ... Inhofe's largest contributor, Koch Industries, owns companies involved in chemical processing and forestry projects. In 2004, Inhofe was named "Legislator of the Year" by the National Association of Chemical Distributors ... Tom Petri's website proudly declares his close ties to Wisconsin "animal agriculture" ... Petri heads the Badger Fund, a political action committee whose top contributor is American Foods Group, which owns slaughter facilities. (Lovitz 2010, 85–7)

Representative F. James Sensenbrenner (R-WI) chaired the committee on the judiciary that oversaw the 2006 hearing. His financial connections in 2006 were through his ownership of stocks in bonds with pharmaceutical companies including Abbot Laboratories, Inc. (over $500,000), Pfizer (over $600,000), and Merci & Co. ($1.3 million) (Lovitz 2010, 85–7).

The AETA was voted through the Senate with unanimous support; thus, a procedure was used to expedite the passage of such "non-controversial bills." On 13 November 2006, the bill was passed by the House of Representatives and was signed by President George W. Bush on 27 November 2006. The language used to defend the bill argued that it offers the necessary power for the Department of Justice to arrest, prosecute, and convict the activists without going through extensive juridical process. In other words, the act allows the federal government, as well as state government, to apprehend and arrest social actors without due process, ultimately denying the accused ecoterrorist access to fair trial. Six members of Congress were present on the house floor when the bill was passed. Dennis Kucinich, a congressman from Ohio, spoke out about how the language of the bill would without a doubt have a chilling effect on the exercise of the constitutional rights of protest (Potter 2008).

The act redefined already state-recognized crimes as federal offenses termed "domestic" terrorism. Combined with the passage of the Patriot Act in 2001, the state was able to surveil, infiltrate, and disproportionately penalize activists that targeted agricultural industries. Direct action activists advocating economic boycott and public protest have faced trumped up charges related to violating the AETA. The vague language around who is protected from what specifically enhances the government's (and corporations') sovereignty to deny civil exercise of the first amendment. The AETA was written and sponsored by financially invested politicians to target direct action activists. Potter argued that the AETA is not specifically targeting eco-activist activists that knowingly engage in illegal direct action. Rather, Potter argues the AETA is meant to instill a chilling effect in activism at large. Aboveground activists assume that the First Amendment protects their right to use legal direct action. The implementation of the AETA, however, demonstrates that legal direct action can also be targeted within the vague and inclusive language of the act.

The AETA is the only federal policy that targets a specific type of non-violent activism, a specific ideological position, and deems it terrorism. It is the only act that criminalizes an expression of freedom of speech based on the ideological motivations of the social actor. Legal scholar Kimberly McCoy illustrates how this act oversteps state sovereignty and targets the actor's motivations in her legal indictment of the AETA (2007, 65). McCoy argues, for example, that we consider the scenario where an angry individual crosses state lines to smash the computers at their partner's laboratory, release the subjects of their research, and spray-paint the word "adulterer" on the wall after learning that they had cheated on them with their research assistant. They might be charged under state laws for crimes such as trespassing, property destruction, theft, or vandalism. But if that same person was driven by an ideological opposition to animal testing, rather than an emotional reaction to their partner's betrayal, and had spray-painted the words "Free the Animals" on the laboratory wall instead of the word "adulterer," they would most likely be charged under the federal AETA as a domestic terrorist for committing the exact same crimes.

The actions – trespassing in the lab, breaking the computers, releasing subjects, and vandalizing the wall with spray paint – are the same. But the ideological motivation to defend animals and challenge the exploitation and vivisection predicated on speciesism defines the latter scenario. Thus, the social actor spray-painting "Free the Animals" is subject to higher fines and increased prison sentencing through terrorism enhancements, as well as the transfer to Communications Management Units (CMU) within prisons. Kevin Olliff (also referred to as Kevin Johnson) is one of the twelve people who have been charged with violating the AETA (Chapekis and Moore 2021). In 2016, Olliff explained the disproportionate sentencing that can result in a terrorist enhancement: "Three years ago, my friend Tyler and I crept onto a squalid and cramped fur farm in northern Illinois and released two thousand mink from their cages to save their lives. Approximately a year later, a man in Fresno, California, crept onto a Foster Farms broiler facility and bludgeoned nine hundred chickens to death with a golf club. As this man was sentenced to 120 days in county jail, I sat in federal prison facing ten years" ("Statement from Kevin" 2016). The AETA relies on a particular type of moral madness in which bludgeoning chickens to death is seen as less egregious than simply opening their cages and releasing them into the wild. The AETA was not only the product of a cultural context, or moral madness, it was the result of a government-corporate alliance: the American Legislative Exchange Council, a lobby firm.

American Legislative Exchange Council

The passage of the AETA and the nepotistic overlap between animal-and-ecology use industries, politicians, and lobby firms and front groups demonstrate the contemporary manifestation of neoliberal capitalism through the ability to interpellate [bad] protest as [eco]terrorism. The targeted legislation simultaneously restricts public access to view and challenge capitalist entities profiting in any capacity off of animal exploitation, while constructing the activists as terrorists. The motivation behind the act relies on capital, both gained through the continued neoliberal structure of these industries and restricting public access to intervene with the practices. Thus the act essentially offers asylum to all animal enterprises, placing them outside of reach from the activist. The ALEC firm advocates for legislation that deregulates animal industries while creating unconstitutional barriers to dissent. Although the board of directors of ALEC is made up of political representatives that are public stakeholders in agricultural industries, and although the Private Enterprise Advisory Council is comprised of significant leaders in the oil, vivisection, pharmaceutical, energy, tech, and agribusiness industries, ALEC maintains that: "The American Legislative Exchange Council works to advance limited government, free markets and federalism at the state level through a nonpartisan public-private partnership of America's state legislators, members of the private sector and the general public" (ALEC n.d.). Powerful groups like ALEC represent the unique sovereignty held by corporations: the ability to inconspicuously institute and enforce industry regulations and the simultaneous hyper-regulation of dissent (Graeber 2009a, 206). ALEC veils the ways in which corporations sponsor repressive laws targeting activists, as well as the ways in which political representatives have backdoor relationships with the very industries they are wielding political power to [de]regulate.

ALEC has found itself in the public eye several times in recent years. Specifically, the documentary film *13th* examined the historical context and creation of the prison-industrial complex. Legal scholar and activist Angela Davis provides a rich history of the interconnections between the carceral system, structural racism, and capitalism. In the film, Davis articulates the unique economic relationship that public policy facilitates between the prison system and corporate interests. As illustrated in *13th*, ALEC was deeply involved in bolstering legislation that would increase arrests and incarceration, while simultaneously ensuring that private prisons also continue to be a massive profit-yielding industry.[12] ALEC has also played a vital role in the Transcanada, Mountain Valley, and Dakota Access pipeline construction. The corporate lobby firm has manipulated the public discourse surrounding not only what legal protections corporations should have, but, in these examples of incarcerated peoples and Indigenous communities, ALEC has also ensured a legal demarcation that denies basic humanity.

ALEC played a key role in garnering support from politicians and ensuring the AETA would pass without resistance. Sovereignty functions within the nepotism of speciesist capitalism and facilitates a deeper analysis of the de-regulation of animal industries in relation to the hyper-regulation of those explicitly challenging them. The media sources and government officials applied the language of terrorism after 9/11 to the AELM. The rhetorical function of ecoterrorism was to naturalize the creation of a federal law that transforms constitutionally protected behaviours such as free speech into "domestic terrorism." The AETA symbolizes a shift in how direct action dissent is interpellated in the terrorism framework that 9/11 provided. Activists within the AELM have faced increased surveillance, infiltration, and federal criminalization for advocating their philosophy and implementing confrontational tactics. In addition to the already hostile sentiment toward the liberation activists, the rhetoric of terrorism following the attacks of 9/11 greatly reshaped the political climate in the US (Chomsky 2004, 219). The AELM has been redefined and demarcated from other social movements through the conflation of activism and terrorism. This is particularly visible in the well-publicized capture and arrests of animal and earth liberationists, in public trials, in the implementation of terrorism enhancements, in CMUs, and with excessive sentencing. Although clandestine underground cells conduct animal and earth liberation acts, the shift in the political climate of dissent since 9/11 has visibly changed the aboveground solidarity movement. The heightened scrutiny permitted through the Patriot Act has created a culture of surveillance. Under the presidential leadership of Trump, the US has seen a dramatic uptick in the rhetoric of terrorism. Specifically, there has been a conflation of "anarchist" and "terrorist."

Combined with the passage of the Patriot Act in 2001, governments can use surveillance and infiltrate organizations recognized under the AETA. The federal government is able to overstep states to prosecute people not only for what they did but also what they thought when they did it. It is widely publicized how the government engages in stalking and surveillance to build cases against activists. According to the legislation, activists can be repressed based on what they thought about an act before they chose whether or not to pursue it.

Within the logic of the AETA, corporations – and the laboratories that house maimed and disfigured animals and inflict physical and psychological violence – are rearticulated as "helpless victims." Meanwhile, animal liberationists attempting to remove animals from laboratories and using their constitutionally promised freedom of speech to pressure shareholders are "criminals" and even "terrorists."

Resistance and Neoliberal Capitalism

The mechanisms of neoliberal capitalism and terrorism rhetoric make it nearly impossible to locate and target *the* central site of power. With an elusive web of corporations, lobby groups and front organizations, and invested politicians, there is no central site of power. These increasingly globalized corporations do not have a central site of power and imagination becomes the site to demand an end to both neoliberalism and capitalism (Graeber 2010, 93). The possibilities inherent in imagination allow for creativity and collaboration amongst non-state actors advancing the critique of neoliberalism. The AELM is faced with the challenge: "To be as militant and effective as possible without losing the moral high ground, without alienating public support, and without diluting the values of freedom and compassion. Animal exploiters have no such burden; they seek out only to oppress and to profit from their violence and terrorism. The state has no such burden; it is an apparatus that monopolizes power and violence and exists primarily to crush dissent and promote corporate agendas" (Nocella and Best 2004, 57).

Eco-activists engage in modes of resistance that articulate the potential for equitable and caring social relations and goods-exchange. Through clandestine networks, they create temporary shared spaces where they exchange ideas and resources through an anarchist principle of mutual aid. Within this framework, direct action is conceptualized as a queer tactic because it disidentifies with good/bad protestor dichotomies to undermine neoliberal capitalism and speciesism. Specifically, the use of home demonstrations relies on a neoliberal logic in order to expose the inherent exploitation and alienation of neoliberalism itself. The next chapter will examine the ways in which eco-activists utilize the strategies and tactics of direct action to demand radical change. Eco-activists advance their critique of neoliberal capitalism through the use of direct action while simultaneously adopting the hegemonic language of neoliberalism. Through the use of spectacle to create terministic screens that utilize a political imaginary, direct action challenges more than just the domination and exploitation of ecologies. Direct action challenges the fundamental ways in which civil society is organized through ideological state apparatuses.

2

Embodied Ethnographies

Therefore, let me warn the reader immediately: there is no particular argument to this book – unless it's that the movement described within is well worth thinking about. This does not mean it does not contain theoretical arguments. Over the course of it, I make any number of them ... What makes this an ethnographic work in the classic sense of the term is that, as Franz Boas once put it, the general is in the service of the particular – aside, perhaps, from the final reflections. Theory is invoked largely to aid in the ultimate task of description. Anarchists and direct action campaigns do not exist to allow some academic to make a theoretical point or prove some rival's theory wrong (any more than do Balinese trance rituals or Andean irrigation technologies), and it strikes me as obnoxious to suggest otherwise. I would like to think that, as a result, the interest of this book might also endure not only for those motivated by historical curiosity, who wish to understand what it was actually like to have been in the middle of these events, but to ask the same sort of questions the actors in it were raising, about the nature of democracy, autonomy, and possibilities – or for that matter, dilemmas, limitations – of strategies of transformative political action.

(Graeber 2009, viii).

In 2016, my partner and I decided to drive a dozen or so hours in order to participate in an anti-captivity demonstration. I felt deeply connected to this campaign, and yet was conflicted about the touristy nature of my participation with it. For years, I had been travelling back and forth to link up with activists and participate in demonstrations. I shared tweets and memes and any other social media posts that would help bolster the campaign. I became friends with the activists I had met in Canada, where this particular campaign was based. The campaign became more than a field site; it became a community for me. As I reflect back on those first few trips across the border, I am struck by how ultimately *ordinary* this extraordinary campaign really is in the larger scheme of the AELM. The structure of the demonstrations, the characters involved, even the scripts that activists use to chant and deliver speeches: it is not unique. It's almost like eating in a franchised restaurant. Sure, they might have some regional foods on the menu and the staff are different. But there is a great deal of creative manufacturing to ensure that the experience is similar for visitors regardless of which location they visit. The End Captivity Now campaign shaped my research in a similar way to how ALA did. I stumbled upon it with excitement and political motivation, I connected with individuals and found solidarity with them, and, simultaneously, I negotiated the tension of feeling like an outsider.

This chapter reflects on how direct action campaigns use public performance. The concept of direct action is one at the heart of anarchist organizing, and most misunderstood by those outside of direct action circles. The first part of the chapter is focused solely on teasing out what direct action is, how it is theorized by activists, and why it is a preferred strategy for revolutionary change. The chapter then dives into my field notes and interviews from that very first visit with folks in End Captivity Now. Over the last decade, I have engaged with and participated in various forms of direct action campaigns. In my own holistic journey as a direct action activist, this was one of the first multi-year campaigns I got involved with. This chapter is intimately linked to the next, providing context on how the research unfolded, and then examining these campaigns through the lens of performance and spectacle.

DIRECT ACTION

Voltairine de Cleyre, a US anarchist, first articulated the term direct action in a widely circulated essay published in 1912 that historicized the efficacy of direct action for resistance movements.[1] Graeber's more recent definition of direct action represents a particularly advanced vision for the remaking of social-capital hierarchies.

> Direct action represents a certain ideal ... It is a form of action in which means and ends become, effectively, indistinguishable; a way of actively engaging with the world to bring about change, in which the form of the action – or at least, the organization of the action – is itself a model for the change one wishes to bring about. At its most basic, it reflects a very simple anarchist insight: that one cannot create a free society through military discipline, a democratic society by giving orders, or a happy one through joyless self-sacrifice. At its most elaborate, the structure of one's own act becomes a kind of micro-utopia, a concrete model for one's vision of a free society. (2009b, 210)

Direct action is not defined here solely by the physical act, but also the ideological underpinnings and symbolic meaning the act represents. Within this logic, direct action is not a label of tactic demarcation, but rather it is an inclusive framework to conceptualize activism (Thompson 2010, 57). Direct action allows for politically repressed and marginalized peoples to reclaim power in the streets through the spectacle of the protest (Shepard, Bogad, and Duncombe 2008, 273). Graeber expands on the significance of direct action as a transgressive experience that empowers an individual to politically engage in a specific action, while participating in a global struggle for liberation from oppressive structures (Graeber 2004, 84). Laura Knaiz defines animal and earth liberation within the framework of direct action as "the use of clandestine, illegal tactics to (1) free animals, (2) educate the public about the oppression of nonhumans, and (3) inflict economic harm on animal enterprises" (Knaiz 1995, 765). Although all actions taken in defence of animals are important, direct action implies there is no intermediary. You are not asking for permission to protest; you are demanding change now. Direct action is:

a core part of the animal liberation movements' tactical and philosophical repertoire, a defining feature of their cultures of resistance – those shared understandings, ideas, and knowledge that inform individual or collective practices of dissent. Direct action can mean mobilizing ideas, knowledge, symbols, and bodies to prevent or support a particular practice or policy (for example, protestors chaining themselves to a tree to keep it from being felled); personal confrontation and property damage (say; a protest outside a CEO's home or the hacking of a company's website); and solidarity with other movements and oppressed peoples (expressing support and allying with other causes). (Pellow 2014, 127–8)

Direct action creates a queer space – i.e., an open space in which people are invited and even encouraged to play with and transgress normative boundaries. Such a space enables politically repressed and marginalized peoples to reclaim power (Butler 2011; Muñoz 1999; Pêcheux 1982). Rather than relying on someone else to make social change, the participants push for that change themselves. These actions are further defined within the parameters of nonviolence, ensuring that acts of property destruction are carefully planned to ensure no physical harm.[2]

The public access to digital media on a global scale has provided a platform for an international solidarity movement focused on animal and earth liberation. A group of clandestine activists can raid a laboratory, capture the grotesque conditions the animals are living in with a GoPro camera, post the video on the internet, and have a communiqué ready to go on the Press Office page just minutes after the action is done. The audience is not limited to a geographic location or political affiliation. Another example of the global reach is with the expansive support systems that exist for political prisoners. The political terrain has been remade through the techno-revolution. Eco-activists that engage in direct action have noted the shift in tactics since the proliferation of the Stop Huntingdon Animal Cruelty (SHAC) campaign.[3]

The SHAC Model

The SHAC campaign emphasized secondary and tertiary targeting, the complementary relationship between public and underground organizing, a diversity of tactics, and the importance of establishing concrete targets with explicit motivations. The SHAC model not only challenges the neoliberal obfuscation of corporate accountability by targeting secondary and tertiary companies, but the campaign also queers the realm of tactical approaches. For example, the SHAC campaign has used tactics that include black faxing (the looped sending of completely black fax pages to drain ink and occupy the line), website defacement and data theft, denial-of-service attack, unsolicited subscription for mailings, services, and goods, and publicizing personal information of targets with the intent to elicit harassment. The notion of secondary and tertiary targeting is simple: target companies that are connected to HLS, but that would rather cease ties to HLS than be the target of a campaign. CrimethInc. Ex-Workers' Collective provides a succinct description: "By targeting investors and business partners of HLS, SHAC repeatedly brought HLS to the brink of collapse, and it took direct assistance from the British government and an international counter-campaign of severe legal repression to keep the corporation afloat."[4]

This model is based on a three-tiered approach that includes "campaigning against customers who provide HLS with an income and profits; suppliers who provide HLS with vital tools to carry out research and financial links such as shareholders, market makers and banking facilities" (SHAC 2012). The SHAC campaign is cited globally as the impetus behind smaller grassroots animal liberation campaigns that utilize secondary and tertiary targeting. One of the sites of research in this book is the WDC-based campaign ALA, which emerged in the mid 2000s and utilized the city's dense population to target individuals. The tactic of secondary and tertiary targeting is particularly useful because it casts a wide net while placing one targeted corporation as the centre nexus.

> Starbucks could easily afford a thousand times the cost of the windows smashed by the black bloc during the Seattle WTO protests, but if no one would replace those windows – or the windows had been broken at the houses of investors, so no one would invest in the corporation – it would be another story. SHAC organizers made a point of learning the inner workings of the capitalist economy, so they could strike most strategically ... The targets do not have a vested interest in continuing their involvement with the primary target. There are other places they can take their business, and they have no reason not to do so. This is a vital aspect of the SHAC model. If a business is cornered, they'll fight to the death, and nothing will matter in the conflict except the pure force each party is able to bring to bear on the other; this is not generally to the advantage of activists, as corporations can bring in the police and government ... Somewhere between the primary target and the associated corporations that provide its support structure, there appears to be a fulcrum where action is most effective. It might seem strange to go after tertiary targets that have no connection to the primary target themselves, but countless HLS customers have dropped relations after a client of theirs was embarrassed. (SHAC 2012)

The relationship between public and underground organizing is also a noted element to the SHAC model. The campaign coalesces the tensions between activists' reluctance to use technology in lieu of shared physical spaces for organizing with the reliance on technology to disseminate literature widely and anonymously. The SHAC websites "disseminated information about targets and provided a forum for action reports to raise morale and expectations, enabling anyone sympathetic to the goals of the campaign to play a part without drawing attention to themselves" (Marut 2009). The diversity of tactics within the campaign addressed the tendency for social movements to experience splinters over divisive tactics. To that end, the SHAC model integrated a limitless array of tactics that inclusively welcomed a broad range of activists. The fourth hallmark of the SHAC model is the selection and targeting of a specific corporation that allows activists to collectivize in a concrete way. CrimethInc. Ex-Workers' Collective reiterates the power of this narrowing technique:

> The fact that there were specific animals suffering, whose lives could be saved by specific direct action, made the issues concrete and lent

the campaign a sense of urgency that translated into a willingness on the part of participants to push themselves out of their comfort zones. Likewise, at every juncture in the SHAC campaign, there were intermediate goals that could easily be accomplished, so the monumental task of undermining an entire corporation never felt overwhelming. This contrasts sharply with the way momentum in certain green anarchist circles died off after the turn of the century, when the goals and targets became too expansive and abstract. It had been easy for individuals to motivate themselves to defend specific trees and natural areas, but once the point for some participants was to "destroy civilization" and everything less was mere reformism, it was impossible to work out what constituted meaningful action. (Marut 2009)

The SHAC model provides a direct action strategy and a series of tactics to intercept both the ideology of speciesism and specific mechanisms of exploitation. Within neoliberal capitalism, agricultural industries function within many ideological state apparatuses and the state apparatus itself that decentralize and veil powerholders. The power held by the industries is thus framed as diffuse rather than concentrated, which makes it difficult to determine whom to target with the demand for radical change. Direct action inspired by the SHAC model acknowledges the ways in which industries are interconnected but allows for individual localized targeting with tangible goals. Rather than lobby for indirect legislation that may regulate the use of animals within the industries, direct action disengages with the legislative process altogether. The economic impacts of the SHAC campaign are a clear indicator in the effectiveness of this tactic.[5] However, to an individual activist, it feels intangible or outside of the scope of reason that they can open all cages or intercept all sites of ecological exploitation.[6] The SHAC model isolates a target and directs all pressure tactics toward said target. This amplifies the façade of accountability that there is an identifiable entity that has been named and shamed for perpetuating speciesism. These tactics queer the spectrum of protest within the realm of animal advocacy by crossing accepted boundaries – by playing with the lines of acceptability and introducing ideas, practices, and forms of dissent and resistance. In many ways, then, the SHAC campaign sits at the cutting edge of direct action and radical social change.

Inaction Is Complicity

Activists in the AELM who endorse illegal direct action claim that any tactics that do not directly intercept exploitation are in fact supporting that exploitation. In other words, if you don't stop it, you are facilitating it. Steven Best, professor of philosophy and animal liberation advocate, has written extensively on the tensions within the animal advocacy movement over the efficacy of direct action. He argues that because the mechanisms of speciesism are "forces hell-bent on exploiting animals and the earth for profit whatever the toll ... the corporate social war against nature," there is a new civil war between the industries and the activists (2004). There are several prominent types of direct action within the AELM, for example: "the Animal Liberation Front (ALF) employs sabotage, Stop Huntingdon Animal Cruelty (SHAC) uses strong intimidation tactics, and militant animal liberation groups such as the Animal Rights Militia, the Justice Department, and the Revolutionary Cells openly advocate violence against animal abusers" (Best 2004). Best critiques those who solely engage in nonviolent civil disobedience to challenge industries of violence by arguing that if one does not stop bloodshed, one is adopting a pro-violence stance by not taking adequate measures to stop it.

Within a moral binary of absolutist terms, activists are either labelled terrorists or freedom fighters. Activists have relied upon historical comparisons that demonstrate the relativism of these labels. Some activists draw literal and symbolic ties between speciesism and other systems of oppression linked to genocide such as racism and slavery, as well as anti-Semitism and the Holocaust (Nibert and Fox 2002; Patterson 2002; Spiegel and Walker 1997). Wiesel stated during his 1986 Nobel Acceptance Speech, "I swore never to be silent whenever and wherever human beings endure suffering and humiliation. We must always take sides. Neutrality helps the oppressor, never the victim. Silence encourages the tormentor, never the tormented" (Wiesel 1986). Direct action activists articulate a similar sentiment in their dismissal of indirect action (such as lobbying and bureaucratic and legislative campaigning) as being implicit in the existing ideologies of speciesism, neoliberal capitalism, and globalization. Alternatively, direct action tactics require little time compared to the bureaucratic processes involved with legal analyses, drafting regulatory policies and reforms, and schmoozing with people behind closed doors. Direct action, as the term implies, directly challenges those in power through time-efficient, cost-effective tactics that rely on activist energy and creativity. Despite the great successes of the SHAC campaign, direct action tactics – and specifically those inspired by the SHAC model – have been the site of debate within the animal and ecological movement broadly.

The use of direct action has been challenged not just by the targeted institutions and state apparatus, but also by activists that claim to be sympathetic to the movement. These challenges claim direct action is violent, ineffective, and detrimental to the movement at large. Within both activist and academic circles, there remains a polarizing debate on the continuum of violence. The direct actions of eco-activists include many illegal tactics of vandalism, property destruction, sabotage, burglary, and theft (of animals) (Grubbs and Loadenthal 2011a; 2011b). Best claims that the critiques of direct action fail to understand political struggle because of the limited rhetoric of *good protestor/bad protestor*. Best states:

> Many critics of the ALF, SHAC, and direct action tactics poorly understand what makes social change movements possible and effective. They rely on a naïve model of political struggle and human nature that assumes rational dialogue can solve all conflicts. They use facile generalizations such as "violence is always wrong" and "ALF actions always get bad publicity" that are flat out wrong. In addition, they consistently misrepresent direct action advocates as naïvely believing that sporadic acts of vandalism and intimidation alone can win animal liberation. Looking at modern social history, it is clear that civil disobedience, property destruction, and violence have been important political tactics for the American Revolution, the abolition of slavery, labor and national independence movements, suffragette struggles, and the civil rights movement. Similarly, the history of the ALF and SHAC shows that break-ins, liberations, property destruction, arson, and intimidation tactics have completely shut down some operations, weakened others, and provided otherwise unobtainable documentation of animal exploitation in fur farms, vivisection labs, and elsewhere. As evident in the 1980s era of ALF-PETA press conferences, the exposes of Huntingdon Life Sciences (HLS), and the summer 2003 attacks on foie gras chefs and restaurants in the Bay area, dramatic sabotage and direct action methods often get good press that reform campaigns cannot generate. This valuable publicity exposes vicious industry practices and sparks important public dialogue about animal wrongs and animal rights. Whereas advocates of direct action such as Paul Watson, Rod Coronado, and Kevin Jonas use inclusive approaches that acknowledge the validity of different approaches in different situations, critics of direct action wield exclusive approaches that deny the need for and validity of a plurality of tactics – both legal and illegal, aboveground and underground. Mainstream "exclusionists" speak ex cathedra as if they alone possess Truth and can infallibly predict which tactic will work. (Steve Best 2004)

The critiques of direct action often privilege nonviolent indirect action as the only effective method to bring about change. This sentiment is echoed in the erasure of illegal direct action in the retelling of successful social movements. The women's suffrage movement in the US, for example, has been captured by historians for over a century. Nevertheless, many accounts downplay the use of direct action from the blockades to the occupations to the gruelling hunger strikes. Rather than accurately cover this history and the effective use of direct action, there remains a dominant discourse surrounding the dichotomized good protestor/bad protestor. Direct action is situated within the construct of the bad protestor, oftentimes publicizing the acts as reckless, disorganized, immature, and violent. Within this critique, methods of property destruction and obstruction are framed as violence. Activists and academics point to the ways in which eco-activists emphasize protecting all forms of life by carefully planning and implementing tactics that only target mechanisms of violence.[7] In addition, defenders of direct action argue that the real violence is being perpetrated by animal-and-ecology use industries and industries that commodify ecological entities. The violent dispossession of resources and habitats illustrate the anarchist principle that property itself is violence through theft (Steve Best et al. 2007; Steven Best and Nocella 2006; Harvey 2004; Proudhon 1840).

The dialectics of effective/ineffective, direct/indirect, single issue/ intersectional coalition, and violent/nonviolent remain the significant splinters within the animal and ecological advocacy movements. These debates become more visibly polarizing between the three overarching tenets of the advocacy movement: the animal welfare movement/ecological conservation movement, the animal rights movement/ecological sustainability, and the animal and ecological liberation movement.[8] I have previously conducted ethnographic studies focusing on traditional animal rights organizations that utilize indirect action such as lobbying and leafletting outside of concert venues. Not only do these groups advocate for small, incremental change, they often publicly condemn direct action taken by eco-activists, regardless of the legality. One example of a tactic that is contested between the welfare and rights camps and the liberation movement is home demonstrations. In 2011, I began attending home demonstrations with ALA and the Occupy Movement. I attended my first home demonstration with the skepticism that had been ingrained in me from years of organizing with the good protestors. The critiques of direct action dominate social movement discourses within the mainstream media as well as in academic disciplines.

HOME DEMONSTRATIONS AS DIRECT ACTION

Academic discourses reinforce the privilege of indirect action by minimizing the ways in which direct action has shaped social change over the
years (Pellow 2014). I was hesitant to engage in direct action after years
of being entrenched in these academic and mainstream discourses. I
began engaging in animal advocacy with the belief that direct action was
too confrontational to gain public support, I thought it relied too heavily
on masculinist and militant rhetoric and was ineffectively aggressive, and
I assumed that these strategies had no real impact on the corporations
they targeted. As an ecofeminist, and an advocate of a feminist ethic of
care, I struggled to see how confrontational acts could contribute to total
liberation (Adams 2010; Donovan and Adams 2007; Adams and Donovan 1995). Initially, I found the targeting of individual corporations and
employees to rely on neoliberal logic that ignored the interconnectedness
of powerholders. As I continued to attend home demonstrations affiliated with the AELM, and as I began networking with anarchists in the
WDC area, and further immersed myself in primary sources from direct
action activists, it became clear something more was going on. The performances, or the spectacle of direct action, did not just refuse to submit
to the *good/bad* protestor dichotomy. In reality, these carefully scripted
and rehearsed performances queered the dichotomization itself and created new and alternative forms of disidentification.

The chants, press releases, proclamations, and tactics are so blatantly neoliberal that it simply is not hegemonic ignorance. I attended
demonstrations organized by several eco-activist campaigns that were
announced through social media. The campaigns spanned across
North America. For archival and legal purposes, many of these
demonstrations were recorded and archived by activists. During the
demonstrations, I took extensive field notes and sometimes my own
video footage. The texts used in this chapter include the transcripts
I recorded from demonstrations outside of corporations and individual homes, my personal interactions with participants and observers,
and website material (including footage from other related demonstrations) from eco-activists. I also reviewed online videos of demonstrations with these campaigns, some of which I did not personally attend.[9]
The SHAC campaign has had a lasting impact on organizations and
campaigns that I have worked with, and the SHAC model continues to
inform strategies and tactics of direct action in the AELM. Despite the
many ways in which you can find footage of these demonstrations, I
have anonymized many of the campaigns, some of the gatherings, and

activists. In some places, I am intentionally vague, obscuring which activist with which campaign said what at what time. The details simultaneously matter and don't matter.

The texts, ranging from my own ethnographic notes to public and private digital communication, queer traditional academic understandings of a social movement. As a form of text, digital "performances" were archived over several years and serve as part of the corpus included throughout the book. The texts analyzed are woven throughout and challenge the incorrect assumptions that informed my naïve assertions that confrontational direct action relied too heavily on masculinist and neoliberal modes of activism. Direct action activists, more specifically, those engaging in a home demonstration, are not simply angry individuals who got a hold of a bullhorn and spent the afternoon taking out their frustrations with the world on one neoliberal subject who works for a vivisection company. The presentation of blame and shame is a rhetorical performance that creates a stage, is led by actors, and relies on a script. These are complicated demonstrations that are filled with tension and contradiction between the more prissy and explicit chants and the methodical proclamations delivered by key organizers. The demonstration attendees rely on different elements of political theatre to highlight aspects of neoliberalism in order to expose it. These tensions became an informative source of text for analysis, because "the best opportunities for analysis arise when it is difficult to see how this coherence has been achieved: where there seem to be logical gaps, logical clashes, and unexpected silences, or disturbances and violations of the presumed default universal structures of narrative" (Hill 1995, 159). Utilizing Jane Hill's optimism regarding inconsistencies in the text, this analysis emphasizes the different rhetorical tactics and their significance in the overall success of the demonstrations.

After carefully reading through the texts of the home demonstrations I attended in 2011, I saw a pattern with the symbolic exaggeration of neoliberalism and, interestingly, a pattern of contradictions between the proclamations and the chants. As linguistic performance, these speech acts are dynamic in their use of voice. I adopted Hill's framework of text analysis and her emphasis on inconsistencies and gaps in coherence within the narrative. Through a textual analysis comparing the proclamations to the chants, I measured these inconsistencies using Hill's concept of voice as she demonstrated with the many voices of Don Gabriel.[10] During one of the confrontational direct actions that took place on the lawn of a specific target, activists created a public performance that highlighted contradictory voices, nuanced by playful chants and confrontational rhetoric. I noted the confrontational chants used during the demonstration, "Their blood, their blood, their blood is on YOUR hands," "Your ticket. YOUR FAULT. Your money. YOUR FAULT," and how they contradicted the individual dialogue activists attempted through the chain-link fence that physically separated them from the customers entering the animal-use park, "Ma'am, why would you want to show your child such cruelty toward those beautiful creatures. Please teach your child compassion" (Grubbs 2013a). Within a five-minute timespan, one activist would shift their voice between aggressive call-and-return chants and more neoliberal performances while speaking with customers entering the animal-use park.

Geopolitical Borders and Embodied Gender Roles

My first border crossing during this ethnographic study was marked by the challenges of intentionality and queering privileged spaces. The US/Canada border crossing became a site of tension between the practical desire to enter the country without any issues and the political commitment to disrupting systems of privilege. My sister and I had taken turns driving for over ten hours, and my daughter, Emory, had just fallen asleep when we approached the border patrol booth. Perhaps because of my various sites of privilege, I had assumed we would breeze through the security check. It was after 10 pm and the border officer seemed irritated to be at work. She shined the flashlight in the backseat and scanned every inch of the car while monotonously reciting a series of questions. I answered quickly and with a rehearsed tone. "Yes, I am authorized to drive the car." "I packed the car myself." "I will be sightseeing and staying at a hotel." As the questions became more personalized to my daughter, I realized her concern was less about our reasons for travel and more about the infant leaving their country of residence. She looked at me with concern, "Where is her other parent? Is he your husband?" When my answers did not satisfy her suspicions, she asked me to pull forward, park in Spot 12, and step inside the building for further interrogation. I woke Emory and quickly ran inside. It had dropped about ten degrees since the sunset, which worsened my discomfort. We got inside and took our place in line with the other precarious border-crossers that were asked to come inside for further interrogation. The officer called me to the counter and began asking a series of questions, "'Does her other parent know that you are entering Canada?' 'Where is *he*?' 'What do you do for a living now?' 'Where are you staying?' 'When will you be returning with her?'" (Border Officer 2013). The heteronormative assumptions embedded in these questions were glaring. As I stood across the counter with my daughter, who has a different last name than me, and my twenty-three-year-old sister, I wondered why they assumed there was a father at all. Without a wedding band on my finger, I also wondered if they read me as married. The border officers had reached many conclusions about me in just a few moments. I rarely wear my wedding band, and intentionally do not wear it when I attend political convergences.[11] There are times that I exploit strategic essentialism by placing my pregnant white body in front of riot cops, but that is in the service of others. I chose not to wear my wedding band while crossing a geopolitical border so as to not rely on and reproduce heteronormative privilege. Gender and class manifest in complicated ways for an activist. As I stood there and thought through how to respond, I could not help but weigh the ideological implications of my answers. Do I challenge heteronormative privilege and lie about my marital status? Does it actually subvert heteronormative privilege or patriarchy to not wear a wedding band when in reality I am, in fact, legally married to a cisgender man? Is it problematic to closet this privileged aspect of my identity and engage in code-switching with these border agents?

Ultimately, I made the practical decision that it was almost 11 pm and I did not want to subject myself to the coercive powers of these officers. I began referring to "her father" as "my husband" and insisted that we could call him in order to verify his approval of my taking Emory out of the country. In a blatant exercise of privilege, the officers never verified my marital status or that the man I suggested we call was her father, nor did they actually speak to said father on the phone. Instead, the officers gave me a patriarchal lecture about travelling without "my husband," made a few jokes about two women driving late at night, and suggested I remember to bring a letter from my child's father granting permission to leave the country prior to the next trip (Border Officer 2013). Perhaps my lecture would have been different if I had appeared less educated, or if I was not a 5'3" slim white woman accompanied by my child and a 5'3" slim blonde woman. It is not accidental how security theatre relies on racialized, gendered, and sexualized processes to give the appearance of safety.[12]

My sister and I had arranged to stay at the home of one of the main organizers, Levi, with the End Captivity Now campaign. Through Facebook Messenger, they provided directions to their house and instructions on how to get in if they were not there. We arrived around 11:30 pm and found Levi on the couch watching television with their housemate. Levi's partner was upstairs changing the sheets and preparing our room. The house was shared between three humans, several cats, and two dogs, and it smelled like fresh basil. There was not a poster to be seen, nor a book or any political ephemera to mark the leanings of those who live there. A quick tour of the kitchen revealed the usual suspects: almond milk, potatoes, tofu, plenty of Asian sauces, and various vegan accoutrements. On the stove homemade dog food was simmering. Two cats under the bed, a dog scratching his ears outside the door, and a little black cat under the nightstand; clearly, we were in the home of an eco-activist. We came downstairs and our host had their phone on the table. Their Facebook application was open, and they seemed anxious. In our exchanges prior to arrival, Levi had mentioned that they had just received a call from their lawyer. Their lawyer wanted to confirm that Levi had been with people throughout the day, as there had been a fire at the office of someone connected to a local animal-and-ecology use industry. Levi's lawyer did not actually suspect their client of being involved, but feared that their client would be falsely implicated. Activists had been targeting this animal-and-ecology use industry for weeks, and just that day had posted something on social media exposing excessive cruelty. The fire seemed like a convenient way to destroy records that documented excessive cruelty. It was notable that one of our first interactions in person was about the threat of legal action based on a (potential) direct action. We talked a bit about the campaign and our excitement to be here and help. Levi was facing a Strategic Lawsuit against Public Participation (SLAPP suit) and the local community had formed a support site. Corporations use SLAPP suits to silence and intimidate activists by threatening them with expensive litigious battles. Activists are critical of how SLAPP suits stifle public challenges to corporations, including Levi.[13]

I struggled between my desire to take advantage of this time to talk in person and the need to put my child to sleep. The lengthy journey from Ohio to this Canadian town had left us exhausted, and my daughter needed my attention. I knew this was a rare moment where I could conduct an interview in-person with a lead organizer who was currently facing significant legal pressure for their activism. My sister took Emory upstairs and tried to put her to sleep so that I could visit with Levi downstairs. The activist and I sat downstairs together and talked about an agenda for tomorrow and how we could help with the pre-demonstration planning. As we were talking, my daughter began to cry. I reluctantly interrupted the conversation and excused myself to go upstairs and put her to sleep. I said that I intended to come back downstairs to talk, assuming she went to sleep quickly. By the time she was asleep, it was 2 am and everyone else had gone to bed. This was one of the first and more critical moments in my research where I was faced with the tension of being a mother-in-the-field. It was one of the earliest moments that I had to choose between gathering research and meeting the needs of my child. My embodied roles were conflicting: the researcher-activist and the breastfeeding parent responsible for childcare. I have never looked back at the decision to go upstairs with my child rather than interview this activist that night with regret. I look back at that moment with reflexivity, as it was a transformative experience that informed the ways in which I understand intersectional barriers to knowledge production (Crenshaw 1989; 1991; Collins 1991; 2006). I manoeuvre both privileged access and barriers to knowledge production, while also struggling to balance the dualities of activist-anthropologist and mother-scholar.

I spent most of the night awake with Emory, nursing and pacing with her, trying to keep her cries from waking up the entire house. Rather than feeling refreshed and ready to gather more data, I stumbled out of the bedroom with a zombie-like gait at 7 am to discover an empty house. My sister and I packed up our things and left the house to find a nearby coffee shop in order to access a WiFi signal. For financial reasons, I only used the free WiFi capacities of my cellular phone rather than network data. I relied on WiFi-based instant communication applications to connect with others while in Canada. I sent a message to our host through Facebook messenger. Looking back, it is amazing how often I used Facebook Messenger, iMessage, and other non-encrypted communication apps. There was a shift in this culture after 2014, when end-to-end encryption applications became more widely-used.[14]

After a few hours of exploring the area, I had not received a message back from our host. We decided to head back to the house and inadvertently ran into Levi leaving the house. They were heading to an office space that one of the eco-liberation collectives had been using as a centralized organizing space. It felt like the invitation to join them was reluctantly extended, but that may have been my own insecurities in this new geographic space. We walked about fifteen minutes while they went into great detail about the campaign and legal issues. The activist was facing legal action for one of the campaigns, and escalation of the lawsuits meant the organizers had to rethink how visible each individual person would be during any given action. I asked if there was an NLG-type organization in Canada that provided free legal defence. They explained that animal advocacy lawyers in the area were already struggling to find professional work, and that this case would be detrimental to those efforts. In some geographical locations, it can be very difficult to find a sympathetic attorney that not only compromises on their fees, but also that provides legal counsel informed by empathy.

Levi experienced both challenges: they had trouble finding an attorney, and the attorney they had secured typically provided a patronizing (albeit well-intentioned) lecture at every opportunity. Though the interaction was not recorded, I made note of a remark that struck me, "You can either get a lawyer that charges very little and agrees with what you are doing, or at least doesn't have anything big against it, or you can use a really good lawyer that you know will win – but will try to give you a lecture about why you should lobby" (Levi 2013). The lawsuit not only brought legal pressure, it also brought interpersonal challenges for Levi. They had received pushback from several friends and fellow activists that compounded their stress level at the time. They felt like the further they pushed the campaign with confrontational rhetoric, despite the lawsuit, the less support they had from activists. In conversation with several activists in the area, there is a divide within the small anarchist community that is even more visible in the animal liberation community.[15] We continued the casual conversation until we reached the office, located within an unassuming office suite.

I took stock of my surroundings: a dark-haired person at a desk repurposing painter's buckets into donation pails, a twenty-something person sitting in a chair to the right was playing on their cell phone, a person ironing recently ink-pressed sweatshirts, a person sitting at the desk across from another person who was covered in tattoos and with a septum ring. After doing a quick survey and some presumptive guesswork, I concluded that most of them were in their early or mid-twenties. One of the people there had just arrived from the US, and runs a punk rock solidarity organization. Perhaps it was the baby sleeping in the carrier strapped to my chest, or the fact that my sister and I entered a closed space the night before their largest demonstration of the year, but not a single person looked up.

After a few moments, we made eye contact with the person who had travelled from the US and they seemed to share an awkward sense of displacement. Both of us had been in prior communication with Levi, and Levi made it a point to introduce us to one another when we had arrived. I went to each individual and offered to help with whatever task they were doing and was met with either silence or lack of eye contact each time. I unstrapped Emory from my chest and placed her on the floor to crawl. After a few minutes went by, I offered to help the person constructing the donation bins and they accepted. As I pulled off strips of tape, I overheard two other people in the room going through Facebook friend requests to confirm the identities of those requesting. Without noting whom they were referencing specifically, they would sporadically proclaim "troll" or "sketchy." Another person said they should delete anyone that doesn't have at least five mutual friends with the organizers. One of the activists mentioned they were hungry, and suggested they place a collective food order at a restaurant around the corner. Once the order was collected and called in, they began debating who would pick up the food. Though my sister and I did not contribute to the food order, and no one had really introduced themselves to us, we watched as they each averted eye contact and did not volunteer to pick it up.

We spoke up and offered to go pick it up their food, knowing it would give us an opportunity to reflect on the awkwardness we had experienced. They began tallying up their individual totals and handed over a pile of bills to use to pay for the order. We walked several blocks, relying on the shoddy directions that they had jotted down for us on a piece of paper. We wandered around in the rain, lost, as we searched for their food. When we reached the destination, we realized they had ordered a carry-out order from a bar. With Emory strapped in the carrier on my chest, I wasn't able to enter the bar to get the order. In what felt like a comical and ironic moment, I had to wait outside with my child while my sister went in to get the food. I look back on that moment as a foreshadowing of all of the times I would find myself stepping aside or sitting out both critical and insignificant moments because of a child.

We returned with their order, but it was approaching dusk. Emory started to fuss, and the cries of a baby were not necessarily the preferred sounds during the pre-demonstration preparations. Without any idea where we were and no cell phone service, we requested that our host draw us a map to use on our walk back to the house. The map was more of a pictorial than an atlas, as they could not remember specific names or turns. I attempted to show my discomfort with navigating our way back without a clear direction and waited to receive an offer for them to escort us. Overwhelmed by the surmounting tasks for the demonstration the next day, they did not offer. With a bit of hesitation, we set off to find our house. We spent over an hour trying to navigate the should-be-ten-minute-walk without any familiar landmarks. Eventually, we stopped into the police station to ask for directions. Once we bypassed the inquiries about why we were in town and whom we were staying with, we discovered the house was not too far. When we arrived back at Levi's home, we found their housemate cleaning up after dinner. They were friendly and welcoming, and seemed surprised that we had walked home alone. I mentioned that the other activists were unfriendly and disinterested in engaging in conversation. They reassured us that we weren't the first person to comment on the unwelcoming nature of these spaces. They asked about the age of my daughter, and said they were interested in having children at some point. This was one of the first times since arriving that someone had intentionally engaged with my child. After a brief conversation, Emory began to cry and required my attention. I took her in the other room to breastfeed, while we also looked for a place to stay. Although our hosts reiterated how much they would like for us to stay, I worried that she might keep them up all night. Given that the next day was such a pivotal event, I did not want to be in the way that night. The first two days in Canada confirmed my insecurities that this ethnographic study would prove challenging, particularly with the personal constraints of motherhood.

Demonstration Day

The following day we gathered with hundreds of others outside of the animal-use park. I left my driver's licence and US passport in the hotel, stuffed $40 in my pocket, and took my cell phone. I chose to not wear any jewellery, pulled my long blonde hair back into a ponytail, and paired my black skinny jeans with a *Support the ALF* t-shirt and sneakers. Emory was dressed in an End Captivity Now sweatshirt that was made the night before, black leggings, and a much smaller pair of similar sneakers. The energy was palpable, with hundreds of activists of all ages gathered along the narrow stretch of grass that faced the entrance and parking lot. I ran into the activists I had met at the headquarters, and also a handful of activists I had met at previous political actions. Several strangers approached me and introduced themselves as "Facebook stalkers" who had seen my comments on the campaign's Facebook page, which is always a weird phenomenon. There was a row of tables set up, each featuring different ephemera and baked goods. One local collective had prepared a series of delicious vegan treats, another group of activists had heat-pressed clothing for sale, and there was a table covered in flyers and leaflets from local campaigns. There was a large pop-up tent stationed in the middle of the grass with an amp, microphone, and a large inflatable animal. The banner for the campaign was prominently hung above the tent. Several activists had set up a sign-making station for activists to create large posters that was adjacent to the kid's area that featured games and art supplies. The organizers encouraged people to arrive in the morning and set up to stay for Caged Entertainment's operating hours. The speakers were scheduled for the afternoon, ensuring the momentum would remain the entire day.

The speakers included Levi, three children, and a hip-hop artist. Levi's opening remarks fostered the sense of community amongst activists and provided legal parameters for the day's events. Levi is a prominent figure with the campaign, well known through social media and public demonstrations, and is a public eco-activist in the area. The proclamation they delivered at the beginning of the demonstration reified this perceived leadership.

I am going to try and make this as quick as I possibly can,
and as painless as I possibly can.
But I need everyone's attention for the next little bit.
And I need people to pass along this information on to others as they
    come in.
So, as most people are aware, I think, at this point,
Caged Entertainment is very litigious.
So that means they want to go to court a lot.
They sued five people at this point
They are claiming damages of a total of $13 million.
One of those people being sued is myself.

In many ways, Levi's proclamations at demonstrations are a departure from their anti-authoritarian politics. During the proclamations, Levi assumes an authoritative role and provides guidelines to other activists. They identify the legal parameters and suggest how activists should interact with law enforcement. Although I saw several women working at the headquarters in preparation of the demonstration, none of these women delivered instructional proclamations to the large crowd. There were, however, many women with bullhorns delivering chants and proclamations to the customers on the other side of the fence. The disproportionate number of women delivering proclamations, a visible and elevated platform at the demonstration, reflects a larger trend in movement organizing to privilege male voices. Additionally, it perpetuates the tendency in many social movements to delegate leadership roles to men and relegate labour-intensive preparation and administrative roles to women.

The demonstration took an interesting turn when the child speakers came to the microphone.[16] Each child provided a different rhetorical argument against Caged Entertainment, though some were more articulate than others. One female nine-year-old child, in particular, described her desire for justice as a "thirst."

My thirst, I thirst for the freedom of certain animals.
There are the animals you think are happy.

You pay a lot of money to go and see.
I thirst for them to be treated well.
You may think of Caged Entertainment as a fun place to gather and
    enjoy a fun day.
But have you seen what they look like up close?
The terror and horror in their eyes
What happens behind the scenes is not what you think.
How they are treated won't be a secret, after you listen
    to me.
Good morning, protestors. (Anonymous A 2013)

At this point, the activists cheer out and begin to applaud. I hear whis-
pers around me from activists that they were surprised to hear a child
recognize these issues at her age. The speaker went on to describe how
the animals are kept at this park, how her teacher is also an activist with
End Captivity Now, and how resolved she was to liberate these specific
animals. She named the owner of the park as the perpetrator of violence
that is responsible and insists that through a financial boycott, the park
can be shut down. This proclamation provided a detailed account of
animal poaching and the artificial (poor) conditions of captivity. The
proclamation both begins and ends with an impetus for change, a call to
action that can satisfy a thirst for liberation.

In contrast to Levi, the child does not insert pauses or use phrases that
elicit a response from the audience. She articulates the unethical treatment
of animals while neglecting to specify specific behavioural commands.
The only command implied is to economically and physically boycott
the park, as her family chose to do several years prior. The proclamation
leaves the audience in awe of her rhetorical devices and emotional matu-
rity. I listen as two women speak behind me, "Now there is an activist in
the making." "I wish I would have been as aware when I was her age." The
women continue to trade surprised remarks about the young girl, focusing
on the emotional appeals in her proclamation. Two other children get up
to speak and also point to their decision to boycott the park after visiting. Each child who speaks had visited Caged Entertainment and became
the voice in their family to insist they did not return. The children also
spoke to their concern for the animals because of their isolation and small,
artificial caged habitats. Interestingly, however, all three children speakers
focused explicitly on Caged Entertainment. The children did not make any
larger arguments about speciesism, let alone authoritarianism.

Between each speaker, there were five to ten minutes of chants and
interactions with patrons of the park. The bullhorns raged as people

screamed, "Your money, *Your fault*. Your ticket, *Your fault*," "What do we want? *Animal liberation*. When do we want it? *Now!*'" and "Hey Caged Entertainment, What do you say? *How many animals have to die today?*" The chants continued as the next speaker prepared. A well-known hip-hop artist addressed, in their lyrics, a range of issues including the displacement of Indigenous peoples, animal and ecological exploitation, and capitalism. On the heels of the young girl's speech, Joban's freestyle delivery was assertive and interspersed with confrontational language: "I think it's so fucking beautiful / That we got so many people here. / Sorry for my language / I forgot. / I'm going to try and keep it family friendly and clean. / I'm a rapper, though" (Joban 2013).

His first piece, "Leaning toward Liberation," abandoned the youthful tone set by the previous speakers. As an advocate of confrontational direct action, Joban shifted the focus from the animals within the park to larger, systemic issues of injustice. In this way, his proclamations reminded the audience, part of whom would not identify as eco-activists, that End Captivity Now critiques not only animal exploitation, but also capitalism, speciesism, and authoritarianism. In the opening lines of the freestyle, Joban uses the anarchist principle and slogan coined by the French anarchist Pierre-Joseph Proudhon, "Property is theft!" (Proudhon 1840):

Property is theft
That's a concept you should get
When you're dropping most your check
On a spot to rest your head.
Little to see the bread
To pay your mortgage and your debt.
So the bankers and the feds don't get your home repossessed.
It's on stolen land.
It used to be the commons.
Before the colonizers came
And started all the problems. (Joban 2013)

The crowd was audibly divided, as some cheered and others began to speak over his proclamation. Seemingly, the activists came together solely to protest Caged Entertainment and did not share the intersectional politics held by End Captivity Now organizers or Joban himself. The proclamation continued to name issues of structural violence and displacement:

Murdering and bombing
Keep the urban sprawling.
More people starving
Just bondin' by buildin' prisons
Border wars don't stop them
So I'm swinging sledgehammers
Till every wall is droppin'
Land is freedom
Property is theft.
Burn all the flags
Until none of them are left. (Joban 2013)

The proclamation concluded with a reiteration of the anarchist principle and a call to property destruction. The proclamation was recorded on video and thus I revisited the gestures and behaviours of others while Joban was speaking. Levi sways to the beat as Joban delivers the proclamation and loudly applauds in between versus. Several activists repeatedly turn toward Levi to monitor their reaction as a sign of approval. At the conclusion of the proclamation, there is a brief pause before the audience responds. The crowd begins to applaud but the tension in the audience is palpable. Without much delay, Joban transitions into another proclamation. The track, "Liberate the Animals," makes reference not only to direct action, but specifically to the ALF and ELF. Whereas the last proclamation stressed intersectionality and the importance of coalitions between movements, the second proclamation was explicitly about speciesism:

Liberate the animals
And the earth too
Free the trees
Free the roots
Free the leaves
Free the fruits.
Liberate the earth
And the animals too.
Free the farm
Free the land
Free them from Caged Entertainment, too. (Joban 2013)

The chorus focuses on larger, systemic issues that the audience does not cohesively share.

While I sat on the grass and listened to the proclamations, I surveyed the clothing others had on and what they had brought to eat.
The demonstration lasted several hours, and people were encouraged to
pack enough with them to stay the entire day. I saw picnics consisting
of packaged products derived from animals, ranging from fried chicken
to inconspicuous sandwiches. There were at least a dozen ALF and ELF
shirts and banners, as well as various slogans indicating an anti-speciesist and/or anarchist politic. Almost every person holding a bullhorn had
political tattoos and facial piercings. The crowd still seemed supportive
of Joban, even when they began talking about terrorism rhetoric and
property destruction:

ELF, ALF
They never caused a death.
To save lives
They take a lot of risks
Liberation of all creation
Is their politics.
But somehow
They are the terror that tops the list?
Come on
Who's really the terrorists?
The slaughterhouse arsonists
Or the slaughterhouse architects?
Would it be terror to burn down Auschwitz?
You gotta give props to the ALF
To SHAC
Smash HLS
And those that invest
No torture, no test.
No one is free
While others are oppressed.
Fight for freedom
Until there's no cages left. (Joban 2013)

The understanding of the proclamation relies on insider knowledge of
eco-activist campaigns and their acronyms, such as SHAC, ALF, and ELF.
The proclamation makes an explicit moral connection between slaughterhouses and concentration camps, and implies that arsonists destroying these mechanisms of death are (similarly to those who destroyed
train tracks during the Holocaust) refusing to accept that eco-activists

are terrorists, and it creates a form of disidentification in which they are freedom fighters. The proclamation returns to confrontational language, another radical departure from the "family-friendly" atmosphere during the children's presentations:

Milk and meat
That's rape and death.
That we eat at our own expense.
We are killing the animals, planet, and ourselves.
Toxic products
We are the toxic problem.
We are the source of the products
And it's our water. (Joban 2013)

The audience, though not necessarily visible to an outsider, was divided into two categories of activists: those there to protest Caged Entertainment, and those protesting this particular site in part of a larger activist agenda against speciesism and/or authoritarianism. Levi, and the collective, were intentional with the selection of Joban as a speaker during the demonstration. As an activist, I am aware of the larger agenda-setting at demonstrations. It is imperative to utilize that space in ways that are both strategic and pragmatic. The children's presentations were pragmatic. They presented emotional appeals that resonated with activists regardless of their own personal stance on speciesism or anarchism. Joban, however, provided the strategic element that ultimately established the ideological agenda of End Captivity Now in this public setting. Their proclamations were direct, explicit, and clearly directed at activists already in support of the ideological agenda. The final proclamation used the metaphor of a blade of grass growing through the pavement to inspire activists facing political repression. The proclamation served as the emotional coda of the demonstration, solidifying for the audience that this demonstration was not simply about Caged Entertainment. The audience is riled at the concept of a growing, unstoppable revolutionary force that will ultimately persevere in spite of attempts to destroy it:

We're everywhere
Hidden like the air
That we breathe together
And we're never scared
The conspiracy is real
They are keeping it concealed

The truth is a virus
These lies will reveal
They paved over paradise
But it's gonna heal
Leaking information is like
Watering a field. (Joban 2013)

The empowering proclamation encourages the audience to "Take a pick-axe to the roads," and insists that anyone can engage with the revolution because, "It's not where you're from. It's where you're gonna go when [the] shit goes down" (Joban 2013). Grass, ultimately, represents the potentiality for revolution in spite of systemic barriers.

Can we overgrow?
Overthrow this toxic overdose?
Open those file doors that keep those undisclosed?
Life revolts, regrows till it shifts.
And this paradigm and system is out of time.
This whole time, the system was out of line.
Mass murder everyday for the dollar sign.
Then through the cracks
Like the grass to the stone
We climb. (Joban 2013)

The audience loudly applauds as the proclamation ends and the crowd is clearly riled up. Joban then leads the crowd in a chant, "Shut it down, shut it, shut it, shut it down." Those who had gotten up and moved to another area during the proclamation had returned to the makeshift stage. The agenda for the demonstration included closing remarks from an international activist who had worked closely with animals in captivity. The speaker, Thomas, had been hyped as the main event.

Before Thomas took the stage, the demonstration broke from the structured speakers to individual chants and interactions with people on the other side of the fence patronizing Caged Entertainment. The organizers dispersed and led the crowd in various chants. The chants, many of which are commonly used at other demonstrations, just slightly modify the words to target Caged Entertainment:

Hey Caged Entertainment, what do you say? How many animals have to die today?
Their blood, their blood. Their blood is on your hands!

Shut it down. Shut it, shut it DOWN.
Give them liberty, End captivity!
Your money, Your fault. Your ticket, Your fault.
What do we want? Animal Liberation!
When do we want it? Now! (Grubbs 2013b)

The chants were directed at anyone on the other side of the fence, but the individual pleas with customers took a different direction. Some children shouted to other children, "You should just go home. The animals are so sad in there," and some adults took a more direct stance, "Don't be an asshole and teach your kids that captivity is acceptable" (Grubbs 2013b). The signs, on the other hand, perform and archive nonverbal communication within the End Captivity Now campaign. The images communicated to those physically present and continue to communicate through digital communities. The signs included humorous references to popular culture, in addition to aggressive attacks against Caged Entertainment and the owner to produce disidentificatory thoughts. Toward the end of the demonstration, Levi was asked by a reporter to identify activists who had travelled far distances to attend, and they pointed my direction. I found the article the next day and was pleased to see that I was among a cohort of travellers who had crossed geopolitical borders for the demonstration. In terms of maintaining my public commitment, the article indicated my justification for the long drive: "Jennifer Grubbs, 28, brought her 13-month-old daughter Emory and sister Samantha, 22, all the way from Cincinnati 'to show solidarity,' she said" (Gordon 2013). The day concluded around 4 pm and Emory had reached her limit with regard to patience. Without a large research budget or couches to crash on, we decided to drive through the night back to Cincinnati, Ohio. We did not encounter any resistance crossing the border back into the US despite the lack of documentation from Emory's father. The inconsistency of regulation, or lack thereof, at the border crossing demonstrates the more obvious manifestations of privilege. Upon reflection, it would seem as though the resistance I encountered entering Canada were clearly an exception to racial, ethnic, cisgender, and heteronormative privilege.

PLAYFUL RESISTANCE

I continued to travel back and forth over the next few years to attend demonstrations with the End Captivity Now campaign. I had watched as the campaign grew, and as the legal pressure facing the activists increased. I was inspired by their resilience and creativity. The posters, the slogans, the scheduled events. The campaign had evolved into a well-oiled machine in a relatively short time span. And yet, I still could not point to anything in particular that was unique or distinct about the campaign itself. I began unpacking the scripted nature of the events and teasing out the interactions I had with folks over the years. Throughout the chapter, the physical and emotional labour that goes into entering activist spaces that are not quite your own, negotiating the gendered embodiment of reproductive labour, and the performativity that takes place within a direct action campaign is nuanced. The next chapter teases out these performances within a queer understanding of both spectacle and play.

3

Direct Action as Queer Spectacle

When taken separately ... [they] all seem to represent a queer edge in a larger cultural phenomenon. When considered together, they add up to a fierce and lively queer subculture that needs to be reckoned with on its own terms.

(Halberstam and Volcano 1999, 154)

Good news! – The U.S. government decided today that because I did such a good job investigating the cyber-industrial complex, they're now going to send me to investigate the prison-industrial complex. For the next 35 months, I'll be provided with free food, clothes, and housing as I seek to expose wrongdoing by Bureau of Prisons officials and staff and otherwise report on news and culture in the world's greatest prison system. I want to thank the Department of Justice for having put so much time and energy into advocating on my behalf; rather than holding a grudge against me for the two years of work I put into in bringing attention to a DOJ-linked campaign to harass and discredit journalists like Glenn Greenwald, the agency instead labored tirelessly to ensure that I received this very prestigious assignment. – Wish me luck!

(The Sparrow Project 2015)

The rhetorical and revolutionary potential of eco-activist direct action challenges the interpellation of fundamental ideologies and practices of capitalism, industrialization, globalization, and the exploitation of ecologies through language, digital practice, and performance. The geographic fluidity of the AELM emulate the globalized corporate powers they challenge. Not only are activists mobile, but campaigns themselves travel and translate beyond geopolitical borders. Because the state-corporate-industrial complex monopolizes access to the social bases of power, particularly violence, non-state actors are always already at a disadvantage to demand radical change. Thus, in order to amplify their perceived power, eco-activists must queer, or re-envision and rearticulate, power itself through the performance of powerful direct actions.

The performance of a public vigil, for example, rearticulates the social and political discourses that do not allow humans to publicly mourn the loss of animal life in laboratories, by exposing, altering, and/or inverting taken-for-granted understandings and practices of vivisection. The vigil, which can entail activists gathering in a public space, lighting candles, and wearing all black, calls into question the precarity of animal lives, through a graphic depiction of animal suffering, and makes visible the invisibility of how speciesism is an accepted part of interpellation of the good citizen (Butler 2006, 22, 46). The vigil further challenges the cognitive dissonance humans use to separate products from persons.[1] The use of public performance as direct action calls into question and challenges a slew of accepted truisms: that human animals are more valuable than nonhuman animals; that "doing one's job" safeguards one from political and/or ethical responsibility; that government and corporate interests are distinct and separate; that legislation is passed for the public good rather than private profit; and, particularly relevant here, that average, everyday people are powerless to change various structures, laws, and customs. Direct action is a queer performance that plays with and transgresses the normative boundaries of society, and it poses an effective, convincing, and powerful critique that queers social/political normativity.

To illustrate a particular form of direct action, this chapter focuses on how certain types of protests can function as spectacle to create terministic screens, within Goffman's metaphor of theatre, to queer the process of interpellation and create disidentificatory thoughts. The performance enacts disidentification through the humour, satire, intimidation, and what Leap refers to as, "the social formation of affect" (Leap 2015, 663). I then discuss the queering of protest as spectacle through direct action and how this demonstrates disidentification. The chapter concludes with a detailed ethnographic account with the Britches Brigade and a discussion of playfulness, a form of disidentification, during home demonstrations as a queer mode of protest.

PLAY AS POWERFUL RESISTANCE

The literature on drag performance and political theatre further contribute to the theoretical framework, as these texts historicize the tactics of direct action and articulate its liberatory potential. Gramsci provided a frame to understand how individuals participate in systems of domination that was further articulated by Althusser. Rosa Luxemburg, however, clarified that although individuals participate in the reproduction of oppressive systems, they are not fools (Glaberman 2012, 31). This analysis extends that sentiment to activists, emphasizing the rhetorical efficacy of play and performance during direct actions such as home demonstrations. Applying Luxemburg's empowering sentiment regarding workers under capitalism, the activists are not fools in their loud, confrontational, aggressive public performances that narrowly blame systemic issues on individual capitalists and vivisectors (ibid.). They are, in fact, creating a public theatre for onlookers to view the conditions in which capitalism, speciesism, and neoliberalism are foolishly accepted and promulgated by the viewer. The fool is the hegemonic viewer. Further, activists recognize the liminality of their direct rescues and vandalism, and still use these tactics to destabilize the perception that these industries are indestructible. The fool is the one afraid to open the cage.

As a challenge to the neoliberal moment, Graeber encourages activists to utilize the political and social imaginary (Gusterson and Besteman 2009, 93). This type of mobilization is predicated on the imagined reality of a post-capitalist and post-neoliberal society. Political theatre taps into this imaginary through the inherent play in exaggerating neoliberal individualism and choice through disidentification. According to activist and performance theorist Benjamin Shepard, play creates "open spaces where new sets of rules and social relations take shape. Play refers to the jest infused with satirical performance that brings joy and lightheartedness to otherwise serious and enraged activism. Here social actors feel compelled to participate in a broader social change drama" (Shepard 2011, 244). Shepard argues that these types of direct actions serve to empower individuals that are systematically excluded from bureaucratic decision-making processes; rather than passively accepting the laws, rules, and regulations made by detached decision makers, people directly participate in the reconstruction of alternative reality. That reality may not be wholesale or long term, but it is, at the very least, the creation of a new now that challenges a targeted grievance. The ability to create and recreate shared realities during a direct action relies on playfulness exemplified by a series of sarcastic and satirical rituals such as collective chants. After destroying hunter towers in Wisconsin, activists detailed the motivation for the action:

We find that when we attack under the blanket of night with masks on we get a lot more done than we ever could standing on the sidewalk with signs. We don't expect our small destructive acts to destroy speciesism, but striking directly at those who murder our non-human relatives feels meaningful, and is fucking fun! We know waiting for 'the movement' to grow is a trap — waiting promotes waiting and acting promotes acting. All there is to do is to sharpen our teeth and get better at attacking domination! (Anonymous L 2020)

The spectacle of direct action queers the ways in which dissent is performed and understood.

As discussed in the introduction, eco-activists are not the first to use play and political theatre, and key theorists used in this analysis have examined political performance through Pêcheux's (as an extension of Althusser) framework of disidentification (Althusser 1971; Muñoz 1999; Shepard 2011; Pêcheux 1982). Although it is outside the aim and scope of this book to recount the complicated history of these strategies, it is sufficient to say play and political performance are part and parcel of most, if not all, contemporary social movements: the Occupy movement, the Quebec student strikes, the anti-Iraq war movement, the global justice movement, ACT UP and the AIDS movement, Abbie Hoffman and the Yippies, etc. (Shepard, Bogad, and Duncombe 2008; Shepard 2011; Shepard 2013; 2011; Shepard and Hayduk 2002; Shepard 2013). Playful demonstrations and theatrical protests create a public space, a spectacle, to challenge oppressive systems such as homophobia, globalization, economic inequality, and health disparities. Direct action, through its boundary blurring of the public and private sphere, brings marginalized issues to such centres of daily life such as shopping districts and residential neighbourhoods. Social movements use play to creatively fuse critiques of social structures with such joyful activities as drum circles, dance, and song. For example, the use of political theatre was an important strategy during the 1980s HIV/AIDS advocacy movement.

Play as Political Strategy

From ACT UP to Circus AMOK, queer activism challenged systems of power with exaggerated mimicry on the public stage of the streets. Circus AMOK organized home demonstrations that targeted defence subcontractors in an effort to challenge the disproportionate government budget for defence rather than public health (Shepard 2011, 258). In effort to queer the anti-war effort, campaigns such as Absurd Response to an Absurd War emerged and relied on a strategic rhetoric of exaggeration. Activists utilized public die-ins and drag races to draw attention to the health disparities and violence disproportionately inflicted on the gay community in New York City. Play, as a political strategy, refers to the playful jest infused with satirical performance that brings lightness to otherwise fiery activism. Drag races, whether they re-enact Judy Garland's funeral or mark the anniversary of the police violence at Stonewall Inn, manage to mix glitter, fishnet stockings, and holistic political analyses of queer repression. While activists mourned those whom they love, they fought to protect those still living. They used play as not only a strategy to challenge the violent social structures, but also to laugh and temporarily suspend their pain. Similarly, the AELM engages in play by delivering elaborate neoliberal proclamations, splashing red paint on fur coats, issuing clever communiqués, seizing poaching vessels at sea, and, even, interrupting a confrontational demonstration with a five-minute-dance-party. These acts, and many more, embody a critique to neoliberalism, capitalism, and speciesism, and, importantly, they allow activists to form supportive, dynamic communities to mourn, grieve, rage, and celebrate with.

The use of playfulness is quite telling in the face of its topic and target – animal abuse and exploitation. Activists utilize the empowering nature of play as an attempt to counter the overwhelming sense of loss of animal lives. Continually witnessing the suffocating reality of animal cruelty and repeatedly protesting outside of a lobster restaurant or a university laboratory is emotionally exhausting. Working with clandestine networks of people, placing trust in others despite the intense vulnerabilities of committing illegal direct action together, produces a particular type of paranoia. Constantly reminding oneself of the millions of animals that are killed dominates the work of an animal liberationist. The power structure is so blatantly controlled by animal oppressors that even the most strident campaign can appear miniscule compared to multi-billion-dollar animal-and-ecology use industries. Shepard elaborates on how a sense of loss can strengthen community: "feelings of loss lingered within a tense struggle to create a different kind of space. People needed a space to come together. I think what drove people to ACT UP … it brought together people who were desperate for some kind of cultural, social, political change, like now. Not tomorrow, but right now. It was a place where a new generation of activists found their voices" (Shepard 2011, 246). The statistics remain glaring to those holding the signs. Every second, every minute, and by the end of the hour, millions of animal bodies have been maimed, raped, and murdered. While activists chant, raid, and torch, the reality of those animal bodies remains starkly at the forefront of their conscience. While the locks are smashed and beautiful animals are removed from their cages, the feeling of joy is quickly replaced by the sobering reality of how many more cages must be destroyed yet remain intact.

The crisis of animal exploitation produces a desperation in which direct action activists are mobilized on the basis of urgency moreso than rhetorical strategy. That urgency, however, does not preclude the AELM from engaging in a multi-pronged approach that scaffolds their strategy and tactics. Perhaps some of the activists attending a demonstration are initially motivated by feelings of urgency and desperation, but that does not embody the movement as a whole. Political theatre relies on the empowering nature of play as an attempt to counter the overwhelming sense of loss of animal lives. Play is a way to combat these negative emotions – it is a cathartic release and a creative re-channelling of one's emotional life. Play enables animal activists to laugh even while confronting egregious acts of violence committed by fellow humans.

While recounting the animal abuses through a megaphone, activists may intersperse a call-and-return chant to lighten the tense atmosphere. For instance, at one demonstration, activists had gathered outside the home of the owner of one specific animal-and-ecology use company to pressure the owner of the company. Not only does this specific company exploit animals for entertainment, but it has also been exposed for excessive negligence and cruelty, keeping animals in unsanitary and unsafe conditions. The demonstration concluded with a remix of Carly Rae Jepsen's (dreadful but catchy) radio hit "Call Me Maybe," changing the lyrics to mock the overarching sense of surveillance and intimidation through song. They sang, "Hey, shitheads, I just met you and this is crazy. But you can't have my number so don't call me. Ever!" The activists' playful remix was directed at the local police that had been present for the entire demonstration. One demonstrator shared a video and commented, "five hours with the PD. We ended it off with a dance party blasting 'Call Me Maybe' into their cars. Don't call me. Ever."[2] The song and dance party were obviously done in jest, which helped create an uplifting and "spectacular" moment for the activists engaged in a long campaign against the company. Again, this was a shift in voice from the aggressive proclamations directed at the owner to the playful singing directed at the police. The activists, through this shift in voice, queered the spectacle of the protest as both confrontational and festive.

Negotiating Confrontation and Humour

The creativity and playfulness of such direct action queers the ways in which marginalized peoples can confront systems of power. SHAC activists, for instance, commonly infuse their chants, proclamations, and printed materials with humour and sarcasm. But this humour and sarcasm are also aggressive and seek to effect serious social change. As SHAC-7 defendant Josh Harper states:

> This was the threat of Stop Huntingdon Animal Cruelty; we saw through all of the social conditioning that tells us that we are too weak to effect change. We went straight to the homes of those in power, challenged them on their golf courses, [and] screamed at them while they vacationed at summer homes. Tooth and nail we went after their profits, and along the way refused to divide and fracture over broken windows or graffiti. Everyone was welcome if they would fight, and I smile so big [that] it hurts when I think of the grandmothers, the punks, the students, and all the other unlikely comrades who marched together in defiance of the false hierarchy that tells us to keep separate and leave the rich to their own devices. We didn't stay in our place. In fact, we recognized that our place was wherever the hell we chose, and the world of finance and animal abuse was rocked as a result. (Harper 2012)

Harper illustrates how home demonstrators blend both humor and creative aggression into an effective campaign. The strategic use of humour, in combination with physical performance, infuses power into play. A playful chant, such as when protestors would shout, "Voldermort owns this zoo," can help to interrupt activists' aggressive proclamations and heated interactions with neighbors.[3] That humor then places people at ease, which can actually aid the persuasiveness of the direct action. The fact that any activist can (more or less) spontaneously create and lead a chant at any point during the demonstration also establishes a more open space. In this way, then, the playfulness of chants reflects a wider goal and vision: to create a more inclusive, bottom-up social order in which everyone, both human animals and other-than-human animals, are able to live freely and joyously.

Subversion or Hegemonic

The concern, as raised by gender theorists with regard to drag performance, is the degree to which mimicry actually subverts rather than reinscribes ideology. This skepticism questions the agency of the activism because "even when self-consciously addressed to the matter of gender, drag can reinscribe dominant ideology – not because it provides an exemplary resolution into that system [as in the literature on ritual reversal] but because the subject of conscious manipulation can never fully enter into the realm of the unconscious" (Morris 1995, 584). Butler interrogated the subversive possibilities of drag performance, though she and other queer theorists remain skeptical of the hegemonic constraints that can hinder this liberatory potential (Butler 2011, 90–5; Muñoz 1999, 89–115; Halberstam and Volcano 1999, 2–7, 35–9). Butler suggests that "drag fully subverts the distinction between inner and outer psychic space and effectively mocks the expressive model of gender and the notion of a true gender identity" (1990, 174). Drag, according to Butler, moves the "reality" of gender into crisis mode, as it blurs the naturalized but artificial narrative wherein so-called "masculinity" is inherently connected to an ostensibly equally inherent quality of maleness, and "femininity" likewise to femaleness (Butler 1990, xxiii). Drag's exaggeration, and therefore subversion, of this pseudo-scientific paradigm of "sex and gender" fundamentally calls into question what actually constitutes "gender" as well as the artificiality of our constructed "knowledge" of gender. Drag consequently opens a space within which the always already shaky realities of so-called sex and gender can be seen as they are: as social creations. This shift in mental frame can serve as an impetus to a radical rethinking of gender as a social construct. Similarly, the exaggeration of neoliberalism within the street theatre of satirical negotiation can shift the way audiences conceptualize their own position within neoliberal capitalism. "Audience" remains a loose construct in the realm of direct action. For example during demonstrations the audience ranges from those passing by on the street, to those watching from within their homes, to those who will view the protest online later that evening. The audience is fluid during direct rescues, lab raids, and acts of sabotage and vandalism. Whether it is the owner of the tree farm, someone who viewed the communiqué weeks later, or a consumer that could no longer patronize a targeted business, the potentiality for change is vast, and the subversion of neoliberal norms is infinite.

Play, and particularly the performance of neoliberal exaggeration, relies on exposing the disjointed relationship between the signifying system (neoliberal capitalism) and the reality (alienated labour and mystified perceptions of individual power) that is facilitated by ideology. The use of play during demonstrations "is part of a larger holistic framework for social change, which includes a clear, well-articulated proposal, an analysis, media advocacy, and an element of freshness and surprise, with a jigger of intelligence, play, and performance" (Shepard 2011, 273). The tactic of exaggeration exposes the ludicrous disillusions of neoliberal capitalism, and it relies on a combination of other tactics as well. Public demonstrations are oftentimes preceded or followed by educational forums such as a teach-in or film screening. For example, ALA collective and Britches Brigade have co-sponsored teach-ins that involved showing a documentary about various animal industries at a community space in conjunction with a punk music show. Other campaigns and collectives have hosted karaoke events that create a space for activists to gather outside of the public demonstration and strengthen community surrounding an oftentimes-shared identification with punk music. These are also great spaces to host fundraisers that support the campaign, animal rescues, and political prisoners. In other cases, organizers schedule a film screening featuring a political documentary and provide dinner prepared by activists or a local Food Not Bombs chapter.[4] It is not uncommon to see an overlap at political events and run into the same people participating in film screenings, DIY shows, workshops, skill-set trainings, and public protests. These events are often insular and exist to solidify rather than promulgate, and thus strengthen internal community and commitments. The public protest, however, creates a spectacle because the intended audience is not necessarily those with affinity politics.[5]

The large demonstration described in the last chapter is just one illustration of how this spectacular use of both private social gatherings serves to solidify a sense of community and political resolve within the AELM, while simultaneously engaging in confrontational direct actions that promulgate a critique of speciesism and authoritarianism to those outside the AELM. The 2013 End Captivity Now demonstration was preceded by targeted memes, tweets, and other forms of outreach shared through digital media. In the days leading up to the demonstration, organizers held a bake sale sponsored by a local anarchist collective, there were merchandise sales promoted through digital media, and punk shows that distributed leaflets condemning Caged Entertainment. These were smaller, in-group acts of solidification, but they do not move the campaign into the realm of the spectacle. The demonstration provided a stage for activists to engage in direct action, providing an alternative screen for individuals to respond to the process of interpellation and subject formation. The mere presence of individuals chanting, shouting proclamations into bullhorns, and storming the gates of the park without paying admission to disrupt a dolphin show all illustrate that something else is possible. Something else is possible when activists can put down their bullhorns and, in the face of an underwhelming presence of cops, begin to climb the chain link fence separating you from rows of cages of beagles, climb the fence, and begin passing animals to activists in a direct rescue.[6] The spectacular moves the audience to question their decision to identify with speciesism, and to possibly reimagine a different relationship between human animals and other-than-human animals. If the locks can be glued, the bioengineering labs raided, and the minks set free, then we can no longer think of these corporations as impenetrable.

PROTEST AS SPECTACLE

Graeber encourages activists to utilize the political and social imaginary in order to challenge the "neoliberal moment" (Gusterson and Besteman 2009). Neoliberalism refers to a new form of "neo laissez faire economics." As activist and author Jason Del Gandio succinctly states:

> [Neoliberalism is] based on the deregulation of free markets and the privatization of wealth. It subordinates government control to the interests of private profit. The government – rather than regulating the market to assure a level playing field – becomes an extension of market activity, the servant of the industries to which it is captive. Neoliberalism provides tax breaks for the rich, reduces spending on social programs and welfare, expands corporate control and eradicates labor rights, environmental protections, drug and food regulations and even national law. The basic purpose is to allow private interests to own and control every aspect of the human, social and natural world. (Del Gandio 2010)

Challenging the hegemonic cruelty inherent in privatizing and profiting from the suffering and murder of other-than-human animals must involve imagining a post-capitalist and post-speciesist reality. Such imagining is facilitated by disidentification, which encourages others to disentangle themselves from current conditions and practices of neoliberalism, the animal industry, and speciesism. The use of direct action, is as a form of political theatre, is one way to facilitate an alternative political imaginary.

The home and public demonstrations, as tactics within the strategy of direct action, conducted by eco-activists often rely upon the use of spectacle to create disidentificatory thoughts. The spectacle can be broadcast and rebroadcast on a variety of stages: television, social media, news coverage, and personal communication. Moreover, the act itself can be entirely virtual. In this way, the stage can be both physical and digital. Pickering expands on the strategic use of mass media:

> We always assumed that the mass media was not on our side. It was expected that our most inarticulate statements would be the ones to

show up in the news, so we tried our best to improve our articulation and speak in soundbites ... Sometimes I would just ignore their
questions and give a pre-rehearsed statement as if it were an answer. In
our case this could work because when a million-dollar building burns
to the ground they don't have a choice but to do a story on it ... Earth
Liberation Front actions were sensational, so we never expected that
the notoriously sensational US media wouldn't sensationalize their
coverage. Reporters are suckers for a big story, and the more radical
we came off, the bigger the story. It was as if they didn't realize that
part of our objective was to get attention and they were giving it to
us, or maybe more that they didn't care because it sold so well ... We
learned to play the rebel card ... They would make a statement about
terrorism or violence expecting me to argue against it, but instead I'd
tell them about how they ain't seen nothing yet. (Pickering 2007, 7)

Pickering collated communiqués in his book, *The Earth Liberation Front:
1997–2002*, and provides a succinct, nuanced discussion about the spectacular use of direct action (without necessarily using that framework).
Eco-activists relied on clearing houses like the NAELFPO and NAALPO
to disseminate their communiqués to a wider audience. As technologies
changed, and we experience a dramatic increase in personal communication devices in our lives, the AELM has wrestled with the tension of
e-activism. The dialectic between online and in-person activism can be
found in many campaigns and collectives. To this end, the End Captivity
Now campaign illustrates the complexities of these discussions in social
movement studies.

Hashtagging the Revolution

The End Captivity Now campaign relied heavily on social media to share
images, videos, and stories through digital communities. The hashtags
provided a linkage to connect these contributions regardless of geographic
location and have even dominated the discourse on Twitter regarding
Caged Entertainment itself. Utilizing CDA to examine how power is conveyed and challenged through digital media, I examined how activists
contribute to the discourse of direct action through popular social media
sites. The integration of direct action in digital media provides another
medium for activists to not only refuse to submit to the good/bad protestor framework, but also engage in digital performances of disidentification outside of that framework. The activists can reimagine the power of
animal-and-ecological use industries through the rhetorical use of digital

media components such as hashtags. For example, the most popular suggestions on Twitter and Instagram for "Caged Entertainment" are those of the End Captivity Now campaign. The commonly used hashtags include: #marchoncagedentertainment, #cagedentertainment, #endcaptivity, and #zoo. The tactic of a social media takeover floods the feed of those following any given industry, individual, or business with counter-images and messages. The Facebook and Instagram accounts for the campaign are both @cagedentertainmentsucks, which of course drives up page suggestions since users often search for "Caged Entertainment." Images may include photos from demonstrations as well as humorous and satirical memes. The memes range from simple edited photographs that have been run through meme generators to professional leaflets posted by activists.

Digital communications, as José Esteban Muñoz describes with regard to the power of drag performance, further extend the representation of the possible within the socio-political imaginary.[7] One profound example of this political imaginary can be found in the Canadian television show *Schitt's Creek*. The show's co-creator, Daniel Levy, has repeatedly explained why he created a fictitious town that seemingly does not have homophobia: "I have no patience for homophobia … it's been amazing to take that into the show. We show love and tolerance. If you put something like that out of the equation, you're saying that doesn't exist and shouldn't exist. We've watched the growth and comfort of people who outwardly live their lives and aren't being feared of being targeted. And it has a ripple effect into people's homes" (Ivie 2018). In the show, the characters' gender and sexuality are not met with hostility or violence, despite the very real threats of both to those who do not conform and challenge the binaries of gender and sexuality. Levy created a town in which such hatred simply didn't exist; if nothing else this provided a temporal space in which marginalized bodies could be seen without this marginalization (Pollard 2020). I am drawn back to Levy's comments whenever I encounter AELM actions and rhetoric that suspends their own marginalization by creating spectacular performances that reimagine another world entirely.

Activists circulate memes produced by various individuals and collectives to creatively engage with campaigns and larger social movements through affect. In some cases, Instagram accounts feature photos of flyers that will be distributed, poster making sessions, and skills sharing workshops.[8] The activists engage in online trends such as "Social Media Tuesday" and "Throwback Thursday" to post comical memes on Instagram that may juxtapose a direct action claim with a photo of an adorable animal. Activists are able to engage in online conversations, debates, and networking through posting images and responding to them. The integration of Facebook, Instagram, Tumblr, and Twitter provide a cross-platform terrain to use multiple forms of digital communication in the creation of a larger, international dialogue. Throughout this ethnography, I wanted to look closer at the ways in which digital media is utilized. If we are to think about direct action as a performance, which this analysis does, then I argue that we can extend this to digital performances. To look closer at these performances, I identified specific account names and their frequent use of symbols such as # and @ to identify key phrases and campaigns. I also used Tag Sleuth, Wordle, and Tweet Archivist to generate word clouds and examine the linguistic analytics.[9]

These digital spaces facilitate a different theatrical stage, one that could mask identities while simultaneously increasing visibility, where activists engage in and discuss confrontational direct action. Digital spaces blur the perceived boundary between public and private, which is commonly noted by activists in their practice of security culture. At one point during this research, a well-known activist posted a public message on Facebook that playfully demonstrates the underlying tension amongst activists to utilize technology as a mechanism of dissent without getting caught:

> US Customs: You are so stupid. You missed my laptop.
> Always ready to flag me and copy my hard drive (the border is a Constitution-free zone), you missed the one thing you wanted despite it comprising at least 15% of my luggage, by volume.
> *Note to data smugglers*: Make your laptop the same size & color as the bottom of your suitcase and you're in the clear.
> (Anonymous B 2014)

This tongue-and-cheek post, which received nearly 100 likes within a few hours, engaged in a public critique of state surveillance. It is again not accidental that activists critique state surveillance in explicit ways (the activist also tagged the airport this occurred in) on a digital media site (Facebook) that archives user data and cooperates with the state to provide data on its users.[10] I have met many activists who use pseudonyms on social media sites. This provides a creative outlet to engage with digital media without the punitive threat of surveillance and harassment. However, anonymization can also empower trolls and fuel suspicion amongst activists. One particular exchange on Facebook sparked a larger debate about how activists should handle personal attacks. The activist posted the following comment and included the private message that someone had sent to them:

> I wake up to comments, emails, messages, like this pretty much every day now. This is a fake Facebook account that was created in February of this year with the sole purpose of harassing me (I know who it is). The joys of organizing.
>
> "Hey asshole I see you crumbled like the fucking little wimp you are. You can spin it but you can't deny you made a deal with [redacted]. Man you are so fucking stupid you are a joke. What story are you going to give about the money those suckers donated to your legal fund which you already spent on yourself. Oh ya and what about your educational fund. Judgment day will come for you and it will be sooner than you think. Have fun asshole." (Anonymous C 2013)

The user comments focused on exposing the individual who sent the message but did not elicit a larger discussion about the accusations. Seemingly, because the activist posted the comment themselves it increased their credibility by disclosing the attack, implying that the claims were outlandish. The post relied on the assumption that because they are sharing the accusation, the accusation must be unfounded.

Digital media is utilized as a way to send instant communication to other activists warning them of potential threats. Specifically, many campaigns utilize Facebook and other sites to share "snitch alerts," and provide information about government informants. One example is a post that appeared in July 2014 in which a collective posted a photograph of an individual with red text overlapping, "HEADS UP. SNITCH [NAME REDACTED] HAS MOVED TO SOUTHERN CALIFORNIA," with the following text in the box above:

> Snitch alert! [name redacted] has moved to Southern California, so activists there should watch out for him. You can learn more about his history of being a government informant and turning his back on activists here: [URL removed]. (Britches Brigade 2014b)

The activist-run site, Indymedia.org, is also the host of direct action announcements, follow-up, and archived video. The extensive archive of video can be used to identify activists that are suspected of working with the government. Many eco-activist websites feature running lists of exposed snitches, infiltrators, and abusers.

Digital media provides a public arena in which activists are account-able to one another. Because I followed the same campaigns closely, I received constant communication from other activists about suspicious activity. In a way, this created a stronger sense of self-awareness of how I would engage with the data I collected in this study. Specifically, I was intentional with my documentation and reluctant to use audio or visual recording devices while attending and participating in direct actions. It would have been immobilizing to my research and activism if I was sus-pected of cooperating with the state or blasted through digital media. At worst, I could have been falsely accused of being an informant, which I am not and never would be.

Exposing Abuse Online

In one post that was shared on Facebook and Twitter, an activist called into question the decision for an animal liberation conference to host a problematic member of the AELM:

What are people's thoughts on this? On the one hand going and speaking out against [redacted] and their ilk at the conference (which I can only assume will happen) might be a good idea and/ or might help sway some of the people going to this conference who aren't knowledgeable about the issues involved or don't know about them (although that could happen without formally lend-ing your name to the conference). On the other hand, it seems like there has been a lot of gauntlets thrown down with people saying they will not go to this conference because [redacted]/[name of con-ference] to drop [redacted] and [redacted] from the conference. To take part anyway and say it is because you don't want [redacted] to divide the movement (which is already very clearly divided) feels a bit like an undercutting of those efforts to me. Am I alone or do others feel like this is kind of a cop out? I find all this especially hard to swallow as [redacted] has been very quick to call out and vilify others for working/associating with people who have oppres-sive politics (which I agree is needed in the AR [animal rights] and Environmental movements), and this is now essentially saying they are going to be involved in a conference that is giving a platform to rampant transphobia. The more I write, the less conflicted I am feeling. I think this is bad on their part. What do others thing about this? (Anonymous D, n.d.)

Interestingly, the activist shared the official speaker announcement from both the campaign's website and Facebook that was being called into question. Several users engaged in a debate on whether or not the campaign should be called out in a more public physical venue. The discussion surrounding de-platforming points to the need for clear, mutually agreed upon principles by AELM campaigns regarding who should be given space and what kind of commitment does the movement have to accountability.[11] In the 1999 film *Pickaxe: The Cascadia Free State Story*, Tim Ream discusses the ongoing issues of sexism with the AELM:

> We were starting to look at the whole way society was organized, the way we as individuals related to the land and the way we related to each other ... A lot of the women were looking at the ways men and women were raised differently in society. And the way men are afforded a privilege in society, many privileges, that women are not afforded. We live in a patriarchal society and we are all conditioned to act that way. It was true in the forest campaign. I mean, men were the ones cutting down the forest. Men were the one profiting from it. It was a man in the White House and mostly men in congress that were making these laws, and when we broke those laws, it was mostly men that took us away to jail. But it wasn't just true in the mainstream society. Within our own campaign, the positions of men and women were quite often different. Women didn't like it and had to fight against it. Men were mostly the ones holding the video camera, and men were mostly the ones that stood in front of them and talked. Every single meeting that we had, every single action that we planned and carried out, there were always issues of male dominance that had to be looked at ... a lot of men had a hard time focusing on that issue. There was a lot of pain in our camp, and there was the excuse on the men's side that forests were falling and that we could look at our deep-seated patterns later, but we needed to get out in the forest and address that issue right now. (Lewis and Ream 1999)

The dire ecological crises are not an excuse to ignore structural injustice and acts of violence within these leftist circles. The tendency to push off addressing inner-movement issues has been referred to by activists as the "after the revolution phenomenon." But there should be a distinction between de-platforming and cancelling someone. Activists that violate shared principles in these sacred spaces should be called in for their acts of aggression and held accountable. The internet has provided a more accessible, safer platform to expose abusers, and a more direct way to collectively hold them accountable. Anarchists reject systems of state-sanctioned violence and thus rely on non-coercive processes to hold those who abuse accountable.

Spread the Word

Activists engage with digital media not just to publicize snitches and abusers, but the internet can facilitate network building and create digital communities. Many of the accounts I followed consistently posted confrontational rhetoric, damning condemnations of vivisectors, and explicit calls to mobilize and engage in direct action. I first learned about Britches Brigade campaign through a Facebook invitation from someone I did not know but whom I shared mutual friends with. Their Facebook events specifically named the campaign, the target, and the event time and place. The event created on social media has symbolic value; it embodies another aspect of the performative nature of direct action. Hundreds of people claimed they intended to attend the event, though only three individuals (other than the organizers) actually attended. Similarly, Britches Brigade used Facebook to mobilize activists for digital activism. In a Facebook post that was also sent out via Twitter, Britches Brigade shared a Pathway to Liberation event, "ABX Air has plans to transport primates from China into the US for labs on June 2nd. Help stop this shipment! Check out the below page, send emails (see the info on the page), and spread the word!" (Bridges Brigade 2014a). In addition to using social media as a mechanism to recruit activists, it can also be used to reimagine and rearticulate the corporate sovereignty awarded to these companies through neoliberal capitalism (elaborated on in chapter 1). The state relies on a neoliberal logic that insists bad protestors are violating deeply held democratic values by engaging in confrontational direct action. In one specific example, the animal-use park Caged Entertainment distributed programs to each customer that described the activists with End Captivity Now:

> Dear Friends, If you have seen protestors outside – we would like
> to explain. They are members of a fringe, radical animal liberation
> front that demands the closure of all zoos and aquariums – deny-
> ing children the opportunity to interact with amazing animals they
> would likely never see in the wild. Children who see and learn about
> our animals are more likely to become their defenders as humans
> continue to encroach on wild habitats. The protestors don't seem
> to care about that nor the fact that every independent investigation

into Caged Entertainment's animal care has disproven any allegation protestors have brought against us. We love and care deeply for the animals in our trust. You will see that today. (Anonymous E 2013)

The program itself is a one-way communication between Caged Entertainment and the public (patrons and protestors). However, activists were able to take a picture of the program and share it through social media to expose the storybook rhetoric that erases the documented violence against animals within Caged Entertainment. The image was shared by several activists and appeared multiple times in my Twitter, Instagram, and Facebook feeds. One activist posted the image with the caption, "This failure of logic will greet every person who grabs a program at Caged Entertainment this afternoon" (Anonymous F 2013). End Captivity Now's post received fifty likes within the first ten minutes and had dozens of comments. The multi-platform structure of social media provides a stage for eco-activists to interrupt the process of interpellation, and it is not as asymmetric as the street corner.

Whereas Caged Entertainment is protected through Canadian law and dominant ideology, End Captivity Now is seen as a threat to the law and the dominant ideology of speciesism. The campaign, however, invokes a particular political imaginary to tell a different story. Online, activists blast images of animal abuse, publicize testimony from ex-employees of the park, and exaggerate the societal rejection of the park in light of these egregious acts of violence. Twitter uses @ to tag handles and # to tag trending concepts and words that link Twitter accounts and words to establish trends. These symbols have been integrated into Facebook and Instagram to also contribute to trends and engage in the process of trending. In looking at the digital media accounts held by the campaigns included in this analysis, there was an interesting rearticulation of power through trends. I used the aggregating site TweetArchivist that integrates Instagram, Twitter, Vine, and Tumblr to gather the most commonly used hashtags associated with Caged Entertainment. The most commonly used hashtags with #CagedEntertainment include #ENDCAPTIVITY, #BLACKFISH, #DIED, #VEGAN, #CLOSING, #ABUSE, #EVIL, and #PROTEST. This is of particular interest because it demonstrates how activists can manufacture the digital discourse through social media. If an individual is curious about Caged Entertainment and follows it on any of the listed digital media sites, they are inadvertently bombarded with these words. Similarly, the most commonly used words associated with @CagedEntertainment include, "ENDCAPTIVITY," "HOPE," "OUT!," "ENDANGERED," "CAPTIVITY," "BLACKFISH," "AVOID," and

"EXPLOITATION-BASED." The digital space, in this sense, also creates an alternative screen similar to the ones discussed in the previous chapter, where activists can disidentify with speciesism itself.

HOME DEMONSTRATIONS

One common tactic, home demonstrations (protests at the personal residences of employees and affiliated constituents of targeted animal/ ecological exploiters) provide a salient example of a spectacular direct action that intends to produce disidentificatory thoughts. The performativity of such demonstrations creates a scene, similar to a theatrical play, in which the grim and hidden realities of vivisection are publicly staged for all to see. Activists, through political theatre, use voice as a central tool in which they utilize exaggeration to create alternative screens as well as alternative presentations of themselves. The modes of subversion, political street theatre and drag, rely on the activists' use of voice in combination with physical bodily performance. The performance of exaggeration does not solely rely on what is said, but also how it is said and how their bodies are presented. Dressed in similar clothes as the observers, you would not necessarily pick the demonstrators out of the crowd (if it were not for the bullhorns and posters). Part of their performance is also wearing some sort of animal liberation swag, whether it is clothing, a button, or a patch on their messenger bag. This can be a discreet signalling, such as a t-shirt with a recognized acronym, or something more blatant, like a political symbol tattooed in a prominent location. Demonstrators are not usually wearing masks or bandanas across their faces; they are dressed casually as if they joined the demonstration ad hoc.[12] In my experience, before a demonstration begins, demonstrators select someone to be the "public relations representative and police liaison." This job can entail holding the demonstration permit, presenting it to the police when they arrive, and engaging people on the street.[13] The public relations representative is not always a predetermined role, but rather given to someone willing to remain calm while discussing issues with those who may not agree with the demonstration. Although the PR rep is attending a demonstration with bad protestors, there is a performative separation between themselves and the activists. They create physical distance between themselves and the activists, engage in a different communication style and posture. If they were assigned the PR role prior to arriving, they may have dressed differently or modified body markers such as make-up and jewellery or concealed their tattoos and piercings.

The home demonstrations I attended, specifically the ones with ALA in WDC, exposed HLS's violence (which is often masked behind corporate walls) and brought this cruelty to the forefront by the garishness of the publicly performed spectacle. During one of the home demonstrations I mentioned earlier, I was holding a large sign that had a picture of a mutilated beagle with the words "This is not my kind of 'science'" written across the bottom. It was during this demonstration that I saw the ways in which performativity itself creates the disidentification. After ten minutes of chanting, a neighbour came outside and began to scream at us. He explained that the person we were targeting had a young baby who was probably trying to sleep, and more importantly, this person we had been shouting at is just a "good person" (Grubbs 2013a). One of the protestors stepped aside and began to engage the neighbour in a conversation. The protestor lowered the tone of her voice; she slowly explained one of the experimentations that the target had facilitated. The neighbour's body language began to shift from anger toward the protestors to disgust at the description of injecting beagles with chemicals. His demeanour began to change; his brows unfurled, his mouth tensed, he audibly sighed. He began shifting, loosening the firm grip his sneakers had on the pavement. The protestor was able to suspend her "proclamation voice" and invoke her "public relations" voice in order to facilitate the neighbour's disidentificatory thought process. The spectacle brought the experimentation out of the laboratory and to the neighbourhood, confrontationally asserting disidentification. Yet, simultaneously, the spectacle relied on the malleability of voice to ease the abrupt interruption of interpellation. This neighbor believed their friend was being targeted, harassed, without warrant. It was the task of the activists to shift the paradigm for these folks and expose the moral madness of speciesism. All the while, the home demonstration *is* a pressure tactic that is designed to confront individuals.

The spectacle of the home demonstration is an attempt to amplify the problem (animal exploitation) and the motivation (profit) by creating an alternative spectacle (one based on truth-telling and the adoption of an ethical relation to nonhuman animals). Demonstrators do this by creating a public performance. The demonstrators use their bullhorns to amplify their message and turn a sidewalk or front lawn into a public theatre. The power of the spectacle lies in its ability to demand attention and render abstract concepts into accessible courses of action. The method is both confrontational and invaluable. As Jean Baudrillard states, "This is our theatre of cruelty, the only one left to us – extraordinary because it unites the most spectacular to the most provocative" (The Spirit of Terrorism 2001, n.p.).

Stages, Screens, and Spectacles

Though Goffman is applied more aptly to how individuals interpret and perform gender, public protest benefits from the framework of theatre. The concept of the self cannot be understood without problematizing the concept of reality through performance. Social actors, in this case activists, create and rearticulate understandings of themselves through performances that are part of a contentious process of co-creating reality through symbolic actions (Burke 1969b; Goffman 1959). Further, activists rely on performance to present themselves to an audience, a public that interprets their own reality through the performance. Goffman argued that theatre serves as a metaphor for how people present themselves to one another based on cultural values, norms, and expectations (1959). Digital media provides an omnipresent stage in which activists are always already performing crafted versions of themselves. In this sense, direct action allows for not only the activist to create a spectacle for the onlooker, but to also perform an idealized version of which they imagine themselves. Amongst activists that are oftentimes ostracized for their physical appearance (political tattoos, facial piercings, asymmetric, dyed hair, DIY altered clothing, extraneous carabiners, and undisguised body odour) demonstrations provide a suspended space to playfully and temporarily reinvent oneself. In the creation of self as an activist, individuals rely on the stage of social media. One must decide what their character will be, which screens they want to engage, and how they will present themselves through physical representations, intellectual and political articulations, kinship networks, and so on. These performances produce terministic screens that produce forms of disidentification.

The activists, through the dialectic of confrontational rhetoric and playfulness, subvert the dominant screens of society, the screens in which most Americans understand social order, by performing a screen in which those do not exist. A world without speciesism is like the small, rural town Schitt's Creek, which exists without homophobia. It is a form of disidentification that is predicated on a political imaginary. When activists release 2,000 minks from a fur farm outside of Chicago, it creates a screen in which those who break the law can get away with it. During many of the demonstrations I attended, I experienced confrontational onlookers that were convinced protestors were breaking the law. The assumed screen was one of complacency, that individuals engaging in public assembly were violating social and legal norms. In attempt to create a different screen, activists happily reminded the angry onlookers that they do not have to bother calling the police because activists themselves had received a permit.[14] On several occasions, neighbours would threaten to call the police, even though cops were already standing right there as part of the city's alleged protocol to attend "approved" demonstrations. Referring back to Althusser and the concept of the ISA/SA social structure, individuals are socialized through institutions to not only fear the establishment, but also revere it. The knee-jerk to use the cops as a threat to dissuade activists reinforces our reliance on a police state. In this sense, activists have the opportunity to create an alternative screen where the establishment is challenged publicly and is forced to show its otherwise-concealed violent hand. In other words, the friendly neighbourhood cops are not just there to "protect our access to first amendment speech," but rather they are there as a coercive reminder of state power. Activists rely on video recordings to capture police harassment, which can be livestreamed through various platforms in real-time.

The demonstrators with ALA began their performance by ringing the doorbell or buzzing an apartment complex intercom.[15] For this example, let's pretend the target's name was Wallace, which happens to be the name of my very, very needy Great Dane rescue. "Hi, Wallace. We spoke several days ago, but you refused to meet with me in person. I wanted to meet with you and talk about your client, Huntingdon Life Sciences." Once the activists confirmed that the "target," an employee of AstraZeneca, was home, the performance began with a series of chants. "One, two three, four. Open up the cage door! Five, six, seven, eight. Smash the locks and liberate! Nine, ten, eleven, twelve. Wallace can go to hell!" These chants solidified the activists' solidarity and reminded onlookers that the demonstration was all about targeting Wallace. In between chants, a few of the organizers gave speeches and proclamations that addressed the target loudly enough for all to hear. One of the organizers took the bullhorn and shouted, "We tried to meet with you, Wallace. We are sure you would not want to be affiliated with the grotesque cruelty that AstraZeneca and Huntingdon Life Sciences are conducting on your behalf." The demonstrators then recounted the horrific vivisection, the thousands of animals ordered from the breeding facility, and the discredited research results from the vivisection that AstraZeneca had engaged in with animals supplied by HLS. The activists, with the aim of maintaining a consistent screen, appeared rational and eager to resolve the issue. The demonstrations intended to make it all look simple: cease relations with HLS and the campaign against you will cease (Grubbs 2013a).

This spectacle invited the audience (onlookers and passersby) to witness the exchange as they exposed HLS, challenged the stereotypical portrayal of violent animal-rights advocates, and mocked many of the taken for granted truisms of global capitalism (for example, that our lives should be based on profit and/or that "the market" equals freedom). The proclamations ensured that the audience clearly understood how many animals were (are) being exploited through HLS-contracted vivisection. The demonstrators did not break from their theatrical characters during the performance; they playfully engaged their audience but turned off their bullhorns when a leashed animal was walked past (Grubbs 2013a). All of this accentuated the heightened sense of spectacle that was being enacted. The activists remained committed to their characters to ensure the audience clearly understood the problem through the terministic screen they had created.

The demonstrators consistently used the first name of the person targeted while repeatedly asking the target to come outside and discuss the situation. Those in the "audience" might have thought (as I once did) that the demonstrators were short-sighted in their faith that such an invitation to talk and discuss the corporate relationship between AstraZeneca and HLS would be productive. A passerby challenged the demonstrators and asked me, "Don't you guys realize this person can't do anything about it? They work for some giant company that doesn't care what one person has to say. They have this job to pay their bills, and if they stand up to company practices then they will just be fired" (Grubbs 2013a). But the demonstrators were not so naïve; they knew full well that the target is unlikely to come outside and even less likely to change their company's practice of animal exploitation. Instead, this kind of demonstration, as queer a performance and powerful disclosure of normativity, rather than a literal political plea, exaggerated the agency of the target and, therefore, highlights powerlessness common to the average person living within capitalism (Leap and Motschenbacher 2012, 6–9). As an additional queering effect, this demonstration highlighted the passerby's implicit understanding of this powerlessness. The onlookers were already aware that corporate sovereignty, as discussed in chapter 2, produces good subjects that, for the most part, are powerless to effect change (Pêcheux 1982, 158; Grubbs 2014a, 246–8). The spectacle, through this alternative screen, called attention to what the onlookers (and the target) already knew, but also forced them to confront the issues and problems of the current system and thereby become more empowered to actually enact social change.

The neighbour that came out to defend the vivisector described above became part of the performance as he confronted his own disidentificatory thoughts while listening to the graphic details of vivisection. The protestors utilize the paradigm of good versus bad protestor in their performance insofar as they can shift their voice to accommodate the onlookers. This dialectic serves as its own respectability politic performance, which returns to the question Butler raised regarding whether drag subverts or reinforces gender. Ultimately, however, the flexibility in their performance queers the dichotomous thinking that protestors must be either good or bad. These campaigns encouraged activists to publicly disrupt exploitative structures through creative means. The use of performance, direct action, and spectacle queers the act of protest that is aimed at primary, secondary, and tertiary targets. Activists creatively engaged in playful direct action while aggressively attacking corporations. The successes of these campaigns, and specifically the implementation of the SHAC model, demonstrate the power in playful protest, and the importance of direct action in the AELM to disidentify with neoliberal capitalism, speciesism, and state repression.

Alternative Screens: Challenging Notions of Science

This particular mode of activism, direct action that targets the exclusively capitalist aims of animal-use industries, provides an effective critique of speciesism. The campaigns against these industries point to how capitalism facilitates the systematic domination and exploitation of other-than-human animals. The rhetoric of pharma-capitalism has interpellated the public, or the good subjects, to believe that vivisection industries can "cure" ailments and illnesses if only individuals raise or donate more money these industries can conduct more animal-based research. The overwhelming powerlessness, coupled with the prolonged uncertainty during the global health pandemic of COVID-19, facilitates a pervasive sentiment that science will save us all. We, as a human society, need scientific research and advancements. But, at what costs to our humanity? Further, how are these vulnerabilities that make us dependent on science manipulated to manufacture our consent with grotesque research practices? The death and destruction that viruses and disease wreak on our lives are visceral. They destroy communities and, ultimately, can steal our own lives. As I prepared this book for publication, I shuffled three of my children through Zoom calls and homework because their school was closed. I've had friends contract the virus and need hospitalization. COVID-19 has brought the entire world to a halt, albeit admittedly not at quite the same pace, or with the same distinct lack of national leadership, as in the US. Although the impacts are distinct in different geographic locations, one universal is that death and illness impact everyone (World Health Organization n.d.).

The history of medical research is beyond the scope of this book, but it is important to note that vivisection has a long history of involving research on marginalized human bodies.[16] But the notion that human life warrants animal death is predicated on the constructed hierarchy that divides and privileges human over animal, referred to throughout the book as speciesism. Confrontational direct action, in response, places footage and photographs in the public eye that capture the conditions in which these animals live: the violent handling and grotesque maiming at the hands of vivisectors. During a home demonstration, the public, those onlooking, residing nearby, and watching coverage of the demonstration on the internet are all confronted with the realities that are veiled behind the corporate walls of animal experimentation through signs, proclamations, and chants (Grubbs 2014c). Further, the footage shared during these demonstrations of inside these closed-off laboratories are gathered through direct action: lab raids. The utilitarian rationales are confronted with what that actually means to excuse the violent vivisection of some to possibly aid others. The utilitarian logic embedded in the vivisection asserts that through animal death we save human lives. However, a glimpse inside the violent laboratories challenge the moral philosophy that this extraneous suffering could be for the good of society. The laboratories may be veiled through security walls and barriers granted by corporate sovereignty, but the onlookers during the demonstration cannot avoid it. For example, I joined a demonstration at the Greater Cincinnati/Northern Kentucky International (CVG) Airport that set up at baggage claim. Travellers could not exit the airport without being confronted with bloody images and damning proclamations held by Bridges Brigade activists. The ability to expose existing acts of violence at the hands of animal-use industries is perhaps one of the more powerful, spectacular components of confrontational direct action. The use of surveillance to capture these manifestations of violence, such as drone footage and access inside slaughterhouses and laboratories, and publicize them in physical and digital spaces has been met with state acts of repression (Potter 2012; 2014; Civil Liberties Defense Center 2012).

Bunnies, Airplanes, and Primates: Britches Brigade

The organizers from Britches Brigade had travelled through Ohio for a demonstration outside the CVG in December 2013. The activists had also travelled to the Gathering for Total Liberation in 2014 to present on a panel about strategic organizing for effective campaigning, the Pathway to Liberation tour, and the international collaboration to end the transport of animals to laboratories. The organizers also led a lecture about building strategic alliances for successful campaigns. In the panel, the organizers discussed why Britches Brigade engages in a national tour to build relationships with other groups within and adjacent to the AELM. The organizers also discussed the ways in which their campaign and actions support a national grassroots network. The organizers then travelled to the Earth First! Rendezvous to deliver a similar talk, and skills sharing. The organizers emphasized that state repression should not and does not deter anyone from being an effective activist.

On 3 January 2014, I participated in a demonstration with Britches Brigade as part of the Pathway to Liberation Tour at the CVG airport that targeted Delta and KLM Air France. My sister, who had travelled with me to Canada and shares a similar politic, was excited to attend the demonstration at the airport. The demonstration was originally scheduled for Thursday, 2 January, at noon, but as the day approached I was unable to find any information on the Facebook page or website. I waited until 11 am and then sent a message through Facebook to get information about where to meet. Thirty minutes later I received a message from one of the organizers saying that the demonstration was pushed back until 3 January at 6 pm. I also received a friend request from one of the organizers on Facebook and noticed that we had several activist friends in common. It is not uncommon to be "vetted" in some capacity before being given more information about a demonstration or gathering. Although I was excited at the rare opportunity to engage in political activism in my hometown, I was also apprehensive about attending a demonstration in a visible location during the holiday (travel) season. At the time, I was employed as an administrator at a private school. My colleagues and supervisor were unaware of my political activism, and this would have been an awkward way to introduce them to it.[17] Ultimately, my solidarity with the campaign superseded the pragmatic concern for workplace discrimination. Perhaps foolishly, though I would make that decision again today if faced with it, I prioritized my reputation amongst activists over my reputation in this particular professional setting. In this sense, attending the demonstration became a political act in and of itself. I wanted to challenge the respectability politics that marginalize the bad protestor, while also challenging the masculinist assumption that these (protest) spaces are not for mothers and young children.

The temperature outside was 18 degrees Fahrenheit, far too cold to bring my child with me. At the time, I was six months pregnant and wore multiple layers to avoid getting sick. After I arrived at the airport, I quickly found the familiar faces of those organizing the tour with their signs in tow. There were several security guards watching them nearby. I introduced myself and met two folks that were travelling with the collective. There were two others that met for the demonstration. Everyone was waiting for another activist, one of the co-founders of the collective, that had gone to get the video camera from their car. When they returned, I recognized them because of their recent arrest for a mink raid. When I introduced myself to them, I mentioned that I had met their co-defendant at an animal liberation convergence in California years prior. This historical connection helped establish my credibility with the strangers.

The activists in attendance were very friendly but did not disclose much information nor ask many questions of me. With the frigid temperature outside, we went to set up indoors. While we were chatting, a Delta manager (dressed in a suit and tie, carrying a walkie-talkie) came over with a grin on his face and asked us to leave the building. We pled with the Delta representative to let us stay indoors because of the temperature but, unimpressed with our cause, he refused. Instead of allowing us to stay indoors where it was warmer and populated, we were taken to a "special spot" that was prepared for us. As part of Kentucky protest laws, activists must obtain a permit in advance. The organizers had done so, and Delta responded by providing a "Free Speech" area outside. We walked outside and saw a 10' x 6' perimeter marked by orange cones. Behind it was a larger sign that the airport had put up. It read: "THE FIRST AMENDMENT requires the Kenton County Airport Board to make certain areas of the Airport available for the expression of protected speech. We understand that the content of the protected speech in these areas may be objectionable, however; the Board cannot restrict or regulate the content of protected speech. The Kenton County Airport Board does not condone or endorse the views expressed in such solicitation areas. – CVG" (Grubbs 2014c). The sign reinforced the sentiment of the airport, security, and local police: they tolerated our presence but clearly did not support it. There were four police offers present, countless security guards, and airport employees nearby during the one-hour protest.

Outdoors, our chants were muted by the sound of rushing wind and passing cars. One activist remarked, "Since we have little access to people, I would at least like to be loud" (Grubbs 2014c). They knew that the demonstration itself would not reach many people in person but wanted the video of the demonstration to posture as if it did. One of the organizers pointed out, "We deliver every video to Delta, so basically this is a way to talk directly to them" (Grubbs 2014c). They had a handheld camera device that allowed them to hold it without it being obvious that it was a camera. Our chants, completely muted by the elements to those indoors, had conjured over the police officer assigned to direct traffic. The cop called over one of the organizers. Sarcastically, the organizer said they couldn't walk over to talk to the cop because that would violate the "free speech zone" we were boxed into. The officer, equally sarcastic, tried to provoke the activists by asserting that we needed to all "tone it down a little." The organizers appeared quiet, were well dressed and unassuming, and could quickly shift from polite to aggressive. As soon as the organizer re-entered the designated area after engaging in a conversation with the cop, they shouted even louder into the megaphone.

As I stood there, I received a text message from my aunt saying, "What is the animal rights protest about at the Delta terminal?" (Grubbs 2014c). I thought it was strange that she had already heard about the demonstration and began to wonder if someone had seen me and was already gossiping. A few minutes later I looked over and saw my cousins and aunt standing at the entrance door to the airport. My sister and I ran over to say hello and explain what we were doing. They had assumed we were there because of our politics but were surprised we were outside in such cold weather. We gave my cousins and aunt some flyers and explained the basic logic of a pressure campaign. She implied that she supported the efforts, and also the ability for people to gather in public spaces and demonstrate. We talked for a few more minutes and then we went back out to participate. After another twenty minutes of chanting, one of the organizers announced that it was now 7 pm and the demonstration was over. In the course of an hour, there were less than a dozen people that passed us by. Unlike the home demonstrations, these demonstrations create a different kind of spectacle. Rather than bringing the demonstration to the doorsteps on an individual, this protest is about exposing corporate practices to the broader public at the place of business. Delta (an amorphous entity) transports primates to be used in medical research. Most travellers at the airport have no idea that Delta does this, but the demonstration changes that. By chanting outside of an airport, the activists are broadcasting Delta's role in this violent industry.

The chants resembled the ones I learned years before with other campaigns, but simply replaced the target with Delta. The performance, in this case, was not for the onlookers. It was for Delta. By recording a proclamation, and speaking directly to an anthropomorphized "Delta," it fit neatly within the SHAC model. Delta ships many things, and their client that uses them to ship primates is just one client. By isolating Delta as a secondary target, they place pressure on the company to cease its relationship with the company that sells chimpanzees for research and assure they will stop being targeted by this campaign. We were all painfully cold after an hour of chanting outside and sighed in relief when we had successfully used our entire timeslot. We chatted briefly before going our separate ways. The cold was not conducive to small talk while standing outside. I tried to mention social circles that we had in common, but the conversations were brief, and the organizers seemed less interested in getting to know me and more focused on getting on the road for the next stop of the tour. The campaign was travelling and in that sense it is self-contained. They didn't ask for my number or even ways to keep in touch. The campaign relied on social media and the internet to publicize events, and also encouraged local activists to connect independently. The campaign, as an eco-activist campaign, did not utilize a hierarchical structure. The organizers planned a national tour, but each city has its own organizers that engage in actions throughout the year. The local organizers are also encouraged to help plan the events that coincide with the national tours themselves. In this sense, I did not expect them to spend time networking with me. Their goal is to provide a space where activists can connect on a local level, link up with an international campaign against the airline, and strengthen smaller collectives.

This demonstration was quite different from the home demonstrations I participated in while in WDC. Those home demonstrations were scheduled throughout the day and followed with solidarity actions in the evening. The densely populated city of WDC is more conducive to multi-site days of action. Britches Brigade did seem to have similar functions in other cities with a larger activist population, and in cities that have an activist infrastructure. Cincinnati, Ohio is a far cry from having any semblance of an eco-activist infrastructure.[18] The model of organizing a national tour inherently means the organizers are transient, exhausted, and do not have the time to get to know local activists before leaving town. Thus, I remained connected to the campaign and organizers through social media, but we did not spend any more time together during their stay in Cincinnati. I connected with a local activist that has organized subsequent demonstrations at the the airline headquarters. Following the demonstration, the organizers posted images and video of the demonstration.

I wondered if they took photographs of the CVG sign or the perimeter marked with large cones. I wondered if they made mental notes of who showed up and ways to reach out again. I wondered what their interest was in the locals that came, or if they had any. It is clear that the campaign is not as focused on pressuring local employees, but rather collating a large number of protests and presenting them to Delta's corporate office. Although it felt like a small demonstration that night, I realized it is irrelevant how many people attend any one specific event. Through creative camera shots and loud bullhorns, the protest is part-and-parcel to a larger video compilation about the consistent pressure the campaign places. It mattered that security had to come twice to request we quiet down, and it mattered that the local Delta staff may contact the airport and complain that they feel unsafe because of protestors. In a sense, the campaign only needs a few activists that are willing to travel and shout. The growing number of local activists mobilizing to host demonstrations and utilize pressure tactics amplifies the scope of this strategy.

The subsequent demonstration I attended with Britches Brigade was outside the ABX Air office. Similarly, the turnout was small, and we spent most of the time chanting to an empty parking lot. Because the demonstration was over an hour away, I had to bring my two-month-old daughter with me to breastfeed. Unlike the demonstration at the CVG airport, however, there were no designated areas for the protest to take place. We simply set up on the pavement outside the offices and began to chant. Employees stood inside the building and peered through the glass walls, and then a black SUV pulled up to the front. We were told one of the targeted employees was expected to leave shortly, which sparked conspiratorial conversations about how the office had created a decoy. The demonstration was scheduled during the end of business hour: 4–5 pm. As the employees trickled out of the office, none engaged with us or looked our direction. We each took photographs, shouted toward the pavement, and headed our separate ways at 5 pm. I had expected the lengthy conversations with onlookers. I had hoped to watch as folks experienced disidentificatory thoughts, and possibly show empathy.

Interestingly, the only interactions I received from those inside the building were stares and finger-pointing at my infant strapped to my chest in a carrier. I regretted not bringing noise-cancelling headphones for her and tried to stay on the end. I had lined up a family member that could meet me if we were removed by police, or if I was arrested and needed someone to take my daughter. We were so utterly ignored that none of that was necessary. I began to wonder what my own political organizing would look like as I continued to live in Cincinnati, Ohio. I missed the vibrancy of direct action campaigns and participating in demonstrations alongside hundreds of people. The adrenaline, the connectedness, that comes from sharing a performative space had seemingly been taken from me when we moved. In exchange for a vibrant activist community, I was using my lunch break to take my baby to a demonstration in a giant corporate park with a handful of people. My changing sense of identity shaped my own interpellation.

CONCLUSION

The dichotomizing and privileging of the human-over-animal boundary
is challenged through eco-activist direct action and it creates forms of
disidentification with ISAs that naturalize speciesism. These actions create alterative screens through a political performativity that attempts to
subvert species boundaries and neoliberal capitalist motives that ultimately alienate beings from one another. Within the artificial confines of
the laboratory, the beagles and rabbits stuffed into wire cages and forced
to endure exploitation are far removed from "scientific rigour." The
emphasis throughout these campaigns is to consistently expose the systematic oppression of other-than-human animals at the hands of human
animals. The AELM publicizes the violent treatment of other-than-human animals and ecologies within animal-use industries and creates a
queer counter public to understand a type of human/animal relation not
reflected in speciesism or neoliberal capitalism.

Neoliberalism, according to Graeber, has become part of the fictional
narrative of US capitalism and globalization. Marx would call it the
opiate of the masses, comparable to religion. Alas, it is during the performance of direct action, the spectacle, that demonstrators expose
the alienation, the powerlessness, the veiled accountability, and overt
frustrations felt by those subjected to neoliberal capitalism through disidentification. The performances purposefully exaggerate the rhetoric
of neoliberalism: rationality, individual agency, free enterprise, market
driven capitalism, and individual responsibility. In turn, those observing,
participating, and targeted are left counting the ways these portrayals of
neoliberalism are ludicrous. In other words, it is not the portrayal that is
ludicrous, it is neoliberalism itself that is ludicrous. Thus, the spectacle
successfully creates disidentificatory thoughts that are critical of globalization and capitalism, undermining all of the euphemisms embedded in
the hegemonic corporatization within the neoliberal moment.

This chapter looks at the ways in which eco-activists refuse to submit to the dichotomy of good versus bad protestor through the use of
direct action to create spectacular resistance as a form of disidentification. The ethnographic data woven throughout contextualize the nuanced
use of voice as confrontation, voice as neoliberal performance, and voice
as playfulness. By juxtaposing home demonstrations with the demonstrations outside CVG Airport and the ABX office, the nuances of these
performances can be teased out. Although the chants are similar, these
were very different. Additionally, my own subjectivities and ethnographic
journey was shaped by a geographic relocation and negotiating domestic

embodiments. I allude to this here but will expand on it in subsequent chapters.

Through textual analysis and ethnographic observation, it became clear these are not merely street theatre of public shaming, but rather they directly challenge the restructuring of global capitalism within the contemporary neoliberal moment. These demonstrations utilize the strategic rhetoric of exaggeration and satire as a mode of resistance. Eco-activists are not unique in their use of political theatre to exaggerate systems of oppression, as evidenced in the history of drag performance in the gay liberation and queer liberation movements. The next chapter moves beyond the rhetoric of protest and interrogates the ways in which the state retaliates by interpellating the AELM's use of direct action as disidentification into ecoterrorism. The use of political theatre may not be exclusive to the AELM, but the dialectic between direct action and political repression as modes of discipline are unique within the construct of the ecoterrorist. Graeber posits that the political imaginary is constrained to only think within the current modes of existence presented: capitalism, neoliberalism, globalization, and authoritarianism. Because eco-activists rely on an anarchist political imaginary beyond the current modes of social relations, the concept of play serves as an essential tool to analyze their rhetorical significance. If we can imagine a world without the monopoly of violence of the state (and capitalism), we can will that world into existence.

4

Disciplining Direct Action

Political language ... is designed to make lies sound truthful and murder respectable, and to give an appearance of solidity to pure wind.

(Orwell 2013)

Over a decade ago, while I was a doctoral student at American University (AU) in WDC, I learned about a graduate student, Scott DeMuth, at the University of Minnesota, who had refused to comply with a federal grand jury. DeMuth was a suspect in a 2004 direct action targeting Spence Laboratories at the University of Iowa. It was in 2008 when his residence was raided in connection to a protest against the Republican National Convention that the prosecutors claimed they found evidence linking him to the 2004 break-in in Iowa. Although his case is a compelling example of how the state targets activist-academics on the left that engage in direct action, this is not why I bring up the case. I have been inspired by several academics that refused to compromise about their own research, such as then graduate student Rik Scarce who (in 1993) served six months after refusing to testify in front of a grand jury about his knowledge of an illegal direct action. What struck me about DeMuth's case was the political and ethical commitment of his faculty advisor, David Naguib Pellow. Pellow spoke out after the government pressured him to provide information about DeMuth and his research participants. He wrote a guest post on the blog *Green Is the New Red*. In one of the essays, Pellow explained why he would not participate in the investigation and said, "I cannot and will not violate the trust relationship that I have with my advisee and colleague Scott DeMuth and with the participants in my research study" (Pellow n.d.; Potter n.d.; Pellow 2014). Pellow received correspondence at work and home from the FBI and worked with trusted lawyers to understand all of the ways he was legally protected. I admired Pellow's commitment to uphold his academic and ethical principles, despite the potential political and professional repercussions.

As I prepared to embark on the ethnographic study that informs this book, I worked with my advisor to conceptualize the project. We talked about research ethics and the possibility of facing legal scrutiny if I did anonymized interviews with ALF activists. I read through reflexive, honest ethnographies where anthropologists grappled with ethical dilemmas. I re-read David Price's book, *Threatening Anthropology: McCarthyism and the FBI's Surveillance of Activist Anthropologists*, and was reminded that the history of harassing left-leaning academics was not far behind us. I wondered, based on this history, to what extent my own faculty advisor would protect my work and those I worked with. I questioned whether or not I could design an academic study that nuanced attention to detail while protecting my activist comrades with intentionally vague ethnographic accounts. The treatment of both DeMuth and Pellow illustrates the insidious ways that we, as communities of activists and practitioners, are constantly navigating political repression. Then I pulled David Graeber's book, *Direct Action: An Ethnography*, off the shelf and I was reminded that this work can be done in politically meaningful ways.

The strategic destabilization of public/private spheres through direct action facilitates disidentification. The state, however, recognizes the magnitude of these threats and retaliates by interpellating disidentification (direct action) into ecoterrorism. In his detailed ethnographic account of the AELM, Pellow asserts, "The most important terrain on which earth and animal liberation activists challenge state repression is the site of discourse around "terror" and "ecoterrorism" (Pellow 2014, 214). The next two chapters, conceptualized interconnectedly, interrogate the relational dialectic between direct action and state repression.[1] Specifically, this chapter examines how the repressive construct of ecoterrorism is used by the state to discipline eco-activists' use of direct action (as a spectacular performance) through interpellation. The next chapter, alternatively, focuses on how activists resist repression through direct action itself.

The AELM is responsible for the direct rescue of thousands of animals from captivity, slaughter, and vivisection. The AELM has inflicted hundreds of millions of dollars in damages to animal-use industries in the last two decades (Loadenthal 2013a; 1010; Pickering 2007; Rosebraugh 2004; Scarce 2006). Direct animal rescue and property destruction effectively threaten animal-use industries: not only do they inflict financial damage, but they oftentimes bring these industries to a halt, even if temporarily. The use of direct action remains a splinter within the overarching animal and eco-advocacy movements and oftentimes faces public scrutiny from those outside the movements. These acts of agitation (resistance) are interconnected to the acts of control (repression) by the state.[2] The physical and rhetorical volley of performative power between the AELM and the state-corporate-industrial complex are a relational dialectic of political activism and repression.

Eco-activists simultaneously feel powerful through direct action *and* repressed through state violence. Activists act and exercise power yet also experience coercive punishment from the state that minimizes their power. These contradictions cannot be parcelled out and fractured from one another because they exist within the totality of a holistic relationship of power and repression. Activists are not able to experience or articulate the power embodied in direct action without resistance, regardless of how symbolically or viscerally the power is experienced. No demonstration, direct rescue, or act of arson exists outside of a system in which the state holds coercive power. Thus, the direct action is an attempt to subvert or overthrow the power of the state through performance, with an understanding that the action alone holds no symbolic value outside of the existing power structure. The praxis of relational dialectics provides the influx terrain in which activists and state actors gain deeper understandings of the needs and desires of one another. The dialectics are continuously in motion, and depend on the changing nature of the relationship. In this sense, the theory of relational dialectic provides a useful way to understand the performative interplay, tensions, and contradictions between the state and the AELM.

Each direct action by eco-activists challenges the state and the systems of capitalism, speciesism, and authoritarianism. Consequently, each challenge is met with actions of the state that both react to and proactively prevent threats to their power. Both the activists and the state engage with power through performance to silence and subvert the other. Despite the significant challenges these non-state actors make, there is an asymmetry of power that monopolizes legal modes of violence.[3] The previous chapter detailed how direct action is used to create spectacular performances that queer this monopoly, providing space for a political imaginary to exist. This chapter, however, revisits the concept of neoliberal capitalism to examine how the state's rhetorical construction of ecoterrorism is connected to statecraft and political repression. As I wrote this chapter, I kept returning to Foucault's extensive history of how discipline and punishment are exercised, interpreted, and inscribed to create biopolitics. Foucault uses the term "biopower" to "designate forms of power exercised over persons specifically in so far as they are thought of as living beings: a politics concerned with subjects as members of a population, in which issues of individual sexual and reproductive conduct interconnect with issues of national policy and power" (Burchell, Gordon, and Miller 1991, 4; Bertani and Alessandro 2003, 239–64; Foucault 2010). In other words, biopolitics is the governmental regulation of all aspects of human life. Foucault astutely describes the arc in which monarchical punishment was replaced with discipline. Thus, disciplinary power "reaches into the very grain of individuals, touches their bodies, and inserts itself into their actions and attitudes, their discourses, learning processes and everyday lives" (Foucault 1980, 39). Specifically, I wanted to examine how monarchical power and disciplinary punishment are used to interpellate direct action as ecoterrorism.[4] After all, the government's rhetorical construction of ecoterrorism (a form of biopolitics) itself is a disciplinary function to stifle dissent (manifest as biopower) (Chomsky 2001, 155; Hoffman 2006, 32; Lovitz 2010, 109; Jackson and Sinclair 2012, 2).

PUNISHMENT WITHIN THE NEOLIBERAL MOMENT

Corporate sovereignty, as facilitated by neoliberal capitalism, not only allows for animal-and-ecology use industries to operate through veiled ISAs, but it also requires the state to use repressive acts to disincentivize dissent. Through the conflation of the good subject and the good protestor, activists are presented with one, nonthreatening form of dissent as effective (Steve Best 2004; Churchill and Wall 1990; Pellow 2014). The rewriting of past liberatory struggles further erases confrontational direct action and the efficacy of bad protests. Foucault and Althusser focused a great deal on the social functioning of power, and its relationship to discipline. In *Discipline and Punish*, Foucault traced the role of governments in shifting modes of punishment. With the birth of the modern prison, Foucault argued, there was a shift from monarchical punishment (the repression of a group through violent public performance) to disciplinary power (the internalization of state power that is reinforced and naturalized through institutions like schools, religion, prisons, hospitals, militaries, etc.). Because there were institutions (for Althusser, these are called ideological state apparatuses) that manufactured docile bodies, there was less societal need for the state to act and appear overtly violent (for Althusser, this is the function of the repressive state apparatus) (Althusser 1971; Foucault 1977; 2010). Althusser expanded on this but focused on the process of subject formation through interpellation. Subjects can be disciplined because they are "hailed," and thus have the agency to accept, reject, or reconfigure through discursive practices of ideology (Althusser 1971, 132, 143–4; Pêcheux 1982, 158). Monarchical power, on the other hand, relies on public displays of grotesque violence to maintain rule through explicit fear of violence. In an effort to discourage theft through fear, the government would gather entire communities to witness someone accused of theft have their hand cut off. The punishment was based on mutilating the body so that the fear of physical pain would instill self-discipline into the soul. In his discussion of the prison system, Foucault expands on the panopticon model put forth by Jeremy Bentham (Foucault 1977, 200–17).

Prisons were built in a circular shape, with a tall tower in the centre. Every prison cell was exposed to the tower, centralizing all surveillance to one specific tower. Tinted windows and obscured architecture ensured the watchtower provided clear views of the entire prison, while making it impossible for prisoners to see in. Prisoners assumed there was always a guard in the tower and became accustomed to constant surveillance. Over time, they began to self-discipline and it no longer mattered if anyone was actually in the tower. Contemporary shopping malls utilize this conditioning through the installation of surveillance cameras. Once a customer is exposed to a few signs that read "Smile, you are on camera" or "You steal, we prosecute," shoppers begin to simply assume that there are cameras omnipresently in place throughout stores. The shopper, thus, is conditioned through the lens of presumptive surveillance. Individuals do not know who is watching, what the store's legal capacities of prosecution are, or even the scope of the camera itself. And yet the shopper behaves as if they are being watched, modifying their behaviour and resisting the urge to steal out of fear of getting caught. The cameras, though omnipresent, appear less violent than would armed security guards in every store.

Within a neoliberal context, the state veils its most repressive actions (read: monarchical) with more insidious, hegemonic forms of repression (read: disciplinary). The dialectic between these two types of punishment: surveillance (subtle and oftentimes invisible) and explicit violence (overt and visible) creates a particularly potent repressive terrain for political activism (Grubbs and Loadenthal 2011a; Loadenthal 2011a; Grubbs and Loadenthal 2011b; Loadenthal 2014). During the Green Scare, targeted legislation such as the AETA, federal grand juries, and the carceral use of both CMUs and terrorist-enhancements form a hybridization of punishment. The amalgamations of these forms of punishment condition activists to engage in protective measures.[5] The collective charges brought against anarchists arrested at the J20 anti-inaugural protests exposed the state's ability to punish indiscriminately and severely. This hybrid of both disciplinary punishment and monarchical power represents a particular type of political repression targeting eco-activists.

DISCIPLINING THE ACTIVIST

The disciplinary power of the state fits within the neoliberal rhetoric of a forgiving judicial system and interpellates bodes that are incarcerated to believe regardless of whether anyone is watching, it will benefit them if they are on their best behaviour.[6] Foucault argued there was both symbolic and physical significance within the body/soul divide during this shift from monarchical punishment to disciplinary power (Foucault 1977, 280–1). The professionalization of power via prisons, parole officers, and probation, have conditioned the soul to behave in ways that allow the state to police through conditioning rather than public displays of grotesque violence.[7] This shift, however, had more to do with cost and efficiency rather than the state's desire to be less violent. The body/soul internalization of power facilitated a shift in the public performance of state violence and the perception that the penal system was capable of redemptive justice (Foucault 1980, 38–40). Several years ago, I was travelling to the West Coast for a feminist convergence. I had packed a few zines and the ALF Primer in my messenger bag. I went through the standard modes of surveillance screening at the airport, like removing my shoes, taking my computer out of the protective sleeve, and emptying the remaining contents in my reusable water bottle. Then I was selected for additional inspection. The Transportation Security Administration (TSA) officer carried my scattered belongings over to a metal table. She instructed me to stand on the plastic mat and turn my palms facing upward. As she put on a pair of blue sterile gloves, she explained that she would be patting down my body. I answered a series of clarifying questions: I did not have "tender" places on the body, I declined being moved to a private area for the screening, and I did not need the instructions translated from English. She then brought over what looked like piece of gauze and wiped the front and back of my hands. After walking away to place the gauze in a detection device, she explained that my messenger bag was going to be opened and the belongings would be examined. I had prepared to travel; I knew that my bags and body were subject to search and was aware my name had been run through security databases prior to my departure. But it was during this "further inspection" that I viscerally felt the state's power. My heart rate began to increase. I felt my face grow hot as I watched my belongings no longer feel like my own in their hands. As the second TSA officer approached my messenger bag, and they pulled out each of the books inside, my hands slightly trembled. I wasn't terrified, per se. I had years of experience with political activism and invested great energy in understanding my civil liberties and rights. I am keenly aware of how my body is always already operating under presumed innocence in the context of racist, heteronormative politics of respectability (Cooper 2017; Hill Collins 2006; 2008; 2005; Higginbotham 1994). And yet, as I reflect on the physical reaction I had to this secondary screening, I reluctantly admit how state power conditioned my actions.

The internalization of how I forewent bodily autonomy and was subject to the state (being subjected to inspection, having my body and possessions searched, the risk of being suspected of having committed an illegal direct action, being handcuffed and escorted into police custody, having my property confiscated, and spending time and resources trying to prove my "innocence") were externalized through the increased heart rate, the sweat, and the shakiness felt in my hands. To paraphrase from Foucault's concept of disciplinary power, as activists we have been conditioned to modify our actions (or conceal them) because of physical fear at the veiled threat of the state.[8] By relying on agencies like TSA, the majority of people travelling breeze through these disciplinary mechanisms without blinking an eye. The state only has to search one person every hour to remind all travellers that they could be searched. Security theatre, in this way, is just that: a theatre. The performance of power, in this instance, is meant to continue the production of docile bodies. Thus, the state is able to wield its power without publicly exposing the ways in which it uses violence in far more invasive ways. There is a general aversion to having civil liberties violated, such as embedded microchips that monitor human movement and active recording devices installed in private spaces, thus governments rely on a more benign mechanism of surveillance. For example, my parents would never consent to the government installing a camera in their home to record their conversations. But they were excited when their Alexa speaker, which uses voice recognition and passive recording, could turn up the music by a simple voice command. In this way, the fetishization of technology has facilitated the proliferation of passive recording devices.

When state surveillance has been exposed in the past, the state swiftly suppressed the information (Gellman 2020; Snowden 2020). Foucault provides a detailed explanation for how the state was able to move away from monarchical punishment that relied on visible acts of violence and instead rely on insidious, omnipresent mechanisms of surveillance. The state, essentially, engaged in a significant public relations campaign to restructure the penal system so that it would embody neoliberal truisms of justice, rehabilitation, fairness, and democracy.

GREEN SCARE CASES

The proactive and reactive measures of the state, however, are tasked with both recouping power while maintaining these disciplinary truisms of neoliberalism. The state selectively delivers coercive punishments to specific activists in order to instill fear amongst society that discourages challenging animal-and-ecology use industries. The selective deployment of coercive punishments within a larger framework of the good protestor fulfill those neoliberal truisms of fairness and justice. Returning to the airport example, the only visible aspects of state power in that exchange were the general and secondary screening. However, the pre-screening and surveillance the state may have used to "randomly" identify me went unseen in that exchange.[9]

Operation Backfire

Operation Backfire demonstrated for the FBI the effectiveness of a multi-department, taskforce-style investigation. Operation Backfire involved the participation of the Bureau of Alcohol, Tobacco Firearms, and Explosives (BATF), the FBI, the Bureau of Land Management (BLM), the US Forest Service, Immigration and Customs Enforcement (ICE), as well as police departments from Eugene, Oregon, the Oregon state police, the University of Washington police, and the Lane County Sheriff's Office of Western Oregon. The cooperation and overlapping state agencies interpellated the activists as ecoterrorists through the performative conflation of an "us" versus "them," that warranted local, state, and federal agencies to work together and utilize surveillance mechanisms reserved for international terrorists.

The FBI identified vulnerabilities in the suspected activists, and approached Jacob (Jake) Ferguson, one of the lead arsonists in these cases, to become an informant. Ferguson had struggled with drug addiction, and his father had been incarcerated throughout his childhood. As part of their plea, Ferguson would trade potential jail time for his role in the arsons if he successfully secured (undercover) testimonies from his peers. Despite the commitment that the clandestine network, "the family," had made to one another, and fully aware of how he was betraying each of his friends (used loosely here), Ferguson agreed to wear a wire and bait them into admitting their participation in the crimes. The federal government followed Ferguson for a year while he helped the government compile evidence that would be used in their subsequent prosecutions.

The multi-departmental investigations dating back as far as 1996 resulted in nationally coordinated police raids on 20 December 2005 that captured seven individuals, Chelsea Dawn Gerlach, Daniel McGowan, Stanislas Meyerhoff, William Rodgers, Kendall Tankersley, Darren Thurston, and Kevin Tubbs. While in police custody, Rodgers, also known as Avalon, died by suicide. He is remembered fondly by activists and honoured in many publications since his tragic death. On 20 January 2006, an additional six people were named in the Oregon indictment: Joseph Mahmoud Dibee, Josephine Sunshine Overaker, Jonathan Paul, Rebecca Jeanette Rubin, Suzanne Savoie, and Justin Franci Solondz.[10] Additionally, Nathan Block and Joyanna Zarcher were tried with McGowan and Paul.[11] Curry's 2011 documentary film, *If a Tree Falls: A Story about the Earth Liberation Front*, features several of the co-defendants, and Ferguson. In the film, McGowan is awaiting trial and reflects on his activism and how the arrest exposed vulnerabilities within activist communities. The disruption of "the family" through betrayal, pressure tactics, and manipulation resulted in a series of plea agreements, some of which were cooperative. The activists faced a total of sixty-five charges that included use of destructive devices, conspiracy, arson, and destruction of an energy facility. In more recent conversations with McGowan, a friend of mine, we discussed the divisiveness of cooperative plea agreements and the long-lasting impacts of that betrayal.

The use of a conspiracy framework and the additional "Terrorism Enhancements," which adds time to a defendant's sentence, served to pressure some individuals into cooperating with state prosecutors in the hopes of differentiating themselves from the larger group. In constructing the charging documents and recommended sentences, the state aimed to overcharge defendants to force compliance and the production of cooperating witnesses. To this end, facing multi-decade jail sentences, six of the eleven defendants acted as "confidential sources" in service of the prosecution. Four of the non-cooperating defendants – Block, McGowan, Paul, Zacher – negotiated plea bargains with the prosecution wherein they pled guilty but were not required to provide information on other defendants. One defendant, Waters, entered a plea of "not guilty" but was convicted at trial.

Operation Backfire, a formative event in the Green Scare, established a precedent for the state to utilize a conspiracy framework wherein a grouping of individuals is collectively charged with a series of crimes they may or may not had individual participation in. While charging documents do specify which individuals played a role in each attack, the conspiracy framework discursively and legalistically links the group together, pressuring those who are less centrally involved to provide evidence against those active individuals in an attempt to mitigate sentencing. The details of who did what, with whom, were gathered by splintering and pressuring individual activists to cooperate with the federal government. The government integrated additional evidence gathered through domestic surveillance and intelligence that had been previously assumed to be reserved for the collection of foreign intelligence. During McGowan's trial, the state uncharacteristically offered him a plea bargain after his defence demanded the prosecution disclose the source of intelligence. While no official documentation has been made public, it is presumed that the National Security Agency (NSA), a single intelligence agency explicitly barred from being used against American citizens, gathered the information used against McGowan. Keep in mind, this was a decade before Edward Snowden's whistleblowing reports that revealed domestic intelligence agencies were working with global intelligence agencies to surveil domestic communication within the US (Snowden 2020).

The investigation coincided with public outrage over President George W. Bush's admission that warrantless wiretapping and NSA surveillance had been used in a number of domestic cases. The assumption is that during this period of heightened criticism on Bush and his use of the NSA, that McGowan's prosecutors were pressured into offering a plea bargain rather than admit in open court that the agency had provided evidence to the prosecution. McGowan was charged with arson and the conspiracy to commit arson for the 2001 ELF actions against Superior Lumber and Jefferson Poplar Farms in Oregon. The presiding judge applied a "terrorism enhancement" (a form of monarchical punishment) to his seven-year sentence, and he was ordered to pay $1.9 million in restitution. While in federal prison, McGowan was incarcerated in a CMU, despite several requests to be transferred to the general population.

Scholar Adrian Parr argues that the public trial and sentencing of McGowan (and "the family" more broadly) was an act of discursive rearticulation: what was once perceived as activism – or perhaps, at most, a basic criminal act – was rearticulated as "terrorism." Likewise, with the AETA, the public is led to believe that protest, rather than vivisection, is violence and terrorism (Parr 2009, 87). In a recent Facebook post, McGowan reflected on his arrest:

Has it really been 15 years? I went to work at womenslaw.org on December 7, 2005 and labeled piles of holiday cards. As I was getting ready to leave for the day, a few beefy dudes asked if I was Daniel McGowan and proceeded to grab and handcuff me. Thus began a very long ordeal that led me to reside in too many places and years of isolation, heartache and bills. My own Pearl Harbor.

I have been off probation for close to 4 years and out of prison for 8 but when I walk by people selling Christmas trees and smell that familiar combo of sap, needles & 50 gallon drum fires, it takes me back in an instant. When I see the monsters that work for the misnamed Department of Justice call young, idealistic people "terrorists," I am right there again, sitting in a cell at MCC trying to stare out the window, blocked by snow, and wondering if anyone knows where I am.

I am forever in debt and appreciative of all the people who had my back, regardless of what they thought of my actions, and showed me love and solidarity throughout this ordeal. It's my hope that eventually, I can make a meaningful contribution to paying it forward for others.

7 of us were arrested that day but only Avalon (Bill Rodgers) matters to me. The rest of my old friends (arrested that day) cooperated and gave information to the state that helped make things worse for me, and everyone else. RIP Avalon. (McGowan 2020)

Fifteen years have passed since the 2005–06 arrests, and there is only one of the alleged co-conspirators left that has not stood trial. Dibee fled after he was subpoenaed by a grand jury, and spent twelve years in Syria, Russia, and most recently, Cuba. He was apprehended in Cuba in 2018, and currently is in Oregon awaiting trial. McGowan and I recently connected to discuss the ways in which repression manifests itself inside of prison. From mail restrictions to guard harassment, the punishments inside can compound and push your release date further and further back.[12] McGowan was released to a halfway house in 2012, only to be taken back into police custody four months later following the publication of an article he wrote for the *Huffington Post* that (rightfully) criticized CMUs.[13] McGowan was accused of violating a regulation that stipulated people that are incarcerated cannot "publish under a byline." After the Center for Constitutional Rights reiterated that this regulation was not constitutional, McGowan was released the next day and sent back to the halfway house in Brooklyn. He was released in June 2013 on probation.

Dibee, now fifty-three, is currently awaiting trial (set for April 2021) in Multnomah County's Iverness Jail. He, along with over 1.4 million people in the US, is locked inside the carceral system during a global health pandemic. They are subjected to additional forms of violence, and the Bureau of Prisons continues to be critiqued for not protecting incarcerated people from contracting the novel coronavirus. He suffered a broken jaw in January 2020, and is currently in isolation with COVID-19. Dibee's capture and subsequent trial will reopen the lasting impacts of Operation Backfire, and more broadly of the Green Scare, on the AELM.

SHAC-7

The legal case known as the SHAC-7 refers to the arrest of seven individuals accused of using their website to incite attacks targeting HLS business partners in Trenton, New Jersey. The original seven people are Jacob Conroy, Lauren Gazzola, Darius Fullmer, Joshua Harper, Kevin Kjonaas, John McGee (McGee's charges were later dropped), and Andrew Stepanian. Undercover investigations had captured HLS employees punching dogs in the face, dissecting live monkeys, and other forms of egregious violence. In March 2006, the six members of SHAC were convicted. They were all charged with conspiracy to violate the AEPA, later expanded to the AETA. Additionally, Conroy, Gazzola, Harper, and Kjonaas were charged with conspiracy to harass using a telecommunications device, whereas Conroy, Gazzola, and Kjonaas were charged with stalking via the internet. Lovitz has detailed the stalking, the infiltration of social networks, and the phone recording that was used to build a case against these in her book, *Muzzling a Movement: The Effects of Anti-Terrorism Law, Money, and Politics on Animal Activism*. The SHAC campaign engaged in a variety of tactics that included information dissemination, demonstrations, and property damage. Unlike the actions of ELF activists in "the family," the SHAC campaign was aboveground. In 2019, Joaquin Phoenix, eco-activist and actor, produced a documentary, *The Animal People*, about the SHAC-7 campaign. Throughout the book, I have pointed to the ways in which the SHAC model informs direct action within the AELM. The film's co-director, Casey Suchan, expanded on why they decided to make a film on such a draconian indictment and prosecution: "The SHAC campaign was strategic and effective and mobilized people globally. It nearly succeeded in shutting down the target of its campaign, Huntingdon Life Sciences, several times. The story that began to emerge was one of how corporations and the government circled their wagons to stop this campaign before it became a blueprint for other activist communities to apply in their own movements" (Lennard 2019).

The high-profile cases of the SHAC-7 and Operation Backfire, taken together with a series of well-known activist convictions mark a particularly visible shift in the state's punishment of eco-activists. In 2004, Luers was extradited from Canada and faced criminal charges connected to two acts of arson (targeting cement-mixing and logging trucks). He received a twenty-year sentence, in 2008, which at the time was the longest sentence an eco-activist had been given for property destruction in which no one was harmed.[14] In 2008, Arrow, who had been indicted by a federal grand jury in 2001 and fled the country, was extradited from Canada and faced fourteen counts of arson and conspiracy. He had been implicated in the attacks by his co-defendant, Jacob Sherman, who took a cooperative plea deal and named Arrow, Angela Marie Cesario, and Jeremy David Rosenbloom. Both Cesario and Rosenbloom took plea agreements, but Arrow did not cooperate and was sentenced to six and a half years in federal prison. Around this time, Rodney (Rod) Coronado, an indigenous (Pascua Yaqui) activist connected to the ALF, ELF, EF!, and Sea Shepherd Conservation Society, was incarcerated for felony conspiracy charges. The year 2006 was not only one of high-profile arrests, trials prosecutions, and prisoner support, it was also when the AEPA was expanded into the AETA.

The AETA as Punishment

Despite the state's reliance on disciplinary punishment, the AETA represented a different kind of punishment targeting those who were challenging animal-and-ecology use industries. Specifically, the state used the AETA to respond to the effective political theatre that AELM cells with the ALF, ELF, EF!, as well as SHAC had been engaging in across the US. After over a decade of notorious direct actions, the state turned to monarchical punishment to discipline the bad activist.

The passage of the AETA created the chilling coercive threat for activists by explicitly targeting not what an activist does, but more so why they do it (Lovitz 2010; Parker 2009; Potter 2011). The heavy reliance on terrorism rhetoric negated the truisms of justice or presumed innocence, and instead tapped into the corporation-as-victim framework. The AETA, as a form of monarchical punishment, makes public how the state protects legal and illegal "animal enterprises." The legislation not only conflates free speech with terrorism in the name of corporate sovereignty, but it obscures specificity with broad brush strokes to target the bad AELM protestor (American Civil Liberties Union n.d.; Lovitz 2010). The legislation increases penalties and prison sentencing, redefines the trial processes for AELM defendants, and carries with it "terrorism enhancements" that have been used to house eco-activists convicted of nonviolent crimes in the highly restrictive CMUs (Potter n.d.). The constitutionality of the law has been challenged repeatedly by activist watchdog groups to no avail.[15]

Hegemonic Consent

Althusser, in his investigation of the reproduction of power, illustrated how individuals participate in their own oppression (Althusser 1970; 2005; Chomsky et al. 1967; Gramsci 1971; 1994; Luxemburg 1900; Žižek 2009). Despite the outspoken critiques by AELM activists and sympathetic legal collectives, mainstream activism was not particularly invested in challenging the legislation. The support for the AETA, on the other hand, was more insidious; it was not epiphenomenal. The public framing of the bad protestor had interpellated dissent in order to manufacture the consent necessary to pass the AETA. In other words, the direct actions taking place throughout the late 1990s and early 2000s were interpellated as direct attacks against neoliberal principles (not individual corporations) such as a free market, deregulation, and increased private sector. Animal-and-ecology use industries were not portrayed as profit-driven corporations that benefit off of violence against animals and ecosystems. Instead, they were framed as symbols of those neoliberal values; the victims of eco*terrorist* attacks. By weaving animal-and-ecology use industries into the fabric of the US economy, their profits were simultaneously woven into the financial stability of the US. The AETA gained momentum as politicians campaigned on the platform of protecting American industries from ecoterrorists. The legislation may have passed in the middle of the night, but the cultural context that enables a law like the AETA to exist is far more of a concern. The cultural context sheds light on why society was/is willing to subjugate anti-capitalist, anti-authoritarian, and anti-speciesist activists in the name of corporate sovereignty.

Hegemonic animal and ecological consumption continue to be promulgated in so many ways; exaggerated nutritional recommendations that justify government subsidies to "meat" and "dairy" farms, costly animal experimentation, deforestation to aid in development expansion, natural gas pipeline construction as a means to jobs, and so on. Consistently, the messages presented through ISA's coalesce corporate and state interests *as* American interests. Simply put, to challenge (or disidentify with) animal-and-ecology use industries is to challenge the state itself. Regardless of whether or not these corporations are under siege by said ecoterrorists, the focus is on manufacturing consent so that repressive laws and tactics are acceptable (Herman and Chomsky

1988). This shift in focus, the construction of ecoterrorism rather than corporate-terrorism, obscures the ways in which the state is culpable for widespread violence and destruction. The interpellation rearticulates the freedom fighter as a terrorist and industries as victims. The state relies on this construction of the *ecoterrorist* to discourage not only direct action, but also the very disidentificatory thoughts they make them possible.

Individuals actively participate in this interpellation of state power through ISAs. These ideological apparatuses rely on the hegemonic consent of the general population to accept and promulgate the unjust and coercive punishments of the AETA. Not only are the industries presented as benign and beneficial, but also the act of protest is stigmatized as ineffective. Individuals undergo a process of interpellation through various ISAs that insists these industries are necessary for sustenance, entertainment and pleasure (Harper 2010).

The general public accepts the ways in which direct action eco-activists have been, and continue to be, marginalized in the overarching advocacy movements. Advocacy movements do not reject the use of animals and ecologies, nor do they incorporate critiques of capitalism or authoritarianism. The advocacy movements, as opposed to the AELM, are focused on improving existing conditions, creating regulations within the current structures, and do not attempt to dismantle speciesism. Advocacy movements differentiate themselves from liberation movements by promoting good protestor tactics like letter writing, ballot initiatives, and lobbying. The good/bad protestor binary is predicated on the general acceptance that some protest can be relegated into the category of bad. Thus, the manufacturing of consent applies not only to what activists can target, but how they can bring about certain kinds of change.

Through the ISAs, the power of the state manifests to produce a spectacle of both monarchical and disciplinary punishment that targets eco-activists through this interpellation as ecoterrorists. The good subjects of neoliberal capitalism and speciesism refrain from home demonstrations or torching a lumber company's office; not only because they fear punitive legal punishment, but also because they, primarily, support (rather than oppose) the normative species boundary of human-over-animal that justifies old growth logging. The state's bigger challenge, however, are the activists that don't support these industries or their practices. The AELM, at its core, believes that governmentality is violent, oppressive, and coercive, and that ecological systems do not exist for human exploitation (Amster et al. 2009; Best and Nocella 2006; Graeber 2009b; Rosebraugh 2004). These activists would burn down a lumber company's office, in protest of the violence these buildings house, rather than lobby a welfarist eco-protection bill. These activists, those in the AELM that engage in direct action, do not rely on traditional social organizing that lend themselves to state surveillance. As anarchist eco-activists, many do not necessarily participate in mainstream ISAs (organized religion, for example) that provide the state with access to individuals.[16] The state relied on the AETA as a performance of power to legalize the interpellation of the bad protestor into the ecoterrorist. The state needed a way to swiftly repress eco-activists that were politically located on the periphery to create fractures inward.

The Green Scare and AETA

In 2006, the AETA provided a spectacular moment where the state used a monarchical punishment to interpellate activists within an overarchingly disciplinary period. The legislation highlights the de facto sovereignty (ability to kill, punish, and discipline with impunity) of both the state and animal-and-ecology use industries. The AETA pulls back the curtain and reveals a punitive, violent governmental practice that is asymmetrically focused on one specific social movement. Despite eco-activists' best attempts, the reality is that there are enough hegemonic good protestors that, by and large no one cares if leftist eco-activists are treated like eco-terrorists. In fact, a chunk of them agreed that "those activists" were bad protestors. Whereas ISAs are constantly engaged in interpellation, which in turn can serve to discipline bodies into compliance, this legislation did something different. The AETA functions more like a guillotine than a shoplifting sign in a retail store.

The blatant violation of (presumed) constitutionally protected free speech and the heavy-handed terrorism enhancements the law included were intended to make an example, a spectacle, out of those that undermine corporate sovereignty. The AETA was an explicit departure from a previously neoliberal performance of discipline toward the bad protestor, and complemented the onslaught of aggressive eco-activist trials. In 2011 when I became active in the AELM, the movement was reconciling this post-Operation Backfire, post-passage of the AETA, with the ongoing violence against animals and humans. I remember sitting with a group of people doing a letter-writing session, and we kept raising questions about the AETA that we could not answer: would it greatly deter activists from engaging in direct action? Would it be overturned? Would it set a precedent for other restrictive legislation to be introduced that impacted other social movements?[17]

It has been more than a decade after the legislation was written into law, and there have only been a dozen activists indicted for either violating (and/or conspiracy to violate) the AETA. The question "How will the AETA impact social movement organizing more broadly, and animal and ecological advocacy more specifically" has been taken up by many scholars, activists, and legal collectives over the last fifteen years since it became law. Data scientists with the Prosecution Project (tPP) have created a multi-variable database to examine political violence in the US. In a retrospective analysis of socio-politically motivated crimes, Chapekis and Moore argue that: "the prosecution of animal liberation extremists was negligible compared to the prosecution of other forms of socio-politically motivated crimes. The relative frequency of animal liberation extremism did not surpass 25 per cent of the crimes in any given year. Additionally, among animal liberation "extremist" crimes, the majority were not prosecuted under the AEPA/AETA, and the number of AEPA/AETA prosecutions per year only surpassed the number of non-AEPA/AETA prosecutions five times in the twenty-three-year span."[18]

When I began this research with the AELM, I argued that the Green Scare itself was a form of monarchical punishment.[19] I expected, throughout my data collection, to see a slew of activists indicted and tried for violating (or conspiracy to violate) the AETA. The AETA was the focus of podcasts, interviews, convergences, and demonstrations as AELM activists, me included, tried to make sense of how this legislation would be used to suppress dissent. However, as the tPP data illustrates, the legislation was not used proportionately to the rate in which illegal direct actions within the AELM took place. In one notable instance, the state indicted four activists in California and charged them each with one count of "animal enterprise terrorism" and one count of conspiracy for participating in a home demonstration (Quigley and Meeropol 2010). The four individuals, Joseph Buddenberg, Maryam Khajavi, Nathan Pope, and Adriana Stumpo, collectively known as the AETA-4, had been indicted after attending a home demonstration that targeted a biomedical researcher who conducted experiments on live animals. Their chants, "1, 2, 3, 4, open up the cage door; 5, 6, 7, 8, smash the locks and liberate, 9, 10, 11, 12, vivisectors go to hell," are not distinct from the many chants I had grown familiar with.[20] The charges, however, were later thrown out by a California federal court judge.

Similar to how airport security relies on the spectacle of searching only 10 per cent of travellers to discipline 100 per cent of travellers, the state only needs the conviction of a few activists to discipline the rest. In this way, the Green Scare should be conceptualized as a hybridization of power and punishment. The AETA was not the watershed moment in political repression that folks expected. This is not because the legislation itself is not scary; it is quite scary. The state, however, needs to maintain a level of tolerance for dissent within a neoliberal logic. I look back at the height of the Green Scare, and question whether or not the decline in illegal AELM direct actions after 2006 was because of a chilling effect from the AETA. In the most vegan sense of the phrase, I am left with a classical "chicken or egg" question of causation. Animal raids, arson, hunt sabs, home demonstrations, and other direct action tactics did not stop after the AETA, and they were already on a decline by the mid 2000s (Chapekis and Moore 2021). But the AETA marked the culmination of a monarchical period, and it provided the government a public form of punishment that disproportionately targeted the AELM. Despite the attempted chilling effect on the movement, it was not the gestalt moment for illegal direct action that the federal government had hoped for. As the next chapter illustrates, the theatrical nature of monarchical punishment, particularly the AETA, is dialectical. The green scare, in some ways, culminated with the passage of the AETA. However, the last decade has illustrated that with repression comes resistance. As many scholars have pointed out, Foucault's notion of biopolitics and biopower is shaped by disciplinary punishment, and that hegemonic discipline is a more sustaining way to generate docile bodies. The Green Scare was most effective not because of the AETA, but because of the cultural context, the biopolitics, that facilitated the passage of the AETA. Similar to 9/11, the AETA was the product of hegemonic consent. The disciplinary use of surveillance and infiltration have proved far more effective to disrupt and dismantle activist cells in the AELM.

SEXUAL INFILTRATION AS DISCIPLINE

Sexual infiltration demonstrates a spectacular hybrid of disciplinary and monarchical punishment. Infiltration is not a new phenomenon. From the Black Panthers to the American Indian Movement to the specific, modern-day case of Red Fawn Fallis, government agencies have always placed infiltrators into activist cells to disrupt and manipulate using biopower. Arguably, the state acts most egregiously toward the organizations they fear most. The US spends hundreds of thousands of dollars on activist surveillance programs, domestically these tend to be run through the DHS. Rather than establish surveillance technologies within activist communities, infiltration relies on the body itself as the mechanism of surveillance. With each exposed infiltrator, and government-paid informant, the sense of invasion intensified during the Green Scare. Within the biopolitics of infiltration, activists are conditioned to distrust one another and feel reluctant to work together. The Panopticon-inspired modes of discipline have morphed, or been manipulated, as the guards are no longer in the tower. They are pretending to be an activist, lying in bed, chanting at demonstrations, and plotting the next illegal direct action with you.[21] EF! activist Chrysta Faye, Coronado's ex-wife, explained how surveillance during the Green Scare impacted their marriage:

> We had our telephone monitored. We had our computers monitored. We were being surveilled by the FBI. They knew where I was at times that seemed totally irrelevant. It does something to your psyche, it truly does ... I think if we would have just been a normal, going to work, doing the 9 to 5, raising kids, things could have been really different, but the amount of trauma that his being an activist brought into our lives had devastating effects. (Brown and Knefel 2018)

The watchtower that was once used to oversee incarcerated bodies has moved into the bedroom and into the private spaces that once felt safe. With the domestication of the panopticon, the process of interpellation operates on a far more insidious level.

There are many examples of notable infiltrators that have been exposed in the last fifteen years, several of which engaged in sexual relationships with activists. The Green Scare ushered a surge in exposed infiltrators and informants, particularly in the US and UK, that had spent years within anarchist, anti-capitalist, and anti-speciesist movements. Although this book is focused on North America, it is worth noting that the UK government has an extensive history of using sexual infiltration. For example, in the UK, Jim Boyling, Bob Lambert, Mark Kennedy, and Mark Jacobs had each made the conscious decision to take on an alternative ego and integrate themselves in leftist political movements with the intention of gleaning information to be used by the government.[22] They fostered friendships, long-term romantic relationships, and, in some cases, produced children with activists while undercover. As these cases were unfolding in the UK, activist circles in the US became increasingly concerned about government infiltration. Specifically, as the AELM in the US grappled with its history of androcentric leadership, toxic masculinity and hyper-militancy, there was a heightened awareness of the presence of government agents operating within activist circles.

The prevalence of government agents within anarchist, anti-capitalist, anti-speciesist collectives has been discussed at length since the Green

Scare began. Rather than revisit the many speculated and confirmed infiltrators, I have selected a few cases to focus on that represent disciplinary trends that the state uses to suppress dissent.[23] Frank Ambrose, "Anna," and Heath Harmon each illustrate disturbing tactics that the government uses to fragment the AELM.[24] The cases reveal the magnitude of surveillance and manipulation of direct action activists over many years. In different ways, each of these people relied on essentialized constructions of gender, heteronormativity, and the dichotomy of the good/bad protestor. They were implanted, physically transformed, to foster trust that would be used to violate and manipulate eco-activists dedicated to direct action.

BETRAYAL AT HOME:
COOPERATIVE WITNESSES

In 2008, I was sitting at a coffee shop in Clifton, Ohio, working on one of the many papers for my graduate seminars. As a newly minted vegan, I had spent that summer living with a mainstream animal rights organization, Farm Sanctuary. While there, I had done extensive fieldwork for my MA thesis. I was heavily steeped in the good protestor rhetoric but also growing disenchanted with the commodification and cooptation of environmental advocacy by Green Capitalism.[25] The clanking of the espresso machine, the sound of cups being lifted and returned to their saucers – the sounds of the café were not particularly distinct. Suddenly the atmosphere changed dramatically as a few people started talking about a local environmentalist who had been arrested. I paused the music I had been listening to and discreetly shifted my chair a little closer to overhear their conversation. I don't remember the specifics of what they said, but I was struck by the fear in their voice. It wasn't until a few months later that I learned who they were talking about. A beloved activist living in Cincinnati, Marius Mason, had been arrested and charged in a federal court with four counts to commit arson and conspiracy to commit arson.[26]

Frank Ambrose and Mason had lived in Michigan and Cincinnati and engaged in direct actions together. He and his then spouse, Marius Mason, had been involved in local environmental and animal liberation demonstrations and teach-ins over several years. They seemed compatible in their quest for justice and community engagement. That is, however, until Ambrose made a mistake and dumped evidence in a dumpster that linked him to an arson. Ambrose had accepted the offer from Agent Shearer in 2007 to become a cooperative witness with the hope of minimizing his own punishment. Ambrose began travelling across state lines, recording conversations with Mason, reflecting on actions they had done together. After months of cooperation with the DHS, the government had a strong enough case against Mason to convict him of the 1999 crimes against the University of Michigan.

Ambrose's sentencing memorandum stresses:

> The single factor most likely to influence the sentence ultimately imposed in this case is the quality and the quantity of open-handed, useful cooperation Frank Ambrose has provided to the government ... The services Frank Ambrose performed for the government are significant and important. But his character, his background, and his personal history are, in this case, especially important to understand in order properly to evaluate his service. Defendant is not a bad guy. (Brady 2008)

The sentencing memorandum reads like a classic apologia, detailing how and why Ambrose now views direct action as "naïve, misdirected, and immoral. And, yes, completely ineffective."[27] According to this document, Ambrose, not Mason, is the victim of seduction. Obviously, this is not true, and it was Ambrose that betrayed the trust and respect of his partner to selfishly increase his own chances of a lighter sentence. Ambrose received a six-year sentence, compared to the nearly twenty-two-year sentence that Mason received, and he was required to pay over $4 million in restitution.

The cooperation with the federal investigation relied on Ambrose's intimate relationship with Mason. On the day Mason was arrested, Ambrose filed for divorce. Mason was threatened with the life sentence or a reduced sentence on the condition that he agree to a full non-cooperating plea agreement. Mason refused to confirm information that Ambrose had provided because it would implicate other activists. Ultimately, Mason admitted to committing a total of fourteen acts of property damage, and received the maximum sentence requested by the prosecution, plus two additional years from the added "terrorism enhancement." Mason's sentence is the harshest prison sentence of anyone convicted of environmental sabotage to date (Support Marius Mason n.d.).

Anna: The Seduction of Entrapment

"Anna" editorialized her transformation into an eco-activist in an infamous interview that appeared in *Elle* magazine in 2008. She entered the leftist scene in the early 2000s and was initially not welcomed into activist spaces.[28] Anna, then eighteen years old, was paid more than $65,000 by the federal government to pose as an activist and develop close relationships with activists. The article, both inaccurate and sensationalist, provided a window into the years she had spent deceiving the people who closely surrounded her. Anna was outspoken about the ways in which she relied on her physical appearance to gain the attention and trust from activists. She talked about how she adjusted her appearance to "blend in" and altered her heteronormative flirting mechanisms to attract the then-nineteen-year-old Eric McDavid. After catching McDavid's attention, Anna would engage him in long conversations that romanticized the direct actions they could commit together. During this tactical courtship, Anna used the promise of sex to bait McDavid into a longer, more trusting relationship. It is not the use of sex and intimacy as ways to build a longer, more trusting relationship that is the issue here. Consensual sex and intimacy can be integral in how individuals deepen their connection with one another. It is, however, incredibly problematic for a government-hired infiltrator to manipulate an activist into trusting her by using the promise of sex to elicit trust. In this way, Anna's ability to infiltrate the movement was predicated on the promise of sex and intimacy.

Anna had successfully garnered McDavid's trust, both as an activist and as a romantic partner. Their conversations became focused on a specific action, one that Anna guided McDavid through step by step. She encouraged him to come with her on a getaway, and they went to a cabin in the woods to prepare incendiaries. Anna took McDavid to the store, explained what he needed to buy, and they then retreated to a cabin to be alone. The cabin, however, was pre-wired with audio and video recording that was owned by the FBI. Anna had romantically coached McDavid, interweaving romance, implied sex acts, and plans for illegal direct action. Once Anna had McDavid on record confirming that he planned to do what they had discussed, and he went into the K-Mart to purchase more supplies, her work was done. The FBI raided the home and arrested McDavid. He never actually committed the act, but based on the entrapped conversations with Anna, McDavid received the maximum sentence of twenty years conspiracy to damage property by fire and explosive.

The Civil Liberties Defense Center attorneys, Ben Rosenfeld and Mark Vermeulen, worked closely with McDavid's partner and director of his legal support group, Jenny Esquivel. They have maintained that this was clear a case of entrapment. The team expressed concern that the government failed to produce all documents in effort to conceal the level of coercion Anna exercised. In 2013, they filed a Freedom of Information Act (FOIA) request for the documents. The defence struggled to obtain the documents, but finally, in the fall of 2014, they received over 1500 pages containing details that had been previously withheld. In total, the government had withheld over 2500 pages with damning evidence that McDavid was entrapped. The documents contained incident after incident of Anna suggesting direct action, offering to assist, making verbal threats when activists would not explicitly describe a hypothetical direct action, and sexual innuendos shared between Anna and McDavid.

It became clear that Anna entrapped McDavid and played a central role in instigating the plans for the direct actions. The government refused to submit 1000 of the pages, however there was enough evidence to reopen the case. In January 2015, Judge England accepted an alternative plea to general conspiracy, one that carried a maximum sentence of five years (Civil Liberties Defense Center 2015). Because McDavid had already served over nine years in prison, he was released forthwith. The plea deal required McDavid to waive all claims for civil damages. The case and release of McDavid call into question the ways in which disciplinary punishment utilize sexual and emotional coercion to entrap activists. McDavid and his support team gave interviews to discuss the case in the days following his release. Rather than simply focus on Anna or the ways in which McDavid was entrapped, the interviews draw attention to the prevalence of this tactic of punishment (York 2015).

McDavid commented, in an interview with Democracy Now!, that he encountered many people who were incarcerated with him that shared a similar experience with government infiltration. The CLDC attorneys emphasized the precedent set by this case and the need to interrogate the ways in which the state relies on infiltration to penetrate activist cells. There are many things that make this case distinct, but one specific aspect is just how public the tactics Anna (and the government) used have become.[29] The public, unapologetic use of Anna by the government not only increased the fear of infiltrators, but it amplified existing misogynism and sexism with the AELM. Within the AELM, predating and coinciding with the Green Scare, men held prominent leadership positions, eco-militancy relied on a valorizing of toxic masculinity, and sexual assault was a concern. Of course, these structural issues can be extrapolated to leftist organizing, social movements, and society more broadly. Government infiltration that relied on sexual violence created a particularly challenging space for activists to grapple with sexual assault by actual activists.

Indigeneity and the Framing of Red Fawn

The construction of the Dakota Access Pipeline (DAPL) brought together two relatively distinct social movements: indigenous autonomy and ecological liberation. Eco-activists have been challenging the construction and use of natural gas pipelines decades (Stover and Center for Biological Diversity n.d.; Joseph 2016). The DAPL garnered international attention in 2016 after it was rerouted near the Standing Rock Sioux Reservation, which would have the pipeline run under Lake Oahe and the Missouri River. North Dakota quickly became the site of the largest gathering of Indigenous Americans in over 100 years.[30] Documentary films like *Awake: A Dream from Standing Rock* and *Black Snake Killaz: A #NODAPL Story* captured the layers of the struggle for autonomy, cultural preservation, water protection, and land rights. The pipeline posed a risk to not only the safety of the reservation's water, but the construction itself would disrupt sacred tribal sites. Indigenous leaders rose to prominence during the NO DAPL campaign as the Sacred Stone Camp attracted hundreds of Indigenous tribes and thousands of activists that opposed the pipeline. The federal government, in cooperation with Energy Transfer, MarEn Bakken Company, and Phillips, was intent on completing the underground oil pipeline that would transport crude oil 1,172 miles.[31] With almost $4 billion at stake, the corporate-government alliance deployed monarchical and disciplinary punishment.

Tribal members held prayers and engaged in nonviolent civil disobedience such as blockades and handcuffing themselves to construction equipment. In contrast, they were met with violence such as police and private security deploying aggressive dogs, high pressure water hoses, rubber bullets, tear gas, and mass arrests (Estes 2019; Simpson 2017). During the Treaty Camp raid in October 2016, Red Fawn Fallis, an Indigenous activist with a history of organizing with AIM, was one of 761 people arrested throughout the 2016–17 NO DAPL campaign. She was accused of firing a handgun three times and resisting arrest. The three charges carried the potential of a twenty-five-year prison sentence.[32] Fawn plead guilty in 2017 to civil disorder and illegal possession of a gun by a convicted felon, and she was sentenced to fifty-seven months in prison. Fallis's case is important for many reasons, but it is notable here for expanding our understanding of disciplinary punishment and sexual infiltration.

Fallis, unbeknownst to her, had been part of a massive intelligence operation that was focused on disrupting and discrediting activists against the pipeline construction. The firearm that discharged during her arrest, for example, was actually registered to Heath Harmon, a member of the Fort Berthold Reservation and government informant. Harmon spent over two months immersing himself in the day-to-day activities at the encampment alongside activists. After successfully integrating himself into the community, Harmon began a romantic relationship with Fallis. The relationship with Fallis had lasted for several weeks prior to her arrest. Even as Fallis sat in the Morton county jail after her arrest, she was unaware that her then boyfriend was actually affiliated with the FBI.[33] On 9 September 2020, she was released after serving all fifty-seven months.

UNDERSTANDING THE DISRUPTION STRATEGY

Will Parrish, journalist with the *Intercept*, provided an extensive overview of Fallis's case. In the article, Parrish summarizes the strategy: "The FBI has long relied on informants, from COINTELPRO to the war on terror, who act not only as observers but as agents provocateur, facilitating acts for which their targets are penalized. After 9/11, according to German, the former FBI agent, the bureau adopted what it called a 'disruption strategy' that involved 'the use of informants as a tool to suppress the activities of targeted groups, even when there is no actual evidence of criminality'" (Parrish 2017).

The state uses informants to disrupt direct action campaigns by not only building criminal cases that target activists, but also by sowing the seeds of distrust amongst them. Informants come in several varieties: government employees who are planted (like Boyling, Lambert, Kennedy, and Jacobs), curious civilians that want to be law enforcement who are hired by the FBI (like Anna), and lastly, activists looking to escape their own criminal convictions and become a cooperative witness (like Ambrose). Again, the use of infiltration and informants is not a new phenomenon, nor is it specific to the AELM. But the onslaught of exposed infiltrators and informants engaging in sexual relationships with activists throughout (and after) the Green Scare have had far more of a "chilling effect" than the AETA could have ever had. These cases, though not an exhaustive list by any means, illustrate a particular disruption technique used to infiltrate leftist movements.

By having others pose as activists and permeate radical circles (sometimes for years) and engage in sex acts with activists, these infiltrators are relying on and reinforcing disciplinary punishment. When the infiltrator's sexual misconduct is exposed, the state dismisses the notion that it is a form of sexual violence by claiming it is in the fight against ecoterrorism. It is within the rhetoric of terrorism that the state argues it justifiably engages in otherwise socially unacceptable behaviour to protect animal-and-ecology use industries (and all they claim to provide) from terrorism. The state's violence is not with physical force or guillotine, but rather it is using sex and biopolitics.

The state relies on sexual infiltration to not only gain access to activists through concealed violations of privacy, but to also fragment activists from one another through the performative functions of disciplinary punishment. Rather than solely relying on the AETA and the prison-industrial complex as a mechanism of violence, the presence of infiltrators in activist circles sews a deep internalization of fear. These mechanisms of violence are deemed acceptable through the retaliatory interpellation of eco-activists as ecoterrorists. The growing sense of distrust amongst activists, particularly those engaging in romantic relationships, is constantly redefining security culture.

Distrust among Us

While attending the Gathering for Total Liberation convergence in Portland, Oregon, I approached a well-known activist who had just given a workshop. I had to leave the panel several times because my then-two-year-old was jumping around and woke up my sleeping infant. I came back in the room after the panel had ended, and walked up to the speaker to introduce myself. As we were talking, my toddler began to scream that she wanted to leave. Without thinking, I said I had to leave and asked for his phone number in order to continue the conversation later. Our interaction quickly turned uncomfortable and he looked at me very confused. His pause caused an immediate reflection on my part, where I realized I had just made a rookie mistake. He eventually responded, "I'm sure we can find ways to get in touch ... I am online."

Throughout the conference, I had several markers that set me aside as different, most visibly my two small children. I was also the only person breastfeeding in the audience at two of the panels I had attended. I took a seat in the back, oftentimes bouncing a sleeping baby or trying to entertain my toddler. My presence, and the gendered politics of reproduction and child-rearing, did not go unnoticed. I interpreted the stares as a sense of distrust, as a reminder that I am not one of them. This followed me that weekend, but, more importantly, it has been a consistent challenge for me, as well as others, throughout my work in the AELM. The insecurity I felt in that space was never affirmed by an explicit comment, and very well could be my own internalized insecurities as a mother active in a movement with anti-natalist folks.

Years later, a colleague questioned how I navigated the sometimes-conflicting roles as an activist academic with kids. They reminded me of my own timeline in these movements and in academia, and the overlap with pregnancy and raising my (still) small children. I laugh recalling this conversation because it was such an arrogant assumption that I needed reminding of the ways in which I am stratified, or suspended, between these conflicting roles. I am perpetually an outsider because of the gendered, reproductive labour inscribed on my body in these settings: not quite professional enough to be an academic with an infant strapped to my chest, not quite radical enough to be an animal liberationist while caring for my children and/or pregnant body, and yet not quite "motherly" enough as a parent because I work full-time and am an anarchist eco-activist. Thus, I find myself internalizing the skepticism and resentment of those I seek community with. The tension between the solidarity and isolation I feel is not the only dialectic in these spaces. There is an ironic sense of paranoia during public gatherings that claim to challenge the surveillance state. While professing solidarity, inclusive politics, and challenging oppression through an intersectional lens, activists and academics alike are constantly border policing in ways that hegemonically reinforce the inability for folks like me to manoeuvre the boundary between "academic," "activist," and "mother."

Grappling with Sexual Assault within the Movement

In 2012, my partner and I were entrenched in a few collaborative projects focused on how the state used sexual infiltration within the AELM. We had prepared a workshop for the NYC Anarchist Bookfair and taken the Chinatown bus from WDC for the weekend. After a lively discussion with activists, one of them pulled me aside and asked to talk to me in private. I asked if my cis male partner should come with us, and they said no. They were particularly moved by our discussion and wanted to continue the conversation about how to support survivors of sexual assault within leftist circles. We spoke in code: no proper nouns, no specific dates or locations, and everything in the hypothetical. Although the vague language lacked specificity to an outsider, I could follow exactly who we were talking about, within what context, and over what time period. What I didn't understand at the time was how these instances of sexual assault connected to the disciplinary punishment of sexual infiltration.

The AELM exists within violent social structures of misogyny, heterosexism, and toxic masculinity (to name a few). The movement, and the activists within it, are interpellated within these oppressive structures. It is far easier to call out the violence perpetuated by the state and corporations than it is to address the violence perpetuated by activists against one another. Although eco-activists strive to reimagine society in ways that are less oppressive, that does not preclude them from participating and perpetrating oppression.

After the NYC Anarchist Bookfair, I continued phone conversations with activists dispersed around the East coast. We talked about accountability processes and how to protect survivors of assault. We reaffirmed a commitment to not rely on law enforcement, and instead used a framework of restorative justice. The biggest challenge we discussed was that survivors do not want to come forward because they are afraid of being called a snitch. Historically, activists accused of being snitches were subject to violence and ostracism from the movement. Bad-jacketing, a common "neutralization" technique under COINTELPRO, is the intentional use of rumours and false evidence to create suspicion around a specific activist. One widely used type of bad-jacketing is snitch-jacketing which explicitly tries to paint someone as an informant (Boykoff 2007, 116–20).[34]

One of the lasting impacts that infiltration, not necessarily specific to sexual infiltration, has on women within leftist movements is suspicion culture, the fear of being bad-jacketed or snitch-jacketed. Women within progressive movements have long carried the guilt of speaking out against male organizers. But suspicion culture does not operate on the concern that speaking out would bring down a righteous hero. Suspicion culture, an inherently disciplinary power, is the fear that you yourself will be called an agent of the state. When prominent organizers have been called out in recent years, smear campaigns have appeared that take aim at the activist integrity of the survivor. Kiera Loki Anderson and Kitty Stryker provide a succinct overview of sexual violence and misogyny within the AELM (Anderson 2015.; 2016; 2018; Stryker 2015). One activist, in an interview with Anderson, reflected on why they were hesitant to go public with their accusations against Coronado:

Besides being called a liar, crazy, psycho, I've been labeled a snitch, an informant, accused of using COINTELPRO tactics, and at one point Rod even accused me of being an agent directly working for lawmakers "targeting my work." That one was actually kinda cute. There's now a rumor going around that I recanted the whole story. There's also an attorney who's been actively creating a climate of fear and threatening others who wanted to talk about it. Not only was I being labeled all these things, but so was anyone who supported me. (Anderson 2016)

Suspicion within the AELM is justified, based on an overwhelming amount of evidence that the state engages in extensive surveillance. Additionally, the state targets women within the AELM who have experienced assault and tries to get them to provide evidence that can be used against other activists.[35] Even when the state pretends to care about survivors of sexual assault, they are not very convincing. Henry, the activist quoted above and featured in a subsequent interview about how she had been approached by an FBI agent, had hired an attorney to speak with the FBI agent. Yoon, her attorney, concluded, "The FBI had weaponized #MeToo to pressure Henry into becoming an informant. To Henry, O'Reilly's call was a clear attempt to prey on her desire for accountability and twist it to meet the bureau's own ends. Henry refused to cooperate" (Brown and Knefel 2018). Disciplinary punishment positions gender and sexuality in complicated ways that continue to marginalize women. Sexual infiltration has not only created a sense of distrust amongst activists, it has perpetuated an unsafe environment where survivors of sexual assault are afraid to hold their abusers accountable without being called a snitch.[36] Sexual infiltration, as a performance of disciplinary punishment, has done more than just create a sense of distrust for activists in romantic relationships. It has also established the ways in which the state uses surveillance in intimate circles that are non-romantic.

Bringing the Surveillance Home

In 2017, I was entertaining my three children, getting them settled for our weekend in WDC, when I received a message from my partner that he, along with everyone else barricaded in the intersection, was going to be arrested. Our communication ceased from that point until he called me, from a borrowed phone, late in the evening the following day, to inform me that he would be dropped off in a few hours. The roughly thirty-six hours between when he had left in the morning on 20 January, until he arrived home around 10 pm on 21 January, were surreal. What we did not know at the time was that the surrealism would take on new levels as the case unfolded.

The state deployed surveillance technology during the anti-inaugural protests, referred to as Disrupt J20, in the US on 20 January 2017. The surveillance of activist gatherings and insertion of infiltrators in the planning stages were a key piece to the prosecution of over 200 defendants arrested and collectively charged in WDC. The anti-capitalist bloc was amorphous, geographically dispersed, and did not have a central organizer or organization dictating the event. The individuals collectivized in a public square, marched down 13th St, and were kettled at the intersection of 12th St and L St. Because of the decentralized, non-hierarchical nature of the gathering, individuals joined the political demonstration at various points along the way. The details of the demonstration have been extensively documented by journalists, and a small number of academics (Lennard 2018; Sugarman 2017; Agency 2017; Loadenthal 2019; King 2018; Sub.Media n.d.).

In coordination with the WDC Police Department, 234 activists were arrested, and of those, 212 were collectively charged with felonies, including inciting or urging to riot, rioting, conspiracy to riot, and destruction of property. Culpability was determined by their presence, and, in a few cases, it was their engagement in planning events that led to their charges. The federal government utilized collective charges to promulgate the notion of collective liability, pushing a clear demarcation between the good/bad protestor. This was particularly juxtaposed to the women's march that took place there the following day. One of the J20 defendants and journalists, Aaron Cantú, articulated the rhetorical strategy via Twitter: "The state shamelessly weaponized the 'good protester/bad protester' narrative in this case. It's time to put it to rest" (Lennard 2018). The contrast between these two protests, and the subsequent prosecution of the bad protestor helped solidify the demarcation of tolerated forms of dissent.

My partner and I intentionally decided not to communicate after he left the house that morning. I had relied on social media such as Twitter and Facebook (specifically Unicorn Riot's livestream) to follow the Disrupt J20 events at various points in the city throughout the day. I watched as police harassed, taunted, and assaulted indiscriminately. When I could, I scanned the crowds to see if I recognized Michael in the sea of black clothing. Like any seasoned anarchist that understands black bloc, Michael had sufficiently camouflaged himself amongst the masses. I couldn't pick him out of the video if I tried. While the kids and I were walking later that day, I noticed a cloud of smoke in the distance. It was rising into the sky from what appeared to be a fire. Hours passed, and I knew activists had been kettled into an intersection. I put the kids to bed that night with a vague explanation that their dad had to work late and that he would be home after they fell asleep. When they awoke the next day and noted his absence, I explained that he would be meeting us later that day. I felt powerless, and was growing concerned that I had not heard anything. But, as parents do, I faked a smile and offered an optimistic estimate of when their dad would rejoin us.

Without any information or connection to those doing defendant support work, I took our three children to the women's march on 21 January 2017. My sister and her partner had driven from Delaware to join us for the march. We walked along the crowded streets of Capitol Hill, flowing from one group of people into the next. We watched as individuals thanked the police officers for their "service" and praised the law enforcement for "helping them" as they blocked streets and violated traffic laws along the march. People posed for photographs with cops, included #bluelivesmatter in their tweets from the day, and celebrities publicly expressed gratitude to the officers while on the constructed platform on the National Mall. I later found out that Michael, shackled and handcuffed together with other detainees, was transported in a police vehicle that went directly through the march. Pink-hat-donning individuals smiled and waved as they neatly parted the crowd in half to let the armoured vehicle pass through. The contradictory performances of resistance and repression, and the erasure of state violence that had occurred less than twenty-four hours earlier, were stark. Here were activists who travelled from all over to attend a women's march in opposition to the regime of Donald Trump, chanting against his authoritarianism and attack on free speech and dissent. Yet, these activists at the women's march made no mention of the detained activists just a few blocks away that had become the first victims of this very regime's repressive tactics.

As I manoeuvred the double stroller and infant on my chest through the crowded streets, I wondered if I could get more information about Michael by showing up at the courthouse. It was close enough to walk to, and there were still hours of daylight ahead to keep the kids busy. With each step further away from the crowd of pink regalia, my surroundings shifted dramatically. Now it was black clothing, septum rings, Chelsea cuts, anarchist symbols, and the smell of free food stationed on a shanty table provided by (and for) supporters that had been camped outside the courthouse. With my trove of children, symmetric long hair, and clear lack of social capital, I was met with hostile looks. I could feel the questions through their eyes, "What are you doing here?" "Why have you come here to gawk at our repression?" I wanted to tape a piece of paper to my chest that read, "MY PARTNER IS ALSO LOCKED UP IN THERE." There were chants like "Fuck the police" and "Let them out," and intermittent cheers as people left the courthouse. With no familiar faces in the crowd, I kept to myself and tried to find some point of entry to get information. I had not heard from my partner in over twenty-four hours at this point, and had no idea if he would be released before we planned on driving back to

Ohio the next day. I needed to coordinate with our hosts, our places of employment, and I had three children asking for an accounting of their father. I needed support, information, and some sense of reassurance that this was going to be okay. Yet as I stood in a crowd of folks providing support to defendants and their loved ones, I felt incredibly alone. I decided to leave my two older children outside with my sister, and I would go into the courthouse with my son in the infant carrier on my chest.

I walked through the crowd, bombarded with skeptical stares, pushing down the urge to shout, "A … Anti … Anti-capitalist … Anti-capitalista." I was suspended in some space between isolation and inclusion as I entered the courthouse. After a patronizing interaction with the cops and security scans, I rushed down the steps to where the activists were held. I was overcome with anxiety as I ran down the hall, bouncing the baby up and down into my chin. I thought once I got into the building, came downstairs to where Michael was held, I would be able to see him. Instead, there were a few people leaning against the white brick wall, and a series of papers taped with names. A stranger approached me with a friendly smile, the first I had received since I got there. They explained that this was the list of everyone detained, with a possible time that they might go before the judge and be released. I told them who I was looking for, and that I was their partner. Their face lit up and said they had known Michael for many years.

I felt a shift in how I was perceived, although nothing had actually changed about myself. It was social capital by proxy. In that space, I lacked many of the physical markers (tattoos, facial piercings, or esoteric symbols) that signalled political affinities in anarchist circles. Despite shared politics, despite my perceived otherness, my partner's long history of organizing in the city resulted in a transferable credibility. Like many instances I had experienced with the AELM, it was my partner and his physical markers that allowed me to gain entry to spaces otherwise closed off. I left the courthouse with more questions than answers, and no clear timeline of how the events ahead would unfold.

When my partner arrived back to where we were staying, after being detained, he was bruised, exhausted, and coughing. His voice was hoarse, and he was starving. He woke me up to say hello, then went to take a shower and put his clothing in the washing machine. After about an hour, he came into the bedroom to kiss each of the kids. We didn't speak much that night, despite the many questions I had accumulated. This would mark a shift in our own relationship, an indefinite period of time where our conversations were constrained by our anxieties and fears. We struggled with the uncertainty of our family as we braced for what would come next. Hundreds of people were detained, and also had their personal items confiscated, including mobile devices and bags, and thousands of hours of surveillance from various recording sites (including from businesses, traffic cameras, body cams, and journalists) were procured around the city.

We would later learn his charges, expanded through a superseding indictment, included conspiracy to riot, rioting, assault on an officer, and property destruction, and carried the potential sentence of seventy years. The state's case against the J20 defendants was symbolic; it was a performative, collective punishment that purported guilt by association. Ironically, here were two anarchist academics who had theorized the complexities of political repression and state violence, and we were perplexed by the possibility that one might be incarcerated for up to seventy years for attending a demonstration. Furthermore, we quickly shifted our tone from cynical to fearful, as the prosecution gained steam in the months following the arrest. Mainstream media outlets celebrated the good protestor who marched on 21 January, while the bad protestors known as "J20 defendants" shifted lower and lower on the news cycle.

The case lingered for eighteen months, with a series of defeats and victories. The defendants were divided into trial groups, generating a range of theories about the reasoning behind each grouping. There were a series of defendant support groups put in place to provide mutual aid, such as funds to cover travel expenses for court, legal fees, and temporary housing, and emotional support and solidarity. The support groups provided a network, a sense of community, for the defendants. The defendants collaboratively crafted an agreement in which they pledged not to cooperate with the state in the prosecution of their co-defendants. Each defendant was asked to sign on to this agreement, a performative and material measure of power against political repression. There are many factors that influence why an activist does or does entertain a plea bargain. For example, the state may have more evidence directly linking them to the charges, they may be on probation, or they may be the sole caregiver for a loved one.

One of the J20 defendants, Dane Powell, took a plea deal and provided context into his decision.[37] Although he was not a part of the mass arrest, Powell was targeted and arrested on 21 January. Powell had recently returned from the Standing Rock Sioux encampment and travelled from Florida with his partner to WDC for the J20 demonstrations. Video footage circulated that showed Powell helping a mother receive medic care for her child after they were hit with large amounts of pepper spray by WDC police. In an interview with "It's Going Down," a digital community centre for anarchist, anti-fascist, autonomous anti-capitalist, and anti-colonial movements, Powell elaborated on his experience just before his sentencing hearing:

> I was arrested for my involvement in the J20 protests in the capitol of the united snakes. I stood as a defendant with others. By the time the smoke cleared, I was looking at 140 years in prison for my actions on January 20th. I took a plea deal, pleading guilty to two of the fourteen charges. After seeing the evidence the government had against me, I knew this was the best route to take while still sticking to the non-cooperation agreement between over 100 of the 214 defendants ... The hardest part of all this for me was having to explain to my crying daughters what was happening to their father. To my children: I love you with all my heart and these walls will only separate us for a short time, but walls of repression could separate all of us forever. Your father only wants those repressive walls torn down. If you have children, make sure they know why you fight before it is too late ... I want comrades to know that I went to jail with a smile on my face. I want my comrades back in Florida to carry on doing the amazing things we have been doing. One thing I can't stress enough is do not ever underestimate the state. Practice the tightest security culture you can implement personally and within your group. They will use everything against you, even if you think there's no way in hell this could hurt you. Don't post shit on Facebook! If you don't want that post from three years ago being shown to a federal judge when some shit goes down, don't post it. (Bloc Party 2017)

Powell also noted the unique form the Support J20 network took, and that he wished he had connected with folks involved earlier. He took the plea after the state presented significant evidence against him and introduced additional charges against him that had the potential of 150 years.

Despite the strong sense of community and constant communication amongst the J20 defendants and supporters, I felt completely removed from it. Although the support groups existed to challenge the neoliberal police state, I could not find a support group with an intentional space for partners of defendants. While I tried to provide stability for my three small children, I came to resent the weekly check-ins, constant messages, and strategic committees that Michael had at his disposal. I couldn't ask questions or discuss the case with Michael, and I had no resources to help me unpack what the hell was happening. It was an odd, conflicting emotion to simultaneously feel sympathy and envy toward a loved one while they struggle in an incredibly vulnerable position. I sometimes found myself jealous of Michael's ad hoc community. There were no encrypted message threads, phone calls, or meetups for me. I didn't have the ability to travel to WDC and stay up late with political kinfolks, sharing our fears and anger. I was at home, keeping the kids distracted, isolated from any notion of solidarity, and frustrated with my partner. The state had won a small, temporary victory during that time.

I began to start arguments with Michael by saying, "How could you not leave the intersection?" and "Well, you kind of seem to enjoy all of these new connections you've made." These arguments did not go well, leaving both of us feeling as if we failed our own political commitments by turning our anger toward the state outward toward each other. We questioned what information we could trust one another with, we siloed our concerns, would go weeks without talking about the case, and we created a bizarre form of doublespeak in front of the children. Whenever a call for a demonstration would come out, I quickly told Michael that I did not want him to go. It was off the table for me to go, because we couldn't have both of us dealing with legal cases simultaneously. I hid the arrest and case from my friends and my place of employment because I feared it would be used against me. The state had effectively disciplined us, and we had begun to discipline one another. Additionally, I had seen yet another isolating side of leftist organizing: the lack of support for those who are co-parents with political defendants.

It took us over a year to have the blow-out fight that would confront the tight grip the state had on our relationship. After missing a menstrual period, I went back through my ovulation calendar to discover the strong possibility that I was pregnant. Early one morning, before the kids had woken up, I took a test that confirmed I was pregnant. Returning to the calendar, this meant an estimated due date would be mid-December 2018. The surprise and joy were quickly suffocated by my anxiety as I realized that Michael's trial was scheduled to begin in October 2018. When he woke up, I told him that I was pregnant and roughly how far along I was. As he looked at me, blankly, I could see his eyes counting the months for a due date. We hugged and said that we would talk about it later. Two days went by, and the tension had only thickened between us. It was not a question of if we wanted another child, it was the fear of how it would work if he was incarcerated by the time the baby was due. We decided to meet at a coffee shop and talk it out while walking.

For over two hours, and almost ten repetitive trips around the winding neighbourhood, we laid everything out there. We shared the times we had felt unsupported, how and what we find ourselves directing our anger toward, the debilitating amount of fear and anxiety, and the questions we know cannot be answered. I felt alone, betrayed that he subjected himself to this risk of incarceration. He felt alone, betrayed that I was abandoning my political commitments and misdirecting my anger with the state toward him. I felt bad for feeling excited about the pregnancy, and he felt bad that he couldn't see past his trial. We decided this pregnancy is what we both wanted, and that somehow, things would work out. A few weeks later, we told our families that we were expecting. I shared some concerns with my mom in a private phone conversation. My mom, who was well aware of the pending trial, reassured me that she babies bring good luck. She felt my pregnancy was a sign that things were going to shift in a positive direction.

Roughly a week after my mom had shared her positive mantra, we travelled to the EF! River Rendezvous. I was in a workshop with Emory, and Michael took Simon and Tevye to explore the forest together. Not only were we deep in the woods with shoddy service, but this was not the kind of space that you play on your phone. I could hear Michael shouting my name from through the trees, getting louder as he ran toward me. He pulled me aside and whispered, "My charges were dropped. It's over."

I paused, tried to find my balance, and smiled. A fuzzy kind of tingle radiated from my toes up to my arms; I felt numb, but in the good kind of a way. Over. The spectacular nightmare was over. He didn't take a plea, which would have meant conviction and jail time. He didn't compromise his political beliefs or invalidate the importance of resisting political repression. We didn't have to explain to the kids why their dad was out of town for several weeks in October, or the possibility that he might not return for an extended period. I wasn't grand juried; our personal lives were not put on display by the courts. Our marriage didn't crumble, despite the immense amount of stress and pressure we felt during those eighteen months. In one of the more egregious examples of political targeting, posturing, and punishment against the left in contemporary US history, the state simply conceded.

5

Disciplining the State

So we used the tactics that were available to us. We didn't have political power. We didn't have billions of dollars. We didn't have the money that HSUS has, the political connections, but sometimes we had a brick, and I think we were justified in using it.

(Klepfer 2013)

My actions were individual acts of conscience and I take sole responsibility for them. The property damage was intended to be symbolic and theatrical in nature, not dangerous or threatening to any individual.

(Mason 2009)

The exposé in *Elle* that featured Anna told a story about how she manipulated, disrupted, and ultimately entrapped an eco-activist. The case had a chilling effect, primarily because the state was able to successful convict McDavid on a conspiracy charge. But McDavid's case was not a total victory for the state. By the time the issue of *Elle* hit newsstands, McDavid's legal support team had begun working on getting him out. Shortly after the magazines were stocked on the shelves, there were reports that they had been stickered with a retraction. One activist with CrimethInc. shared: "This month, as every month, I tromped over to Borders to purchase the new issue of *Elle* magazine. But when I opened the magazine, I discovered a sticker pasted across one of the articles ... This sticker was in every single copy of the magazine in the store" (Collective n.d.).

The sticker, stuck overtop the article in each of the copies in the bookstore, read:

Following consultation with federal agencies, we at *Elle* wish to retract this article. Not because of the stream of factual inaccuracies beginning in the second sentence (there has never been a CrimethInc. Convergence in Athens, Georgia), but because in the current political climate it is irresponsible to even pretend to give a fair hearing to radical anti-capitalists. Even if Anna's story is a cut-and-dried case of entrapment, we have to understand this as a necessary defense of our free market freedoms.

Not to say that we are not concerned about the environment at *Elle*. On the contrary, the global environmental crisis offers unprecedented opportunities to promote sustainable fashions (98), give the meat industry a makeover (245), and renew faith in this country's discredited electoral process (104); even the color green itself is making a comeback (72). Consumer capitalism may be threatening life on earth, but there's simply no other option – that is, not unless you're willing to join the ranks of the eco-terrorists. (Anonymous G 2008)

The previous chapter provided an extensive (but not exhaustive) overview of the ways in which the state uses disciplinary and monarchical punishment to interpellate activists. Political repression, specifically during the Green Scare, is both performative and material. The tactics are not particularly novel: surveillance, infiltration, turning activists into agents of the state, targeted legislation, physical violence, incarceration, and even assassination. Because these tactics have existed for generations of social movements, activists have become quite creative in their fight back against repression and have adapted to the new technologies. As Foucault astutely points out, "Where there is power, there is resistance, and yet, or rather consequently, this resistance is never in a position of exteriority in relation to power" (Foucault 1990, 95).[1] Thus, we cannot conceive of punishment without conceiving of it as a dialectical performance.

Direct action, particularly illegal direct action, is an effective challenge to the state's monopoly of violence. These acts of resistance create a spectacle that queers the retaliatory interpellation of disidentification. Damaging and destroying property. Liberating animals from a laboratory. Tearing down fences and releasing animals from farms. Sabotaging a hunt. These are different types of monarchical punishment that interrupt interpellation. Direct action blends monarchical punishment and disciplinary power through spectacular events, such as the lab raid, where the activists create an alternative panopticon that instills corporate fear.

Tim Lewis, eco-activist and filmmaker, reflects on the impact of the Superior Lumber arson, "When the big bad bully gets hit in the stomach and feels a little something, maybe a little fear or whatever, that felt good," and later in the film we hear from the owner of Superior Lumber, "After the fire, for a long time, you really looked over your shoulder. We put alarms in our homes, and things like that, things that before

we hadn't thought about" (Curry 2011). This type of disidentification
challenges the perceived power of the state and shows how corporations can be disciplined. Individuals working for animal-and-ecology use
industries question, or disidentify with, whether or not they are actually
protected by the state from so-called ecoterrorists. The (neoliberal capitalist) social contract between employees and animal-and-ecology use
industries is broken when an individual becomes the target of a pressure
campaign. For example, a home demonstration targets an employee of a
corporation, holding the individual accountable for the collective corporate actions. The individual turns to the corporation for protection, but
the corporation cannot protect them without capitulating to the activists. Pressure campaigns isolate and focus on individuals, and they foster
disidentificatory thoughts where that individual questions what the corporation is doing to protect them from harassment. During the sentencing hearing for eco-activist BJ Biehl, a cacophony of mink farmers took
turns sharing how activism impacts mink farming. They claimed it had a
"ripple effect," that the entire industry had been affected by the ALF, and
that they were being "held hostage" by fear of ALF raids.

Eco-activists foster this disidentification through direct action, and its
performative spectacle of discipline, to challenge the state's reliance on
good versus bad subjects. The spectacles disrupt the truisms about species,
capital, and authority while proposing an alternative political imaginary in
which animal-and-ecology use industries are not just or wholesome. The
spectacular arson, for example, subverts the state's presumed monopoly of
monarchical punishment, and asserts power over these industries. As the fire
burns, the corporation, a symbol of neoliberal capitalism and speciesism,
capitulates. This is the performance of monarchical punishment, but the
power of direct action lies in its disciplinary function. Reflecting back on the
End Captivity Now campaign, Levi shared how direct action effects change:

> Eight years! Three days after this, the first business day, [redacted]
> announced regulations would finally be coming for captive marine
> mammals after fifty years as an industry and fifty years of protest. Those
> regulations later ensured there would never be another captive Orca in
> Canada after Kiska and created significant new barriers and costs to
> importing/exporting and keeping captive marine mammals. We never
> got to the end goal of shutting the park down, but the collective effort
> and energy of this day was a highwater mark that changed the shape of
> captivity for marine mammals in this country. As always kids, remember
> that it was direct action – one of the largest acts of civil disobedience for
> animals in this country's history – that got the goods. (Levi 2020)

Throughout the chapter, I weave between participant-observation ethnographic fieldnotes, legal documents and activist archives, interviews, and activists' use of social media to gain in-depth understanding of how activists challenge speciesism and respond to political repression. I use selected ethnographic notes to demonstrate the tensions (and beauty) inside AELM activist spaces before focusing on three case studies that illustrate how the AELM disciplines the state, and, in some cases, responds directly to repression. Peter Young, the first activist convicted for violating the AEPA, has spent more than twenty years agitating and advocating for animal liberation. His use of direct action, followed by decades of press support for the ALF, illustrates the aboveground ways eco-activists use disciplinary power. The second case study, Walter Bond, charged with violating the AETA, provides an interesting discussion about the spectacle of the courtroom and inflammatory rhetoric. The third case study, Eric King, highlights the ways in which prison support for political prisoners is vital in undermining the state's use of the prison-industrial complex.

Over the years, I became engulfed in political prisoner support networks, eco-activist trials and sentencing statements, workshops on security culture, communiqués, direct action campaigns, and the creative world of spectacular political theatre. Peggy Lautenschlager, the USAO that questioned Peter Young's co-defendant, Justin Samuel, began a federal grand jury hearing like this: "Okay. First, I have a personal question to ask. Does one pronounce it vegan or veegin?" to which Samuel replied, "Depends on the person. Different people, different ways," and Lautenschlager continued, "There's no preferred pronunciation?" and Samuel responded, "No," to which Lautenschlager concludes, "Okay. We'll move on then" (Federal Grand Jury Hearing 2000). The courtroom is a theatre, and it is up to the activists to expose the absurdity. Consistently, respondents shared how important solidarity is within the movement (Grubbs 2013b; 2014c; 2014b, Anonymous H, Anonymous I). The state relies on biopower to create docile bodies, and in this case, good activists. But, if the bad activists can stick together and maintain consistent pressure on the state by engaging in direct action, there won't be any need for good activists. As the saying goes, direct action gets the goods.

DISCIPLINE IN ACTIVIST SPACES

The first time I heard Coronado, one of the most influential animal liberationists, speak at an activist convergence, I was in graduate school.

He was giving a talk about activist strategies and indigenous cultural preservation. He was focused on Wolf Patrol, a conservation effort that supports Citizen Monitoring Programs where community members take an active role in witnessing and documenting public wolf management practices (Coronado 2014). He seemed to always have a crew of people around him, almost like a celebrity following. His reputation is complicated within the AELM, as discussed in the previous chapter, but his legacy is undisputed. His activism in the AELM dates back to the late 1980s and includes sinking and scuttling whaling ships as a crew member of Sea Shepherd Conservation Society, committing arson attacks on research facilities, releasing mink from a research farm, damaging property connected to animal abuse, and publishing some of the most prolific, useful manuals and literature that are still circulated today. Coronado is credited with the zine *The Final Nail*, a primer that includes tactical advice and the most comprehensive, up to date database of fur farms in the US. In 1996, *The Final Nail #1: Destroying the Fur Industry* was released and widely circulated throughout the AELM. The primer is credited with the dramatic increase in fur farm raids in the mid-90s. Dean Kuipers provides a detailed account of Operation Bite Back, a series of ALF actions that targeted mink farms and researchers, and Coronado's prominent position as an ALF spokesperson (Kuipers 2009). In 2013, *The Final Nail #4* emerged online, and it situated itself within the Green Scare: "In a time when the climate in the movement has shifted from offensive to defensive, from a conversation on what we're going to do to stop them to what they're doing to stop us, from a time of ALF actions at a rate of one every two weeks to one of movement-wide paralysis inspired by rampant fear-mongering, *The Final Nail* represents a return to the essence of the ALF and the warrior model: the where, the how, and purpose that transcends all obstacles and fears. To the rebirth of *The Final Nail*, and swift death of the fur industry" (Anonymous J 2013). Coronado approaches issues of animal liberation as an indigenous member of the Pascua Yaqui nation, and brings an intersectional lens to issues of sovereignty and animal use. He has remained at the forefront of the AELM for his actions, his roles a spokesperson and advocate, his public instructional lectures, and the ongoing political repression he faces.

ELF COUNTRY: THE PACIFIC NORTHWEST

I remember the first time I watched the film *Pickaxe: The Cascadia Free State Story* by Tim Lewis and Tim Ream. I was nineteen and taking an Environmental Communication course with Stephen Depoe. The film tells story of the 1996 anti-logging campaign at Warner Creek, a federally protected forest in southern Oregon. There is a rich history of eco-activism throughout the Pacific Northwest because of the concentration of Redwood trees and other exploited ecological resources.[2] I recalled the opening scene from *Pickaxe: The Cascadia Free State Story* as we drove Interstate 5: "The government wasn't going to solve our problems. So I decided to come out here to Eugene, Oregon ... when I got out here and I saw the rivers and the big trees, and the mountains of Cascadia, I fell in love with this place. And when I saw the clear cuts and the tree farms, I was sickened. They are far more prevalent than the natural forest" (Lewis and Ream 1999). In many ways, travelling to the Pacific Northwest was a sacred journey for me. The mountains and rivers called to me, along with the activist communities.

I arrived in Seattle in June 2014 with my partner and our two children: our then-four-month-old daughter, Simon, and two-year-old daughter, Emory. As we struggled with the car seats and luggage through the airport, I felt the physical realities of my anthropological baggage. Similar to the trips to Canada, around the Midwest, and to local demonstrations, I chose to travel with my children for the six weeks of data collection across the country. Although I frame this decision as a choice, the physical, financial, and emotional demands of parenting constrained my agency to "choose." Simon was exclusively breastfed and nursed on demand. Emory relied on me for emotional and physical support and had never spent more than twelve hours away from me. Truth be told, at that time the only night I had slept apart from Emory was in 2013 when I stayed in hospice by my Papa Simon's bedside before he passed away. I am intentional about gathering ethnographic data that reflects my own lived experience and reflects my identity within this movement. Thus, these stories write motherhood into academic activist literature, and highlight the embodiments of gendered labour and reproduction.

Similarly, the decision to publicly care for my children while engaging in activism and academic research contributes to the larger socio-political project focused on disrupting traditionally male-dominated androcentric spaces (Adams and Donovan 1995). During this six-week period, we drove an average of 100 miles per day, stopping frequently at anarchist worker-run businesses, infoshops, demonstrations, convergences, and academic conferences. During the first two weeks alone, we drove over 1,400 miles from Stanwood, WA, to Klamath, CA, to Seattle, WA, stopping throughout the way. We then flew to Denver, CO, and drove from Ft Collins, CO, to Albuquerque, NM, to Denver, CO. We detoured up logging roads, drove through ELF-targeted ski towns, and got lost in

the forests that forever etch their way into your psyche. I began to understand what the activists meant when they signed so many communiqués
with, "The elves are watching."

Gathering for Total Liberation

The first planned stop was Portland, Oregon, for the Gathering for Total
Liberation convergence held at a college campus in town. The convergence organizers stressed that this was not an academic conference, nor
was this solely a skills-based series of workshops. The convergence was a
hybrid of tabling, presentations, workshops, and roundtable discussions.
The list of presenters included direct action activists, lawyers, university
professors, and eco-activists who had been previously indicted and/or
convicted, as well as students who wandered in for the free food provided
by a local collective. Many of the activists in attendance were travelling to
the EF! Rendezvous in the coming week, making the convergence one of
the earliest points of contact with my research participants during the trip.

I debated whether or not I should make my first appearance at the convergence with my children. I decided to have my partner go inside alone
and report back whether or not the space was conducive for children.
After a few minutes inside the building, he emerged and reassured me that
we would feel comfortable and helped take the kids from their car seats.
Emory was potty-training, and we had this ridiculous portable toilet in
the trunk to help ease the process. We have this picture of her going to
the bathroom just outside of the convergence, perched on her potty in
our rental car trunk. I remember laughing to myself and thinking, "If only
I could leave all my shit outside too," as we trekked in with an arduous
amount of kid stuff. I put Simon in a cloth wrap, clinging her close to my
body, so that she could sleep or breastfeed at her discretion. Emory, on the
other hand, was eager to explore her new surroundings. She was dressed
in a pair of jeans and a black t-shirt that read "I am vegan and I love you,"
made by the local vegan company Herbivore. I surveyed the room and
noted the prevalence of dark clothing, patches, and tattoos.

Perhaps I'm dating myself, but I also scan the room for septum rings.
By late 1990s, septum rings were one of the more visible markers within
the intersecting communities associated with punk and anarchism. The
cultural significance and popularity of septum rings has changed a great
deal in two decades, and there is a less politicized association with the
piercing today. However, there is an entire generation of those folks that
were young enough to participate in the 1999 shut down of the World
Trade Organization (WTO) in Seattle that shaped the younger generation

emulating this nostalgic body modification and ephemera. Although I don't have any of these obvious markers (political tattoos or facial piercings) my partner has both a prominent anarchist tattoo and a septum ring. The visual culture within the AELM, though contested and not exclusively marked by these ephemera, represents a particular aesthetic overlap of anarchist and anti-speciesist culture.

I wandered into the tabling room and made my way around the small space by stopping at each table. In one of the most uncomfortable moments of my research, I reached the table of a prominent eco-activist. I had met them before and heard them discuss the practice of elective sterilization as a way to combat ecological destruction. I was aware of this divisive politic when I approached them wearing my infant child in a wrap. As I discussed earlier, I do not often wear jewellery and intentionally do not do so during political actions. However, that day I had worn an heirloom ring on my fourth finger on my left hand, commonly known as the ring finger. I had forgotten to remove it prior to entering the space. I caught them looking at the child wrapped around my abdomen, and then their eyes immediately travelled to my hand. Their nose scrunched and clearly conveyed their disapproval. They turned away, closing off the opportunity to speak with them. As I walked away, I slowly removed the ring from my finger and put it in my pocket. Again, I was left feeling ostracized in a space in which I so deeply wanted to belong. Although there was no verbal exchange, I found myself narrating an explanation in my head as I stood there.

My mother had been given the ring by her grandmother, my great-grandmother. The ring was a symbol of gratitude from my great-grandfather to my great-grandmother. As Jews living in Nazi-occupied Poland, they were displaced from their home in the 1930s. My great-grandfather had been taken as a prisoner of war and held in a detention camp. My great-grandmother, worried about his survival, sold the few pieces of jewellery she had smuggled with her during their expulsion. She used the money to purchase bread rations and would illegally sneak food to him in the camp. Years later, my great-grandfather was able to save enough money to purchase her some small, second-hand jewellery to give as gifts. The diamonds most certainly are unethical, and the symbolism of love as a commodity is no less problematic here. But, for me, the ring symbolizes resistance and resilience. In that space, at the conference, none of that mattered. I felt shame and was annoyed with myself for even bringing it. I suppose this contradictory moment captures the ways in which I wrestle with deeply personal inconsistencies. But it also captures how tenuous our sense of belonging can be within any given space.

A few tables down, I recognized two activists that I had met at a demonstration with Bridges Brigade. The activists were presenting later that afternoon and had also been listed presenters at the upcoming EF! Rendezvous. We spent a few minutes chatting, and they passed along flyers, stickers, and posters to bring back to Ohio for the demonstration that was scheduled in August. I dropped the materials off on a table and headed into the next panel.

Don't Be Paranoid, but They Are Listening

The panel featured two eco-activists who had been arrested for direct action activism and/or conspiracy to do so. I still had Simon asleep on my chest, and my partner carried our toddler as we attempted to blend into the back of the room. The presentation was held in a multipurpose room that had a series of board games tucked into a corner. I grabbed the game "Apples to Apples" and removed the top. Within minutes, hundreds of red and green cards littered the floor. Rather than receive friendly smiles or reassuring nods from the attendees, their glares conveyed their indignant sense of "I wonder if she will clean that up." I didn't, and instead I waited until Emory was engrossed enough in the cards for me to take notes during presentation. The presenters focused on the role of surveillance in the AELM as both a disciplining and performance of the state. The first speaker, a well-published author and highly regarded activist, challenged the presumed power of the state and surveillance:

> Don't be afraid. The government doesn't know shit. Know your rights. You don't have to talk. Remember to keep teaching that over and over again. Apple, Google, and other companies know far more than the US government, and for now that information is siloed so even if they will sell the information in the end. It is all about the *perception* of fear. Political prisoners that get released often struggle with PTSD. Make friends with people who have resources in your community. Lawyer up! (Anonymous H 2014)

Their remarks highlighted how the state's efforts to interpellate eco-activists fit neatly within the good versus bad protestor dichotomy. The presenter critiqued the state's retaliatory attempt to interpellate direct action eco-activists as ecoterrorists. The power of the state, according to this presenter, is merely a perception that they insist we challenge. The second presenter, someone who worked with the NAELFPO, challenged the ability for the state to gain incriminating information through surveillance but stressed the physical and psychological impacts of the perceived surveillance.

In this sense, the presenter relied on a traditional reading of Foucault's disciplinary punishment and the conditioning of the body (Foucault 1977, 104–5, 215, 280). But rather than reinforce the social conditioning of the state, the presenter emphasized the ways in which activists can manipulate the media and hold the state accountable through the Freedom of Information Act (FOIA). Ultimately, however, the presentation seemed suspended between the tension of denying the state's effective use of surveillance and reifying it through sharing stories of repression. The presenter reflected on their own experience with surveillance. Specifically, the US Postal Service had delivered mail with stamping that revealed it had been intercepted, scanned, and archived by the FBI. The story was used to illustrate how activists can counter the impacts of surveillance through the use of strategic media:

Use the media. You can manipulate the media to help release documents. You should utilize the FOIA. People are now using it in the movement to expose bad stuff. I used FOIA to receive the photocopies of all of my mail that was scanned and photocopied by the federal government during the 30-day period. If you get something, you sue and appeal and follow it all the way through. People tend to be afraid of the media – but we should use it to tell these stories of surveillance. I reached out to journalists to tell my story because it's a closed case. In other cases, the government is ready to indict and convict, but this was not the case for me. I worked with a journalist to get 3 things out there: represent anarchy in a decent way, make me look reasonable, and make the FBI look like fools. I wanted to demonstrate a clear "us" that is against a surveillance state. We can't deny that the media is an important tool and two years after my story, Snowden releases all these documents. We can make the FBI seem like the out-of-control entity they are, but we can also show that we don't buy the story. I didn't want to be distracted by surveillance and make a stink when I noticed mail surveillance. But then looking back I admit I underestimated the power of repression. (Gathering for Total Liberation 2014)

The convergence featured several panels that focused on security culture and provided perspectives on how activists can work in solidarity with one another to challenge state authority and speciesism. Although the convergence was held on a university campus, the panelists used accessible language to address practical issues with organizing, ways to engage in solidarity work, and how to access community resources.[3] Several days later, we travelled from Portland to northern California to attend the EF! Rendezvous.

Earth First! Rendezvous

The EF! Rendezvous organizers did not release the location of the convergence to the public until a month before the gathering. The location was given as coordinates, making it pretty difficult to navigate. The EF! Journal released the following, "The Rondy is an annual gathering of biocentric revolutionaries, hosted by Earth First! This year the Rondy will be July 1–7, in Southern Oregon, near the coast (location to be disclosed closer to the event)" (Earth First! 2014). EF! hosts gatherings in the spirit of temporary autonomous zones (TAZ), a widely cited anarchist concept articulated by insurrectionary anarchist Hakim Bey. A TAZ creatively challenges property and the role of the commons, providing a physical space to disidentify from not just the good versus bad protestor paradigm, but also the authoritative functions of the state (Bey 2003). In these spaces, the physical and digital divide is widened, and people co-create forms of disidentification that invoke the existential questions and framework put forth by Bey:

> Are we who live in the present doomed never to experience autonomy, never to stand for one moment on a bit of land ruled only by freedom? Are we reduced either to nostalgia for the past or nostalgia for the future? Must we wait until the entire world is freed of political control before even one of us can claim to know freedom? Logic and emotion can unite to condemn such a supposition. Reason demands that one cannot struggle for what one does not know; and the heart revolts at a universe so cruel as to visit such injustices on *our* generation alone of mankind ... The TAZ is like an uprising which does not engage directly with the State, a guerilla operation which liberates an area (of land, of time, of imagination) and then dissolves itself to re-form elsewhere/ elsewhen, *before* the State can crush it. Because the State is concerned primarily with simulation rather than substance, the TAZ can "occupy" these areas clandestinely and carry on its festal purposes for quite a while in relative peace. (Bey 2003, 96–9)

The camp was set up as a suspension of geopolitical borders, state regulations, and authoritarianism.

The gathering was not a cohesive group with one agenda, but rather a series of agendas that overlapped and diverged on specific issues. Many of the distributors featured literature on the ELF and ALF, as well as CrimethInc. and Green Anarchy. The sessions provided skills trainings, anonymous spaces to network and build activist communities, and workshops providing legal counselling. Many of the activists looked familiar from various political actions, including demonstrations in Ohio.

After locating the specified area through Google Maps, we planned the route. Unlike the Gathering for Total Liberation or other convergences held on college campuses, the Rendezvous is specifically geared toward activists. The gatherings provide trainings in direct action tactics, networking for aboveground and underground activists, and a space to engage in dialogue to advance social justice aims. As we drove the winding roads of the national forest, our cell phones lost service. The directions from EF! were based on landmarks, which oftentimes underestimated the timing to reach each site. The guidelines suggested attendees leave identifying information (such as photo identification and credit cards) at home. Drivers were encouraged to use precautions to avoid unnecessary stops from law enforcement. Before we realized the campsite was approaching, we noted two unmarked federal cars parked aside the road.[4] A few minutes later, we passed another unmarked vehicle with the United States Department of Agriculture (USDA). We slowly drove by with the windows down and heard the nervous barks of a dog in the back of the USDA SUV. The directions mentioned that there would most likely be various forms of law enforcement present along the journey, and that a concentration of them should indicate the site is imminent. As expected, we turned the corner to find at least six vehicles stationed at the base of the camp. We drove past the entrance one time, making note of each vehicle, and then turned back to enter the EF! campsite.

The long and narrow path led to a pop-up umbrella tent with three activists sitting in lawn chairs. The handwritten sign read Earth First! Rendezvous and a series of photocopied handwritten maps sat in a pile. One of the activists came over to the car to greet us and peered inside the car. I watched as their eyes travelled throughout the car, while another activist seated in a lawn chair noted our licence plate. My partner got out of the car and walked over to the table to get a map and say hello to the other activists. He came back to the car a few minutes later and we drove into the forest. The campsite was located about ten minutes off the state route, deep into the forest. Along the dirt road there were hammocks and single-person tents sporadically placed.

Despite the explicit requests to not bring companion animals, there were several dogs adorned with political bandanas and black dog clothing, oftentimes accessorized by a subset of transient anarchists called crust punks (Parmar, Nocella, and Robertson 2014). I watched as a dog lunged toward an activist passing by, and the activist turned to scream and hit the dog. I was struck by this violent act, and it served as an orienting event in this contested, shared space for activists who clearly do not have the same anti-speciesist politics. As an anarchafeminist, I struggle with the masculinist and misogynist tendencies within crust punk culture, and the overlap it can have within the AELM. The cars were directed to park in a centralized area. We pulled into an empty spot and noticed cars had their licence plates covered with towels and rags. Some cars had their front and back plates removed. The cars ranged in make, condition, and age, reflecting a relatively diverse representation of economic classes present. The Rendezvous had started a day earlier, making our late arrival visible with our clean car in a sea of dust-covered vehicles. I got out of the car, again tucked Simon in a cloth wrap close to my chest, and took Emory by the hand as we ventured out.[5]

The map explained how the spaces were designated, illustrating how the organizers understood concentrations of people to use specific areas. The different populations were stationed throughout the forest: general camping, family camping, medical tent, Cascadia Kids Tent, kitchen, session spaces, and the Trans and/or Women's Action Camp (TWAC). The EF! Journal had pinned papers with solidarity calls to the board asking for donations and announcing actions specifically in Bay Area. The dirt paths each led to specified areas and had makeshift signs and pathmarkers indicating the intersecting areas.

Shortly after arriving, I befriended a few people, one of whom was with a small child, and another had noticed me at the Gathering for Total Liberation. They were on their way to the TWAC for a swim in the lake, and suggested I come along with my daughters. With Simon wrapped on my chest and Emory in tow, I set off with them to find the "watering hole." As I trekked along the path, I noticed the Rose McCarthy Memorial Way sign tacked on a tree, the signs addressing inclusivity and safe spaces, and a large board listing terms and definitions including "white privilege," "cultural appropriation," "racism," and "Indigenous." The smaller board offered sign-up slots for attendees to volunteer to assist with kitchen duties, cleaning, childcare, and site management.

Along the walk to the lake we discussed our activist backgrounds and what brought us to the rendezvous. Another person had their daughter present and described how they had hitchhiked across the country to attend, and that they were not sure how they would get home. I was introduced to others as "Jenny," but everyone else was introduced by their chosen pseudonyms such as Glitter and Leaping Lizard. When I introduced myself as Jenny, I was met with confused expressions and skepticism. I could tell they were wondering why I chose not to use a pseudonym. It was a magical moment in the forest where Emory was able to get lost in play with another child. Glitter and I exchanged stories about activism, parenting, and mundane things like popular culture. I suppose that I, too, got lost in conversation with another adult and it was its own kind of magical moment for me in the forest. After a long walk through the TWAC, we were unable to locate the swimming area. We heard shouts through the trees, and one of the activists said they had heard "men's voices" and we grew uncomfortable moving forward. We turned back and headed to the next series of sessions that were slated to begin. As we approached a more populated area of the forest, they expressed an interest in sticking together when we returned to the base camp. Although we didn't explicitly say why we felt more comfortable together navigating the sessions, I interpreted it as a sense of solidarity as caregivers. We found a clearing and sat down for the children to play while we listened to the panel.

The panel focused on security culture, a recurring theme that was also prevalent at Gathering for Total Liberation. The speaker, a lawyer representing the NLG, facilitated a series of role-playing activities to provide legal trainings. The speaker took turns role-playing, moving between "the activist" and "the law enforcement officer," acting out scenarios to demonstrate the legal rights of protestors. At the end of this demonstration, they reiterated, "Three things: Don't talk to cops. Don't trust cops. Cops are like wild animals" (Anonymous I 2014). The third piece of advice, conflating wild animals to cops, felt out of place. I chose to avoid debating this speciesist metaphor. The participants wanted to know more about the ways in which they can protect themselves at convergences such as the one they were currently at. One activist described the ways cell phones can be used for surveillance and suggested it be a requirement that all batteries are removed. Another activist spoke out and challenged this tactic claiming that people can simply bring a backup power source.

The conversation became contentious when another activist shouted that the only effective way to avoid cell phones being used for surveillance is to lock them in a metal box at the beginning of each gathering. Clearly, cell phones were problematic in these spaces. Unlike the other activist gatherings and direct actions that I had attended, I intentionally left my cell phone in the glovebox of the car. It was challenging to not use my cell phone or camera, especially with the rich ethnographic data and elaborate infrastructure that was available during the rendezvous. This posed a challenge when I was finally able to write down my observations at the end of the day. I knew going into this research that I would have to recall the specific physical surroundings using memory. The final role-playing scenario was a "stop and search" between an activist and a law enforcement officer. The NLG representative probed the participant with invasive questions, each with an insinuated threat. When the activist began to answer one of the questions and address the speculation, the NLG representative loudly said, "STOP!" They began to explain that you do not have to answer any questions and the only vocalization you should make is to request legal representation. The panel wrapped up and we made our way back to the kitchen area for lunch.

The food had been prepared by a collective that provides large-scale meals in activist spaces, but I couldn't tell which of the trays of food were vegan. As a vegan, this made it a little trickier for me to discretely make a plate of food. I found a piece of bread and slathered on some peanut butter and brought it back for Emory. While we were sitting there, two activists quickly walked past and were shouting to one another. I overheard as they questioned the choice to host the Rendezvous in the Siskiyou National Forest, which was Native land. Given that the US was colonized by European settlers through land and labour theft from indigenous peoples, I wondered where they expected the Rendezvous to occur that was not on colonized land. Land acknowledgments are one way to intentionally recognize and pay respect to the stolen land that we call the "United States." They slowed down and continued their conversation within earshot. I listened as they went on to discuss the prevalence of "dread locks" worn by white people in the AELM. Right around the time that septum rings were on the rise in punk anarchist circles, locks became popular amongst white activists. For some, it was the crossover between the fading hippie culture of the 1980s, whereas for other activists it was the crust and gutter punk culture that informed their decision to lock their hair. Through overhearing, I learned that they had attended a talk earlier that day that focused on white privilege and cultural appropriation, and a white woman had defended her decision to wear her hair in locks. They disagreed with her defence and discussed the ethical dimensions and implications of this blatant example of cultural appropriation. They glanced over and awkwardly paused when they noticed I had been listening. In effort to ease the discomfort, Glitter and I joined the conversation.

We chatted about identity and the problems with concepts like authenticity. The conversation about locks and how racism shapes the larger discourse around hair in the US shifted to a broader discussion of the tendency to call out and ostracize someone that violates shared principles rather than calling them in to accountability processes. Calling someone out reinforces the tendency for activists to police and discipline one another. I disclosed that I oftentimes feel ostracized for my appearance and gender performance. One of the activists laughed and said, "Yeah, I'm sure when you walk into a room people think 'Hey, there is Activist Barbie!'" The other activist laughed and admitted they thought that when they noticed me earlier. I took it in jest and laughed along with them, despite the awkward reminder of my perceived otherness. The conversation trailed off shortly after that and they left to attend a tree-sit workshop.

Performing Anarcho-Primitivism

I began to notice a rotting smell close by and got up to locate the source. There were two women, each in their mid-twenties, seated nearby working with the dead carcasses of squirrels. Although the smell was putrid, I moved closer to overhear the conversation. Two men came to sit down next to them just as I made my way closer. The two women began to explain that they were working the hides of squirrels they had hunted in the forest. The women both wore jewellery made from bones and feathers and one of the men was wearing a fur skirt. One of the women offered the men a cup of tea, made with the brains of the squirrel. After a brief conversation about how to make squirrel brain tea, they began to discuss the possibility of trading animals. Although one of the women had just slaughtered two elks to make her bedding at home, she was interested in trading her remaining two elk.

This same woman went on to describe her hunting and skinning practices as an art form, and she stated that she could survive in the woods, unlike most of the people there. This particular interaction was a departure from the intersectional conversations at Gathering for Total Liberation but fits within an anarcho-primitivistic politic.[6] I found myself on the other side of the coin, judging these two women for (what I perceived to be) their appropriation of Indigenous practices. If I cringe at the archetypal label "activist Barbie," then I cannot turn around and call these women "hipster survivalists." Although I think I just did.

Sharing a Carrot

Another conversation of note was with a couple someone directed us to that also had an infant. There were not many children in attendance, so it seemed like lots of folks wanted to connect the few child caregivers with one another. The couple had also travelled from Ohio, and coincidentally one of them was pursuing a PhD from a university in Ohio. We shared a few words on struggling to survive on adjunct wages and the instability of the academic job market and exchanged stories of participating in political actions with a child. This was one of the few conversations I had with another activist in which I discussed my research at length and received a positive response. The other couple also disclosed their legal names, and we exchanged contact information. In a farewell exchange, Emory watched as the mother ate a raw carrot with a fresh green stem. Emory, enamoured with the carrot, asked if she could also have one. I walked away from the exchange with a delightful sense of camaraderie, and Emory walked away with a delicious carrot.

Exiting Camp

The exit from the Rendezvous was not without its own excitement and dose of security culture. As we pulled down the dirt road to exit, we noticed a long row of state and federal vehicles. The vehicles represented the USDA, local sheriff's office, United States Forestry Service, and two unmarked cars with plainclothes officers in them. When we stopped on the dirt path so that I could take a picture of the cars, an officer shouted, "No blocking the road!" We began to drive forward toward the state route but noticed there were several officers walking into the forest. Moments after getting on the main road, my partner indicated he wanted to go back into the campsite.

Initially, I resisted the decision and questioned how we would provide assistance. In an exercise of empowerment, my partner began to list off a series of services that we would be able to provide, including: an extensive knowledge of our legal rights, two cell phones capable of recording video, a vehicle to transport an additional person, and the ability to provide forewarning before the site is searched. After my initial hesitation, we turned back around and drove into the site. We rolled down our window, revealing our two small children strapped into their car seats in the backseat, and listened closely to the officer's conversations. One of the officers walked by the car and dismissively asked me if this was a Rainbow Gathering. I wanted to reply, "Nope, just a bunch of people gathering together and planning ways to challenge your arbitrary power as a pawn for the state." But I thought it was best to hold my tongue. We kept on driving until we reached the pop-up welcome tent and activists in lawn chairs that had greeted us upon our first welcome. My partner got out of the car and explained that there were about fifteen officers at the foot of the entrance road and that an additional five officers were walking on foot into the forest. The activist explained that today alone, twenty people had been stopped and searched in their vehicles and one person had been arrested and subsequently released. We were given the okay to enter the campsite again and let the organizers know what was going on.

We parked in our earlier parking spot and I waited with the girls while my partner went to find some of the organizers. After he located them, I watched as their interaction progressed. They reached for their two-way radio devices and a few minutes later another organizer came running down from the TWAC. After ten minutes of conversation and strategizing, the officers made their way to the parking area. Two officers stood with my partner and the organizers while three officers dispersed into the camp. One of the officers walked the aisles of the parking area and appeared to be looking at each individual vehicle. The conversation lasted less than ten minutes and then Michael walked over to me and said the situation seemed diffused. The officers claimed that they heard there were fireworks in the forest, and that they were simply there to remind them not to use them. The visit was one of many during the EF! Rendezvous and a rather unsuccessful attempt to intimidate the organizers. While I was waiting in the car, I watched as several individuals stood in a circle and passed a joint with potent marijuana around. Activists scoffed as they walked by and did not appear concerned in the least. On our drive home down the mountain, we noted an additional law enforcement vehicle with the USDA SUV parked behind slightly off the road. Emory waved goodbye and held tight to the Smokey the Bear binoculars someone had given her at the convergence.

DIRECT ACTION AS DISCIPLINE

The dialectical praxis between activists and the state within the contemporary moment continues to evolve through technological advances. The technopower (the internet, smart phones, d/encryption, surveillance devices, etc.) available in tandem with direct action tactics, provide significantly destructive mechanisms to subvert statecraft (Chomsky 2005; Virilio 2012; Žižek 2008; Zuboff 2020). The creative strategies and tactics that activists use expose the tenuousness and vulnerability of state power in the physical disruptions of animal-and-ecology use industries. Furthermore, these efforts undermine the hegemonic foundation of disciplinary power itself. The anarchist rejection of governmentality, capitalism, and coercion, coupled with the anti-speciesist rejection of animal and ecological exploitation, utilize direct action to create a spectacle that expose the fragility of state power without consent and produce disidentificatory thoughts.

When activists walk into the headquarters of a multinational corporation in Cincinnati, Ohio, dressed in black clothing, glue the locks to an office shut, drop two sixty-foot banners, and hang from a zip line strung between two buildings to protest the company's sourcing of palm oil, the audience is confronted with the contradictions of state power. Employees, onlookers, activists, and the targets themselves are witnesses to the performance of disidentification that interrupts hegemonic power. The employees of the company must reconcile feeling unsafe despite the heavily policed fortress, onlookers must reconcile distrusting the effectiveness of security, and the Cincinnati residents must reconcile why activists would challenge the highly regarded local company.[7] The activists credited their ability to penetrate security during the day to technology, a destabilizing mode of protest that disrupts the state's monopoly of surveillance. When Potter announced the Kickstarter campaign to purchase two drones in order to capture aerial footage of factory farms, the state's monopoly of violence is challenged.[8] When SHAC activists hack into the email accounts of HLS executives and leak internal documents, power is disrupted. When activists release 500 mice from a laboratory and widely distribute a communiqué, power is disrupted. Bodies are disciplined to behave in particular ways, and when they step outside of that, power is interrupted.

Peter Young: The Jetsetting Terrorist

In the fall of 1997, during a two-week period, over 8,000 mink and fox were released from six different fur farms in Iowa, South Dakota, and Wisconsin. Additionally, the breeding records were destroyed at all of the farms. A Wisconsin mink farmer, Linda Zimbal, had followed Young and Samuel into town after she saw their red Geo Metro driving by. The mink ranch network had relied on a phone tree to alert farmers to be on the lookout for this car. Zimbal called the police, and they were pulled over and questioned. But, because the cops didn't have a search warrant at the time, they were released before the car was searched. Both Young and Samuel left town quickly, and each fled the country before they were indicted by a federal grand jury in 1998. They were indicted on two charges of "Animal Enterprise Terrorism," and four charges of "extortion by interfering with interstate commerce." Although Samuel was extradited to the US from Belgium in 1999, Young evaded police for seven years until he was arrested in San Jose on shoplifting charges. Because the definition of extortion had changed, the prosecutors were forced to drop this charge. Young pled guilty to conspiracy to release mink from six fur farms, as well as the release of 2,400 mink from one fur farm in Wisconsin. Young was sentenced to two years in federal prison, and his mandated community service specifically stated that it could not benefit any other species than human. While incarcerated, Young published several prominent essays and was in communication with scholar Don Liddick. Liddick published a conservative book focused on eco-activism and included several of Young's letters and addresses to the court. Young makes an explicit connection between straight-edge vegan music, such as Earth Crisis and Vegan Reich, and his politics. He was articulate, passionate, and unrepentant about his actions in every communication. In his address to the court, he condemns the state:

> This is the customary time when the defendant expresses regret
> for the crimes they committed, so let me do that because I am not
> without regrets. I am here today to be sentenced for my participation
> in releasing mink from six fur farms. I regret it was only six. I'm
> also here today to be sentenced for my participation in the freeing
> of 8,000 mink from those farms. I regret it was only 8,000. It is
> my understanding of those six farms, only two of them have since
> shut down. I regret it was only two. More than anything, I regret
> my restraint, because whatever damage we did to those businesses,
> if those farms were left standing, and if one animal was left behind,
> then it wasn't enough. I don't wish to validate this proceeding by
> begging for mercy or appealing to the conscience of the court,
> because I know if this system had a conscience I would not be here,
> and in my place would be the butchers, vivisectors, and fur farmers
> of the world. Just as I will remain unbowed before this court – who
> would see me imprisoned for an act of conscience – I will also deny
> the fur farmers in the room the pleasure of seeing me bow down
> before them. To the people whose sheds I may have visited in 1997,
> let me tell you directly for the first time, it was a pleasure to raid
> your farms, and to free those animals you held captive. It is to those

animals I answer to, not to you or this court. I will forever mark those nights on your property as the most rewarding experience of my life. And to those farmers or other savages who may read my words in the future and smile at my fate, just remember: We have put more of you in bankruptcy than you have put liberators in prison. Don't forget that. Let me thank everyone in the courtroom who came to support me today. It is my last wish before prison that each of you drive to a nearby fur farm tonight, tear down its fence and open every cage. That's all. (Liddick 2006, 87)

Young dismissed the state's punishment and created a spectacle in the courtroom. Over the years, he has been an advocate of direct action and ran Animal Liberation Frontline: Covering Animal Liberation Above the Law, Warcry Communications, and published primers (some under different names). He not only disciplined fur farms by raiding and releasing animals, but his unapologetic rhetoric facilitates and inspires new activists to engage in direct action. He uses exaggeration to mock the terrorism rhetoric used against him, and even ran a website (which was later published as a book), "The Jetsetting Terrorist," which documented all of his encounters with security agents at airports.

Young's book, *Liberate: Stories and Lessons on Animal Liberation Above the Law,* collates years of communiqués in one place. The communiqué explicitly calls out the state and reasserts the monarchical power of the direct action by stating that attacks like this will continue until the industries cease to exist. In 2014, following an act of sabotage, a chemical abrasive was put in the fuel system of a mobile slaughter truck operated by Warts Custom Meat Cutting in Washington. The communiqué, published by the NAALPO, illustrates this type of punishment:

There is nothing humane about turning a living-breathing animal into a lifeless commodity in order to satisfy frivolous human desires. The so called "humane meat movement" is not about respecting the "welfare" of non-human animals, but about masking and normalizing a culture of violence and exploitation directed towards sentient non-humans. This is an act of solidarity with the pigs and cows that are slated to be killed by this company and with all the victims of animal agriculture.

Until the last slaughterhouse truck is idled and the last butcher's blade is snapped. ALF Freedom Summer 2014 has officially commenced. (North American Animal Liberation Press Office 2014)

The activists articulate their threats to the state not only with the specta-cle of direct action, but also through the communiqué. The activists that are caught, entrapped through infiltrators, or implicated by cooperative witnesses have the ability to issue monarchical challenges to state power throughout their legal proceeding. Young is an example of an eco-activ-ist that continues to engage with state power through a rhetorical dia-lectic of performing repression and punishment as disidentification. He continues to inspire eco-activists, and his primers have been referenced by direct action activists like Olliff and Tyler, who were both released from prison in 2017.

Unrepentant Activists: Walter Bond

In 2010, I watched as the trial of Walter Bond, an ALF activist known as "the Lone Wolf," unfolded.[9] His essays and courtroom addresses were spectacular; he was unrepentant and condemned the state and spe-ciesism. In his 2011 essay titled "I Am the Lone Wolf," he specifically addresses the Green Scare. He argues that the concept of "Green Scare" is a moniker that is used to silence activists, and that to even call it the "green scare" gives it power. From the walls of his prison cell, Bond pro-claimed that activists should act collectively and without fear. In other words, they should disidentify with the state's interpellation into eco-terrorists within the Green Scare.

His writings, however, illustrate how his struggle with this disidentifi-cation evolves as he laments that he "acted without fear" and trustingly told his brother about the arsons in Colorado and Utah. He signed his essays with the pseudonym The Lone Wolf and advocated the impor-tance in acting alone.[10] The tension between the collective and the clan-destine is evident in political prisoner reflections that simultaneously claim there is power in collectivity and that the reactionary punishment of the state is ineffective, while also lamenting that their peers deceived them. Activists outside of the prison-industrial complex rely on perfor-mance to posture a nuanced solidarity network and security culture.

Bond, notably a problematic person in the AELM, used his prosecution and time incarcerated to rhetorically challenge the state. Bond's author-itative voice was initially perceived as anarchistic, antagonistically and unapologetically demanding a capitulation of state power. As the years progressed, Bond's rhetoric became increasingly fascistic and problem-atic. In 2020, Bond and Camille Marino, another animal liberation activist, launched a website the "Vegan Final Solution," claiming they had started a new movement that promotes third-positionist fascism, and they advocate murder of those called "traitors" or "useless" in the struggle for animal liberation.[11] The obvious link to Nazism with the "final solution," compounded by his explicit calls for violence against humans, was enough to elicit strong pushback from AELM collectives. Despite all of this, he warrants analysis here. I include this caveat and context because, as an anti-fascist, I strongly believe in the tactic of de-platforming. Although I focus on his early rhetoric in this chapter, I have chosen not to include his more recent writings to minimize the platform he has here. For the first few years of his prison sentence, Bond was heralded by many within the AELM for his spectacular performances in the courtroom, taking heroic direct actions in defence of the earth and animals, and advocating anarchist anti-capitalism organizing. His unrepentant stance was amplified within the AELM as a performative pushback following the massive state efforts to repress activists with Operation Backfire. He provides one case study into how activists discipline the state both materially and rhetorically.

In 2011, Bond, faced multiple indictments and symbolically transformed the courtroom into a stage to discipline the state. He was first tried and convicted in Colorado for burning down a sheepskin factory, before facing trial in Utah later that year. In Colorado, Bond received the minimum sentence allowed by a Colorado court, five years, and three years of probation. Through bombastic rhetoric, he utilized his trial and sentencing hearing to publicly denounce the state and speciesism.[12] The judge made several references during the trial to Bond's intelligence, she acknowledged that she had read all fifty letters of support sent from activists, and she also took the time to encourage Bond to focus on writing rather than illegal acts. Similar to Young, Bond begins his speech with an acknowledgment and rejection of the expected apologia. He says:

> I'm here today because I burnt down the Sheepskin Factory in Glendale, CO, a business that sells pelts, furs and other dead Animal skins. I know many people think I should feel remorse for what I've done. I guess this is the customary time where I'm supposed to grovel and beg for mercy. I assure you if that's how I felt I would. But, I am not sorry for anything I have done. Nor am I frightened by this court's authority. Because any system of law that values the rights of the oppressor over the downtrodden is an unjust system. And though this court has real and actual power, I question its morality. I doubt the court is interested in the precautions that I took to not harm any

person or by-stander and even less concerned with the miserable lives that sheep, cows and mink had to endure, unto death, so that a Colorado business could profit from their confinement, enslavement, and murder.

Obviously, the owners and employees of the sheepskin factory do not care either or they would not be involved in such a sinister and macabre blood trade. So I will not waste my breath where it will only fall on deaf ears. That's why I turned to illegal direct action to begin with, because you do not care. No matter how much we Animal Rights activists talk or reason with you, you do not care. Well, Mr Livaditis (owner of the Sheepskin Factory), I don't care about you. There is no common ground between people like you and me. I want you to know that no matter what this court sentences me to today, you have won nothing! Prison is no great hardship to me. In a society that values money over life, I consider it an honor to be a prisoner of war, the war against inter-species slavery and objectification! I also want you to know that I will never willingly pay you one dollar, not one! I hope your business fails and you choke to death on every penny you profit from animal murder! I hope you choke on it and burn in hell!

To my supporters, I wish to say thank you for standing behind me and showing this court and these animal exploiters that we support our own and that we as a movement are not going to apologize for having a sense of urgency. We are not going to put the interests of commerce over sentience! And we will never stop educating, agitating and confronting those responsible for the death of our Mother Earth and her Animal Nations. My vegan sisters and brothers our lives are not our own. Selfishness is the way of gluttons, perverts and purveyors of injustice. It has been said all it takes for evil to conquer is for good people to do nothing. Conversely, all it takes to stop the enslavement, use, abuse and murder of other than human animals is the resolve to fight on their behalf!

Do what you can, do what you must, be vegan warriors and true animal defenders and never compromise with their murderers and profiteers. The Animal Liberation Front is the answer. Seldom has there been such a personally powerful and internationally effective movement in human history. You cannot join the A.L.F. but you can become the A.L.F. And it was the proudest and most powerful thing I have ever done. When you leave this courtroom today don't be dismayed by my incarceration.

All the ferocity and love in my heart still lives on. Every time someone liberates an Animal and smashes their cage, it lives on! Every

time an activist refuses to bow down to laws that protect murder,
it lives on! And it lives on every time the night sky lights up ablaze
with the ruins of another animal exploiters' business! That's all Your
Honor, I am ready to go to prison.[13] (Bond 2011a)

Bond's performative punishment of the state was not only his direct
actions, it was also his unrepentant speeches in the courtroom. He rhetorically refused to identify with the disciplinary function of the state.
In the opening paragraph, "I guess this is the customary time where I'm
supposed to grovel and beg for mercy ... but I am not sorry ... nor
am I frightened ... And although this court has real and actual power,
I question its morality," Bond challenges the ways in which neoliberal
capitalism places disproportionate value on profit in relation to the lives
of other species (Bond 2011a). Throughout the speech, Bond frames the
current legal-political landscape as a capital-driven system that supports
violent exploitation, whereas his own actions fall within a trajectory of
liberation activists who act ethically to destroy an unethical society.

He echoes Young with the following syllogism: society has immoral
practices toward other species, laws supporting these practices are tied
to profit for the state, therefore it is justified to defy society and the laws
by disrupting these practices and profits because they are immoral. Thus,
if you agree that society has immoral practices toward other species, and
you agree that these practices are facilitated by and profited off of by the
state, then the state supports immoral practices. The syllogism challenges
the neoliberal logic that the state acts with the public's best interest and
draws attention to the ways in which the state creates and enforces laws
based on profit rather than ethic. The logic, then, contributes to disidentificatory thoughts as the audience questions their own support for these
immoral practices and the complicity of the state.

Bond symbolically shifts the traditionally repentant practice where
the convicted demonstrate remorse during the sentencing hearing. Bond,
however, uses the words: oppressor, unjust system, sinister and macabre
blood trade, gluttons, perverts, and purveyors of injustice to describe the
state and animal-and-ecology use industries. Conversely, he addresses
his supporters, the "Vegan Warriors" and "True Animal Defenders," and
encourages them to continue to act with urgency and with disregard for
the law. He does so by valourizing his acts within a context of war.

He states: "Prison is no great hardship to me ... it is an honor to be
a prisoner of war, the war against inter-species slavery and objectification!" He concludes the speech with a final rallying call for the ALF:
"you can become the ALF. And it was the proudest and most powerful

thing I have ever done ... don't be dismayed by my incarceration. All the ferocity and love in my heart still lives on ... every time an activist refuses to bow down to laws that protect murder ... it lives on every time the night sky lights ablaze with the ruins of another Animal exploiters' business" (Bond 2011a). The final sentence, in many ways, is monarchical. Metaphorically, it is a linguistic guillotine that cuts into the disciplinary power of the state. Rather than request mercy or special consideration, Bond indignantly declares in martyrdom, "That's all Your Honor, I am ready to go to prison." The declaration undermines the disciplinary function of the state, explicitly asking for the punishment that will elevate his status to prisoner of war within the AELM.

The US Attorney's Office issued a statement on 11 February 2011, after his sentencing, wherein the state responded to Bond's speech to interpellate his rhetoric into ecoterrorism. The statement focused on Bond's criminal history with arson to depoliticize the act in claiming, "His claimed 'cause' is mere pretext: The evidence in this case demonstrates that he has a history of committing crimes involving fire before he ever began advocating animal rights" (US attorney's office 2011). Rather than respond to the ways in which Bond challenged the disciplinary power of the state, the USAO asserted that the sentencing "sends a strong message that violence is never an acceptable road to change in our democracy ... arson is a violent crime that often results in catastrophic loss of life and property" (US Attorney's Office 2011). The statement concluded by invoking the rhetoric of terrorism: "Preventing and pursuing domestic terrorism – those acts of violence committed in furtherance of a political or social agenda – remains one of the top priorities of the FBI ... this sentencing demonstrates again that the FBI and Joint Terrorism Task Force partners remain dedicated ... to work together to bring justice to those who would resort to acts of violence" (US Attorney's Office 2011).

The narrative of the state does not acknowledge the critique of speciesism or capitalism found throughout Bond's speech; however, it does use neoliberal rhetoric to interpellate Bond through performative power. They use terms like gratified, dedicated, determined, justice, and victim to describe the interagency collaboration between the ATF, FBI, and local police as well as the sheepskin factory in Glendale. Bond is described with phrases like "using violence," "history of committing crimes," and "destroy a business," to demonstrate a justified use of disciplinary punishment.

Bond was then extradited to Salt Lake City, Utah, where he was tried and convicted of two additional arsons claimed with the ALF. In October

2011, Bond delivered a speech to the court that followed a similar unrepentant disregard for the state. In the months between the two trials, Bond gave interviews and delivered a keynote speech to an animal liberation conference that I had attended in Long Beach, California. Bond utilized this social capital as a valorized political prisoner and was featured in many prominent activist venues. His speeches, particularly his courtroom addresses, served to solidify and mobilize eco-activists to engage in illegal direct action without fear of the state. The second speech delivered in court in Utah undermined the state's formulaic expectation for a remorseful defendant to plead with the state. Instead of apologize for his actions, he utilized this classic rhetorical use of apologia to mock the state:

I'm here today because of the arsons I committed at The Tandy Leather Factory in Salt Lake City, and the Tiburon Restaurant in Sandy, Utah, which sells the incredibly cruel product foie gras. The U.S. Attorney wants to give me the maximum sentence and beyond, not because of my "crimes," but because I am unrepentant and outspoken. My intuition tells me that this court is not going to show me mercy because I became "suddenly sorry." So instead of lying to the court in a feeble attempt to save myself, as I'm certain many do when they face their sentencing day, allow me to tell you what I am sorry for.

I am sorry that when I was 19 years old I built two slaughterhouses that are still killing Animals, even now as I speak. I am sorry that Tandy Leather sells skin that has been ripped from the dead, and often live bodies of such Animals as cows, ostriches, rabbits, snakes and pigs. I am sorry that the leather tanneries that supply Tandy Factory, poison the earth with dangerous chemicals. I am sorry that the restaurant Tiburon profits from the force feeding of geese and ducks until their livers explode, so that rich people can then use that as a paté for crackers and bread. I am sorry that they make a living from the dead bodies of wild and exotic Animals. I am sorry that we live in a day and age where you can rape a child or beat a woman unconscious and receive less prison time than an Animal Rights activist who attacked property instead of people. I am sorry that my brother was so desperate to get out of debt that he flew from Iowa to Colorado just to get me in a taped and monitored conversation for reward money. I am sorry that I am biologically related to such a worthless little snitch! I am sorry that I waited so long to become an Animal Liberation Front operative. For all of these things, I will always have some regret. But as far as the arsons at the Leather Factory and Tiburon go, I have no remorse.

I realize that the laws of the land favor a business' ability to make a profit over an Animal's right to life. It also used to favor a white business owner's ability to profit from a Black person's slavery. It also used to favor a husband's ability to viciously attack his wife and act on her as if she were an object. Those who broke the law and damaged property to stand against these oppressions were also called "terrorists" and "fanatics" in their time. But that did not change the fact that society progressed and is still progressing along those lines. So today I'm the bad guy. That is just a matter of historical coincidence. Who knows ... perhaps a less brutal and less violent society will one day exist that will understand that life and earth are more important than products of death and cruelty. And if not, then to hell with it all anyway! Whether my supporters or detractors think I'm a freedom fighter or a lunatic with a gas can makes no difference to me. I have spent years verifiably promoting, supporting and fighting for Animal Liberation. I have seen the Animal victims of human injustice – thousands of them – with my own eyes and what I saw was blood, guts and gore. I made a promise to those Animals, and to myself, to fight for them in any way I could. I regret none of it, and I never will! You can take my freedom, but you can't have my submission. (Bond 2011a)

The second speech also refuses to identify with the [dys]functions of disciplinary power used by the state. Bond challenged the neoliberal trope of rehabilitative justice by calling out the USAO. He claimed that it was not his crimes that would be judged in handing down a sentence, but that it was because he is "unrepentant and outspoken ... this court is not going to show me mercy ... instead of lying to the court in a feeble attempt to save myself" (Bond 2011b). In an interesting dialectic of performativity, Bond disidentifies with disciplinary power while being interpellated within it through the judicial proceedings that legally reify the construct of ecoterrorist. He recognizes the "hailing" and attempts to suspend the interpellation momentarily through this performance.

The second portion of the speech relies on apologia to shame the state and animal-and-ecology use industries. Bond does not apologize for his actions; rather he is "sorry" for the ways in which speciesism and capitalism naturalize the violence of foie gras. The speech queers the rhetoric of apologia itself, forcing the audience to question who is shaming who here, given the presumed protocol of this type of speech. He created disidentificatory thoughts amongst his audience, treating the courtroom as a theatre and stage, by using poignant rhetoric such as:

killing, sells skin ripped from the dead, poison the earth, and force feeding to describe Tandy Leather and Tiburon. Bond also apologizes for being related to his brother, an accomplice in the sting operation that led to Bond's arrest, and whom he characterizes as a worthless little snitch. Bond apologizes for the unjust function of the legal system where those who commit violent acts against humans, "receive less prison time than an Animal Rights activist that attacked property instead of people ... I realize the laws of the land favor a business' ability to make a profit over an Animal's right to life" (Bond 2011b).

Bond creates a moral trajectory between eco-activists and those who broke the law during slavery to protect African-American people, those who fought against the objectification of women under the law, and those who have been called "terrorists" or "fanatics" during their time. He argues that the illegality of his crimes and the label of terrorist are simply historical coincidence that will not stand the test of time. The speech concludes, again, with a refusal to submit to the power of the state: "You can take my freedom, but you can't have my submission" (Bond 2011b).

Bond was one of the first individuals convicted of violating the AETA, and he utilized the vast network of eco-activists to promulgate his rhetoric far and wide. Several environmental activists that have been arrested have spoken out against direct action, or specifically the direct actions they were arrested for, and publicly questioned the efficacy of property destruction.[14] The remorse may be a public performance rather than an outward retrospective reflection, but they serve to reinforce the state narrative of a rehabilitative justice system. It also reinforces the power of the state by demonstrating a level of submission required from activists to re-enter society. It is as if homo sacer is allowed to rejoin the general population only after a thorough disavowal of his crimes.

Resisting Repression inside the Prison: Eric King

Eric King, a vegan anarchist activist currently serving a ten-year sentence for one count of "using explosive materials to commit arson of property used in or affecting interstate commerce," is a heartbreaking example of how repression inside of prison (an already repressive institution) disproportionately targets the unrepentant. King, an unrepentant activist that was arrested and charged in 2014 with attempting to firebomb a government official's office in Kansas City, MO, has faced ongoing harassment inside of federal prisons. After the murder of Michael Brown, King had travelled to Ferguson to participate in protests with the

M4BL. During his sentencing hearing, King unapologetically mocked the legal proceedings, "This court is a farce. I stand by what I did. I'm happy I did it. I'm sorry that I got caught. I would have loved to attack more government buildings" (King 2016).

Although King was not arrested for actions specifically connected to the AELM, he faces targeted repression because of his vegan anarchist (particularly anti-fascist) politics. His unwillingness to submit to the discipline of the state has elicited ongoing harassment. King has "since remained outspoken against the prison system. Exposing abuses and standing tall in the face of constant attacks and repression" (Anarchist News 2019). King continues to be subjected to physical violence at the hands of correction officers and perpetually held in isolation and stints in the Solitary Housing Unit (SHU). While incarcerated at FCI Florence, King was attacked by a CO and sustained injuries that went ignored while he was tied to a 4-point restraint for eight hours. The attack and subsequent indictment were later covered in a statement:

> Eric was indicted yesterday for his own assault. He faces up to
> twenty years in prison for being attacked and beaten. By a guard
> who feels safe dragging prisoners off camera and attacking ... Being
> brought up in the federal court system, a court system that is built to
> crush as a much more effective machine than any other in our country
> ... We need folks to write Eric letters, print articles, short stories ... hell,
> print books. We need folks to donate, hold fundraisers, we need to be
> prepared. We need folks to show up at court appearances. We need to
> show the state we won't let them bury our friend ... We need help,
> Eric needs help. With love and rage – EK support crew.
> (Anarchist News 2019)

The Eric King Support Crew is calling upon activists to demonstrate their own disidentification with the state by showing solidarity for political prisoners like King.

The global health pandemic of COVID-19 has exposed the obvious vulnerabilities of people that are incarcerated, and prisons continue to have some of the highest concentrations of positive cases in the US. Most state and federal prisons revoked volunteer access to prisons in March 2020 and have not restored visitation access. Despite all of the violence King is subjected to, he remains committed to "a world free of domination and oppression" (*Support Eric King* 2020). His lack of remorse, and his articulate critiques of fascistic state regimes, minimize the perceived power of the state. King, in many ways, embodies *homo sacer*: someone stripped of bare rights, given a lengthy prison sentence, punished with repeated stints in the SHU, and denied medical care. But his disavowal of the system that imprisons him, his explicit critique of how the state supports violence, and his refusal to identify with the neoliberal rhetoric of rehabilitation show there is more performative power than simply exerting state power over King's body. King demonstrates a particular articulation of disidentification that performs monarchical punishment from a position of power. King and other activists alike have the ability to challenge the state through these public condemnations that remain prolific outside of prison.

PRISON JUSTICE WORK AND
ABOVEGROUND DISCIPLINE

There is significant overlap between the AELM and the much larger prison abolition network. There are many prisoner support networks within the AELM (such as letter writing groups, book to prison groups, fundraising campaigns) and solidarity actions. These groups provide material support to activists in a range of political movements that share a critique of state-sanctioned violence. Prison support work is one illustration of the ways in which activists disidentify with the state, and, specifically, disidentify with the interpellation into ecoterrorists.

Prison justice work is one way for those outside of the carceral system to provide material support. Sending postcards, interacting in a prison classroom, or fulfilling book requests are ways that activists foster disidentification with the prison-industrial complex. In my capacity as an activist and assistant professor, I facilitate the Prison Justice Initiative (PJI) at Antioch College. The PJI is steeped in the vibrant abolitionist community of Yellow Springs, Ohio, and is acutely connected to anti-racist work at the Coretta Scott King Center for Cultural and Intellectual Freedom.

Going inside the Prison

In this capacity, I run Antioch's Books to Prisons project, established by the brilliant Emily Steinmetz, and teach courses inside a women's prison in Dayton. We host bookpacking events where volunteers respond to letters from people that are incarcerated. The most common requests are technical guides, travel books, and legal zines. As you tear the envelope and read a handwritten letter from someone locked in a cage, you are given a glimpse into their severely restricted, heavily surveilled world. Sometimes you receive a request for legal aid, or a xeroxed copy of someone's life story that they have mailed to prison justice collectives more broadly. If you look closely at the postage, you can determine that they used their one provided stamp that month to make that particular book request. Sometimes the letters are written on, or the envelopes have been opened and resealed by prison employees. There is a massive network of leftist collectives that do this sort of work, fulfill book requests from incarcerated people. The NAALPO is one example of a central repository to find support sites for political prisoners, as well as addresses for currently incarcerated eco-activists.

In addition to the Books to Prisons project, I facilitate mixed-population courses inside Dayton Correctional Institution (DCI). My courses are made up of campus students and students who are incarcerated. Before I bring the campus students inside the prison, I meet with both groups of students separately. We map and unpack the ways they will experience interpellation. Campus students submit to a background check by the Ohio Department of Rehabilitation and Corrections, which provides a challenge to the undocumented students on campus. Each visit, they bring their state-issued identification, are subject to search, and must follow the strict dress code for visitors.

The incarcerated students must receive approval and clearance from the correctional officer (CO) in charge of volunteer programs. If they receive a disciplinary action, or at the discretion of a CO, they can be removed from my courses. I carefully select the course material and look for texts that challenge the state but do not put the incarcerated students at risk of disciplinary action. The warden can set arbitrary restrictions on content, and those restrictions are not clearly communicated to the volunteers. One student shared that they had been placed in the SHU for having Robert Greene's *48 Laws of Power*, and was later disciplined for having a copy of Alexander's *The New Jim Crow: Mass Incarceration in the Age of Colorblindness*.

The institutionalization of these punishments – regulating their ability to communicate with people outside of prison, censorship of what materials they can receive inside the prison, and their inaccessibility to those outside of prison via restrictions to enter – interpellates those engaged in prison justice work. Prison justice work involves active listening and decentring yourself to meet the material needs of those most vulnerable to the prison apparatus. As a prison abolitionist, it is uncomfortable and destabilizing to continuously have to interact with COs and prison employees. But, to echo Foucault again here, where there is power, there is resistance. Within the AELM, activists work collaboratively and collectively to raise commissary funds, publish accounts of grotesque abuse and neglect inside the prison, purchase books off of wish lists, pressure state-level Department of Corrections and the Federal Bureau of Prisons, contribute to legal funds, and so much more.

Solidarity as Refusal

As a form of refusal, these support networks acknowledge that although the interpellation performed through punishment by the state (incarceration) exists, so too do the continuous acts of direct action. Political prisoner support networks, in this way, are not repentant. The celebration of direct action is a rearticulation of power and punishment in which the interpellation of disidentification is visible, and activists are able to retaliate against the state. Aboveground activists engage in solidarity through social media to publicly align themselves with the illegal direct action, disidentifying with the presumed power of the state aimed at targeted AELM activists. Prisoner support websites, Twitter feeds, Facebook forums, Instagram pictures, activist trainings, conference papers, book chapters, and even baked-goods fundraisers are public performances that challenge the disciplinary function of the state through disidentification. In this sense, activists rely on direct action to create the spectacle of monarchical punishment, punishment by the sword, to undermine state power and capital through destruction.

Every time an activist knowingly breaks the law to liberate an animal or destroy property, the public is reminded of the potentiality of revolutionary change. Similar to how the monarchy would execute someone in public to instill fear in the citizens and remind the public that the government possess power over all life, eco-activists use direct action as an exposure of monarchical power to create disidentificatory thoughts. These activists use monarchical power as a way to remind the public the state is not all-powerful. It is not impossible to penetrate. They [activists] can pull back the curtains and expose the violence behind speciesist capitalism and utilize the internet to spread this exposed violence widely through undercover footage inside agri-vivisection industries.

Property destruction presents a unique challenge to the state's reliance on disciplinary punishment, particularly when the activists go un-captured. Clandestine activists issue damning communiqués that undermine state authority and call out the state-corporate-industrial complex. Further, these acts disrupt the social contract between corporations and the state in which neoliberal capitalism is predicated on. The de-regulation of industry and global trade agreements attempt to restore or renew the social contract between corporations and the state. The public performance of direct action activism demonstrates a hole in this contract, and the possibilities of how interpellation can be resisted. The state is weakened, unable to protect animal-and-ecology use industries from arson, a cyber attack, or a raid. Thus the state must perform monarchical punishment and retaliate to illustrate that it still has a monopoly on a violence that guarantees the social contract of capitalism. Further, the state relies on the dichotomy of good versus bad protestor to interpellate eco-activists as ecoterrorists deserving of monarchical punishment.

SECURITY CULTURE

As elaborated on in the last chapter, the use of infiltration and informants within social movements has created ripples of distrust amongst activists. With the increased technopower available to activists challenging the state there are also increased ways for the state to exercise power through political repression. The state-corporate-industrial complex relies on ISAs to naturalize the state's monopoly of violence through speciesism and neoliberal capitalism. The state also has coercive mechanisms of punishment like the prison-industrial complex to demarcate which types of dissent (against which entities) are a crime rather than responsible patriotism. Laws such as the AETA are a legal manifestation of the social contract between the state and animal-and-ecology use industries that interpellate eco-activists into ecoterrorists. Eco-activists have been critiquing the way capitalism and speciesism have dictated laws for centuries (Proudhon 1840; Kropotkin 1897; Goldman 1911; Bonanno 1987). Activists are tragically aware of the ways in which the state manipulates activists in order to undermine their efforts in the Black Power movement, the AIM, and anti-nuclear movement, to name a few (Davis 1983, 2013; Churchill and Wall 1990; Della Porta 1995; Della Porta and Fillieule 2004; Churchill and Vander Wall 2002; Price 2004; C.D. Morris 2010). However, the proliferation of digital media requires a level of social encryption that has is lagging. Security culture proliferates leftist circles and is predicated on the omnipresence of technology.

Securing Activist Spaces

While attending the 2018 EF! River Rendezvous, my partner and I went through a checklist of security measures before entering the forest for the convergence. We left our wallets at home, locked our driver's licences in the glove box, took all political insignia out of the car that we had been travelling with, and only brought one cell phone. When we arrived at the campground, we also left the cell phone locked in the glove box. I resisted the urge to take pictures of the beautiful forest, and also could not stop to take written notes. Whenever we met someone new, they were introduced by their pseudonyms, and I had learned over the years not to ask biographical questions. Similar to my experiences at the Gathering for Total Liberation convergence, 2014 EF! Rendezvous, and large gatherings, I censored each interaction by sticking to vague questions and vague answers whenever I met someone.

The first workshop I attended at the 2014 rendezvous was on security culture itself. Two attorneys from the NLG presented on the legal protections of activists in the US. Seated in a loose circle between the tall trees, scattered blankets, and makeshift chairs, the activists discussed a series of security concerns. Phone and email encryption, forcible removal from a blockade, and stop-and-searches of your vehicle were among some of the exercises that I participated in. There is a palpable climate of suspicion in these convergences that makes it difficult to forge honest, new connections with individuals. My role as an anthropologist, in many ways, may have been seen as threatening to the security of the culture. It created a moral and practical dilemma while gathering data in the "field." I negotiated the tension between maintaining credibility as an activist and protecting the identities of those I worked with, while being fully aware that I was in these spaces with the intention of extracting ethnographic notes for research.

Activists are constantly faced with the challenge of expanding their connections while not appearing predatory, trusting in their peers but minimizing their vulnerability, and ultimately advocating collectivity despite engaging in autonomous clandestine direct action. The volley of punishments between the state and eco-activists attempt to discipline one another through performative power. The state utilizes a hybridity of disciplinary and monarchical punishment to repress activists, however technology has provided a new terrain for dissent. Eco-activists are able to identify and blast the images of infiltrators through social media campaigns to expose them. Activists use social media to expose cooperative witnesses, suspected infiltrators, and to train one another in ways to resist state surveillance. There are entire websites dedicated to exposing government infiltrators, cooperative witnesses, and individuals accused of committing sexual violence.[15] The rapid, wide-reading ways in which someone can be exposed in leftist movements are only possible through technology. Activists can expose the state's use of monarchical punishment through social media in ways that challenge even the most apathetic individual's view on speciesism. Activists can educate one another, including justice-focused legal centres such as CLDC, about encryption to resist wiretapping, grand jury indictments, search warrants, and security culture itself. These workshops do not even require a physical space that may increase individual vulnerabilities, but rather can exist solely online on encrypted sites. Within this constant exchange of power between activists and the state, eco-activists are particularly effective in their performance of monarchical power to undermine speciesism and neoliberal capitalism.

Activists Talkback Online

Through social media forums such as Facebook, Twitter, Tumblr, and Instagram, activists engage in talkback. I became an active participant in these online forums, particularly in the days before and after large demonstrations. Activists are able to posture, knowing these mediums are heavily surveilled by the state, and undermine the state's use of disciplinary and monarchical punishment. In the preceding chapters, I explored the commonly used hashtags on Twitter, the playful Facebook posts, the powerful declarations accompanying photographs on Instagram, and the ways in which these rearticulate power. Within such a tightly protected interpersonal security culture, there continues to be tension in activist spaces about using social media. I used CDA, in combination with utilizing narrative as a tool for analysis, to examine the ways in which individuals utilize the internet to (re)create their identities as a rearticulation of power.

The internet provides a platform for social actors to anonymously express their politic. Some activists conceal their identity in the communiqués they release following a direct action, while others rely on the public nature of their social media accounts to maintain status and credibility within the movement. Activists face the punitive powers of the state for advocating anarchist and anti-speciesist political leanings, whereas the state relies on anonymity and deception to gain authenticity and credibility as a provocateur in anarchist and anti-speciesist circles. This dialectic of visibility and anonymity is one of the marked tensions between activists, oftentimes debated through public forums at convergences and academic conferences.

Conclusion

The performance of monarchical and disciplinary punishment, particularly through interpellating eco-activists as ecoterrorists, represents a powerful sentiment; direct action as disidentification successfully challenges fundamental ideologies that undermine state power. Although activists remain fearful of targeted legislation such as the AETA, police violence, and surveillance, activists are also aware of the ways in which direct action eco-activists have been successful. These campaigns continue to claim victory against the state-corporate-industrial complex through illegal direct action that forces the state to violate its performance of a fair and just juridical system. These activists are targeted *because* they pose successful challenges to both state-sponsored capitalism and the monopoly of violence. The AETA was a direct response to the state feeling legislatively powerless against a growing tide of eco-activists, particularly SHAC, ALF, and ELF. The interpellation of disidentification as ecoterrorism suggests there is something that the state feels particularly threatened by. The rhetorical and revolutionary potential of direct action pose a threat to those industries most profitable for the federal government. The state's social contract with animal-and-ecology use industries protects these capitalist entities, but it is challenged with each arson, laboratory raid, and each time the letters ALF are spray painted across the walls of a slaughterhouse.

The state is expected to perform the disciplinary functions of a punitive justice system that guarantees each citizen a trial in which they are innocent until proven guilty. The state must also perform the neoliberal functions of disciplinary punishment in order to maintain the façade of freedom of speech and assembly. The state must furthermore uphold its contract with the targeted agri-vivisection industries. Thus, the state engages in illegal surveillance of activists, hires individuals to entrap activists, and passes targeted legislation that creates disproportionate sentencing to place ecoterrorists in CMUs within prisons with Al Qaeda operatives.[16] These tactics demonstrate that the state still does utilize monarchical punishment to deny citizens the right to free speech and assembly. The J20 case exemplifies a hybridization of both disciplinary power and monarchical punishment. The state was willing to reveal its violent tactics but garnered public consent by constructing its target as the bad protestor, an Antifa-terrorist. However, the tactics of monarchical punishment used by the state beg several moral questions. How can informants and infiltrators that manipulate activists and engage in sex acts be held accountable? Why are government employees that intentionally deceive activists and engage in sexual relations not held accountable? If an activist who engaged in sexual relations with a government infiltrator became pregnant, is the state then liable for child support? The ways in which eco-activists utilize tactics that emulate this performance of disciplinary and monarchical punishment further disidentify with the interpellation of activism as ecoterrorism.

Conclusion

By the time the fire burned itself out the next morning, all that remained was a 12-foot-long banner that read: "If you build it, we will burn it."

(Schorn 2005)

Welcome to the struggle of all species to be free. We are the burning rage of this dying planet ... The war of greed ravages the earth and species die out every day. ELF works to speed up the collapse of industry, to scare the rich, and to undermine the foundations of the state ... We show the enemy that we are serious about defending what is sacred. Together we have teeth and claws to match our dreams. Our greatest weapons are imagination and the ability to strike when least expected ... 1000s of bulldozers, powerlines, computer systems, buildings and valuable equipment have been composted. Many ELF actions have been censored to present our bravery from inciting others to take action. We take inspiration from Luddites, Levelers, Diggers, the Autonome squatter movement, the ALF, the Zapatistas, and the little people – those mischievous elves of lore. Authorities can't see us because they don't believe in elves. We are practically invisible. We have no command structure, no spokespersons, no office, just many small groups working separately, seeking vulnerable targets and practicing our craft. Many elves are moving to the Pacific Northwest and other sacred areas. Some elves will leave surprises as they go. Find your family! And let's dance as we make ruins of the corporate money system ...

(Earth Liberation Front 1997)

I gave birth to my fourth child on 21 December 2018. Prior to his birth, my partner and I brainstormed potential names. We wanted to continue the Jewish tradition of naming him in honour of a deceased relative. Even after combing through our collective list of ancestors, we had nothing we felt committed to. Earlier in the pregnancy, I had travelled to Baltimore with the kids to visit my sister living on the east coast. We ventured into a worker-run leftist bookstore, Red Emma's, for some lunch. While we browsed the shelves, I came across a biography about an anti-fascist who had famously resisted oppression in Europe. I decided to buy the brick of a book and learn more about this inspirational figure.

As the US became swallowed up by the vitriol of Donald Trump, and as acts of violence targeting anti-fascist organizers, Black people and people of colour, queer folks, and Jewish people increased, I found myself returning to the biography I had picked up at Red Emma's. In the face of violent repression and fascism, Buenaventura Durruti had turned to direct action. Durruti, an anarchist, advocated for leaderless resistance and mutual aid. He travelled from one community to the next, listened and learned what they needed, and provided material support in their resistance struggles.

The early months of my pregnancy were riddled with fear and uncertainty. Even after we learned that my partner's charges were dropped, it would be another month until we heard from his lawyer to confirm the charges could not be brought again. Not only had I been interpellated, but I felt like my then fetus had been interpellated as well. We wanted to give him a name that was an act of disidentification. Durruti, our fourth child, was named in honor of Buenaventura Durruti.

Eco-activists engage in physical and digital direct action to challenge the state's interpellation of good versus bad subjectification through spectacular performances that create disidentificatory screens. The dialectic between physical and digital activist spaces, the use of terministic screens, the role of the stage, and the performative functions of protest are negotiated through anthropological discourses of power, resistance, and performativity. As the political backdrop changed throughout my research, I adapted the manuscript to follow the organic evolution of the AELM into the contemporary moment.

Initially, I had intended on conducting in-depth interviews with activists throughout the data collection period. After receiving a few negative responses from activists when I requested an interview, and in the face of a growing fear of state surveillance, I decided to revisit the notion of interviewing. Instead of in-depth interviews with individual people, I found myself engaging in informal conversations, loosely structured, with many activists over the years. Through a flexible, mixed-methodological approach, the book builds on my participant-observation ethnographic studies and incorporates digital media as text. The research was guided by a central inquiry: how is leftist resistance strategized and actualized within the ideological, social and economic [super-] structures of the state and neoliberal capitalism, and how does such a positioning impact effective activism from the left? To address the questions, I integrated the data gleaned from both physical participation and digital engagement in activist spaces.

Similar to how the data collection led to a re-examination of my selected methods, the process of aggregating data led me to performance studies. I had originally relied solely on queer theory as a way to articulate the disidentification facilitated through direct action, but later found that queer theory also provided a useful lens to examine the performative function of political action that rearticulates and reimagines the revolutionary potential of eco-activist direct action. Throughout the analysis I primarily focused on ethnographic events, activists' use of digital media to organize and publicize political action, to engage in national and international networking with activists, and disseminate information to a wide audience necessitates the multi-sited analysis used throughout this study.

The use of CDA and a queer linguistic approach facilitated the focus on how power is negotiated through language, and how ultimately; the oppressed can use language in social justice aims. Activists engage with digital media to strategize and actualize anti-authoritarian and anti-speciesist critiques as a form of disidentification. They do this because it facilitates an international, anonymous stage to reimagine structures of power. The intricacies of voice during the performances of direct action demonstrated a constant renegotiation of aggressive language, playful tones, public relations, and educator. CDA provided a useful framework to incorporate these sometimes-contradictory voices that challenged structures of power (speciesism and neoliberal capitalism).

When activists converge in public spaces to organize or engage in political theatre, the social labour of finessing new members or interrogating the authenticity of one another has already been filtered through the screen of digital media. There were many instances in which activists in a public space approached me and disclosed they recognized me from something on social media. In a particularly telling moment, a stranger approached me at the grocery store in WDC and asked how a specific activist was doing. Although the space was not necessarily marked as political, the stranger recognized me and felt a sense of connectedness through digital media. But we had never met.

The ideological, social, and economic [super-] structures of the state detailed in chapter 1 map the interwoven institutions of power facilitated by neoliberal capitalism and speciesism. The political economy of the state functions as an interconnected nexus of legal, political, corporate, and medical industries that ultimately reify and extend dimensions of sovereignty. The concept of corporate sovereignty illustrates the ways in which the ideologies of speciesism, capitalism, and neoliberalism naturalize political repression through the passage of industry-vanguard legislation such as the AETA. These legislations and subsequent legal trials of activists serve a performative function as disciplinary punishment, relying on the rhetoric of fear to fragment activists from one another. The conditions in which eco-activists engage in confrontational direct action are extrapolated within the structures of neoliberal capitalism and speciesism themselves. As discussed in chapter 2, eco-activists face disproportionate financial penalties, prison sentences, and mechanisms of surveillance to silence dissent. These mechanisms of repression have drawn the attention of the NLG, the CLDC, and other legal collectives aimed at protecting First Amendment rights.

The political economic terrain of neoliberal capitalism described in chapter 2 calls into question the processes of interpellation that construct protest as terrorism. Specifically, the construction of the eco-terrorist relies on a "hailing to" and acceptance of speciesism and neoliberal capitalism. The examination of this construction contextualized the subsequent chapters that focus on the dialectical relationship between eco-activist direct action and state repression. The analysis in chapters 4 and 5 provides a close examination of how the performance of direct action creates a spectacular screen in which activists, targets, and onlookers can disidentify with interpellation. Each public convergence I attended featured at least one panel discussion addressing technology and surveillance. Although activists utilize digital media to advance their aims of radical social change, activists are also astutely aware of how these technologies are being used to fragment them from one another. There is a growing literature on the ways in which digital media is revolutionizing social movements, both in creating advancements and debilitating challenges. For example, the Earth First! Rendezvous featured panel discussions about surveillance which also provided tactical trainings in cryptography, hacking/hacktivism, and security practices regarding the use of cellular phone.

The trainings serve a performative function, as they undermine the state's monopoly of violence and use of surveillance through a refusal to submit to the paradigm of good protestor. Activists are able to effectively challenge the state through performances that facilitate a disidentification that allows them to deny the asymmetric distribution of power. For example, activists establish temporary spaces that suspend the overwhelming violence perpetrated against other species and demand the (unfathomable) capitulation of neoliberal capitalism and speciesism. Direct action engages with the political imaginary through creative political theatre and facilitates disidentificatory thoughts through comical, humorous, satirical, and emotional performances that make the impossible seem possible.

The research illustrated, interestingly, that the interplay between the state and eco-activists did not adhere to the initial theoretical framework I had proposed. Preliminary research and personal experience had pointed to the state utilizing the technopower of surveillance through Foucault's concept of disciplinary punishment to silence dissent by interpellating the bad protestors into ecoterrorists. As chapter 4 demonstrates, although the state does rely on this traditionally theorized mechanism of power, and the state does interpellate the bad protestor into ecoterrorists, the state also engages in very public displays of grotesque violence through sexual infiltration and a punitive prison system that exercises de facto sovereignty.

This hybridity of state power is used to punish activists for engaging in anti-authoritarian and anti-speciesist direct action. But upon close analysis of this volley between direct action and political repression, it became clear that activists were relying on direct action *as* monarchical power. Critical scholars have already begun to examine the ways in which the state actively represses social movements. This study, however, provided a unique lens to examines the ways in which direct action activists are actively resisting the hybrid use of disciplinary and monarchical punishment. Chapter 5 examines the ways in which confrontational, playful, and satirical performances not only create disidentificatory thoughts with onlookers, but the performances also queer the state's monopoly of violence through monarchical punishment. The state focuses on how they can interpellate the bad protestor into the ecoterrorist; meanwhile eco-activists are rearticulating the very meaning of terrorism through spectacular protest. Rather than accept the repressive construct of ecoterrorist, eco-activists encourage brick throwing, refuse to grovel during sentencing hearings, and publicly support political prisoners who are labelled ecoterrorists.

The integration of performance studies made space for the creatively crafted political theatre that publicly punishes the state, interrupting the attempt to interpellate eco-activists as ecoterrorists. Direct action, from its inception to its implementation to the rhetorically crafted communiqué disseminated, relies on a symbolic appropriation of the guillotine. As the flames radiate off the slaughterhouse, as the beagles are carried over the laboratory fence, and as the undercover footage of vivisection is displayed on the digital screen, speciesism hangs from the gallows and is severed from the paradigm of good versus bad. The paradigm itself is queered, forcing the audience to disidentify with omnipotent power of the state when confronted with activists that refuse to submit, the altruistic values of science when face-to-face with photos of maimed beagles, and ultimately, the rhetoric of terrorism. The potentiality for revolution, then, feels palpable to eco-activists. Through disidentification, activists create alternative screens that politically reimagine the currently commodified relationship between human animals and ecologies. This disidentification, facilitated by the performance of direct action, talks back to the state's reliance on interpellation in powerful ways.

Direct actions have an implicit threat: fear us because we will be back. Although the actions only temporarily sever these structures of power and may not create sustained disidentification, they create a lasting financial impact. Further, the ability to engage in political theatre in these temporary spaces serves to solidify the resolve of activists that are otherwise overwhelmed by the loss of other-than-human animal life and state power. Eco-activists disrupt the truisms of neoliberal capitalism by creating alternative screens that expose the ways in which people are exploited by said truisms. By playfully exaggerating the truisms during a home demonstration, for example, the truisms themselves appear ludicrous to the onlooker. The spectacle facilitates disidentification by allowing the onlooker to participate in the performance.

Voice becomes the central tool in which the demonstrators utilize exaggeration. Similar modes of subversion, political street theatre and drag, utilize voice in combination with physical bodily performance. The performance of exaggeration does not solely rely on what is said, but also how it is said and how their bodies are presented. Dressed in similar clothes as the observers, the demonstrators can perform respectability through conforming to the societal norms of protest. Specifically, during home demonstrations in densely populated areas, activists may forego the use of black bloc and dress as if they joined the demonstration on their way to brunch. As an anarchist principle, these collectives are not organized through hierarchical leadership. However, there are pragmatic horizontal organizing practices used to ensure someone participating in the political action will serve as a liaison to both the public and law enforcement. Their performance of exaggerated neoliberalism is not only embodied in chants and proclamations, it is further articulated through dress, communication styles, posture, and bodily presentation.

This analysis contributes to social movement theory within anthropology, and specifically to the growing discourse surrounding neoliberalism. Over the years, it became clear these direct actions were not solely political theatre of public shaming, but rather they directly challenge the restructuring of global capitalism within the contemporary neoliberal moment. These demonstrations utilize the strategic rhetoric of exaggeration and satire as a mode of resistance to facilitate disidentification. The paradigms in which the state relies on to interpellate audience members are exaggerated to the extent that it is both laughable and tragic. Through the viewing of these paradigms as laughable and tragic, audience members begin to question their complicity with them.

The AELM is not unique in its use of political theatre to exaggerate systems of oppression, as evidenced, for example, in the history of drag performance in the gay liberation and queer liberation movements. Despite the historical trajectory of its utility, the use of play and performance in the AELM is understudied within anthropology. Social movement studies have focused more broadly on hierarchal animal advocacy groups, ignoring or dismissing the revolutionary potential of the AELM. When political theatre is discussed, it has focused on the racist and sexist campaigns by PETA (rightfully so). But collectives such as SHAC, ALF, ELF, and ALA remain outside the scope of anthropological discourses on social protest. But what would an environmental anthropology look like that takes seriously the powerful ways that illegal direct action advances social justice? How can we confront our complicity in moral madness and take to task the ways speciesism informs our academic pursuits?

Throughout the book, the ethnographic texts demonstrated the significant rhetorical functions of performing both disciplinary and monarchical punishment against the state. From the unapologetic rhetoric of Walter Bond during the sentencing hearings following his arsons claimed by the ALF to the mink raids in Minnesota, eco-activists utilize monarchical punishment to challenge the state. There is a gap within social movement literature that overlooks the theoretical contributions of direct action activists that identify as anti-speciesists. The erasure of these particular eco-activists has meant a discursive erasure of these critiques and actions. Within the neoliberal university, there are deep investments in animal and ecological exploitation (such as genetic bioengineering labs, vivisection, toxicity testing, and military). This book is part of a larger intellectual political effort to incorporate eco-activist direct action into anthropological discourses on resistance. Admittedly, I leaned into the AELM with my own assumptions about direct action based on years of indoctrination into the good/bad protestor paradigm. I expected these direct actions to be frustrating and merely reinscribe neoliberal individualism through naming, shaming, and blaming. But, like many others in the AELM, I was disillusioned from a decade of being the good protestor.

My own scope of analysis was hindered, initially, through these assumptions and they almost kept me from attending at all. Inspired by Graeber, I challenged myself to think outside of existing modes of protest and tap into the political imaginary. The political imaginary, in this case, involved subjecting myself to potential arrest and public embarrassment. In the populated areas near my own home, I stood with these activists and chanted, proclaimed, and engaged onlookers. I dressed in casual clothing but sported a pro-vegan shirt and button on my messenger bag. I allowed myself to be videotaped and was photographed by corporate-hired private investigators throughout the day. I speak publicly in support of direct action, contribute to legal defence funds, and travel to skills-sharing convergences when I can.

Future research should continue to include direct action, regardless of legality, within the spectrum of both strategies and tactics analyzed. The state would rather repress and punish activists than take seriously their critiques of speciesism. Anthropologists must be willing ask more questions, challenge hierarchical boundaries, and respond to the crushing crisis of our ecosystem. This ethnography carved out space for several important conversations within the field: direct action as strategy, intersectional eco-activism, anarchist culture, and reproductive labour within social movements. There has been a historical devaluation of qualitative research that not only acknowledged the researcher's subjectivities, but also explicitly embraced them.

Reflexivity is a powerful methodological approach that contextualizes the unique contributions of the researcher. The obscure subjectivities that become hidden in the rhetoric of objectivity lead to speculation and distrust between research participants and the researcher. The violent history of vulnerable populations being exploited in the name of scientific progress and academic research serve as constant reminders that research has political and ideological ramifications that extend far beyond the specific study. Future research should interrogate the methodological approaches to ethnographic research with activists that are both transparent and empowering. Critical scholarship should be held accountable to advance aims of social justice through praxis-based research. Specific to this book, future research should include academics that do publicly endorse confrontational direct action as an effective form of resistance. Reflexivity, in this case, provides a methodological explanation to address the assumptions and interpellated paradigms brought to the table by the researcher. The researcher can then interrogate their transformation or disidentificatory thoughts, allowing for a more transparent engagement with the discourse.

In the final months of the ethnography, End Captivity Now issued a statement that the campaign was defunct effective immediately. The announcement specifically referenced the financial and social pressures that have been exacerbated by legal pressure. Several of the collectives that I worked at have either gone inactive or disbanded. Under Donald

Trump's presidency, my own activism has shifted. I remain committed to the AELM and dismantling speciesism from an anarchafeminist perspective. But the focus of state repression has shifted. When I began this work, we were in the throes of the Green Scare. Or so we thought. By 2014, there was a downward trend of AELM direct actions and ecological advocacy had made its way to the mainstream. Thanks to a few successful documentaries, there was a growing public discourse around issues of sustainability, animals, nutrition, and so on.

On the other hand, presidential rhetoric under the Trump administration has focused on what he calls the "radical left" and "Antifa." Future research should examine the language the state uses to describe these social movements. Specifically, it would be useful to understand what words are used in relation to "Antifa" and "radical left" in presidential speeches, tweets, and other public appearances. Similar to how the ecoterrorist was constructed as the bad protestor during the Green Scare, Antifa is constructed as the bad protestor in the contemporary moment. Future research should continue to examine this rhetorical construction, and how it is functioning as a form of discipline.

The focus in this book on performativity provided a particularly useful frame to engage with direct action activism. The combination of performance studies and linguistic analysis, coupled with a close engagement with activist literature, facilitated an inductive analysis that incorporated local modes of communication to uncover the ways in which eco-activists engage in direct action. The transdisciplinary approach integrated rhetorical theories within communication, performance studies, and anthropological discourses to examine the symbolic use of political theatre as a mode of protest. Future research should foster an integrative approach that does not rely on the constructed boundaries of academic disciplines. Where one discipline falls short, another discipline may provide a complementary lens to expand the analysis. Specifically, the study of direct action facilitates a transdisciplinary framework that values symbolic, satirical, humorous, and aggressive rhetoric that lies at the intersections of various social movements. Activists engage in coalitional politics and have integrated the strategies and tactics from other movements that benefit from collaboration and creative appropriation. Academics, similarly, can benefit from a collaborative and creative exchange that rearticulates fragmented discourses into interdisciplinary dialogues.

The use of participant-observation in this ethnographic analysis facilitated a level of imagination that required anthropological play and performance. The proclamations and chants were not literal, nor were they meant to endorse the façade of agency in neoliberal capitalism. The rhetorical nature of these protests is playful, constantly mocking the rhetoric that interpellates us all as subjects within neoliberal capitalism and speciesism. As an audience seated in front of the stage in which eco-activists expose the fallacies of individualism and capitalism, we are then supposed to feel sadness and repulsion when the demonstrations provide graphic proclamations detailing vivisection.

We, as an audience, are meant to laugh at the childlike chants and reappropriated versions of pop songs that mock the police. Disidentification is an intended response to the performance and it is met with the challenge to act upon those disidentificatory thoughts. Affect is a necessary and powerful tool for revolutionary change. Similar to how the performative spectacle of drag challenges the static construction of gender and pushes it into a state of crisis, so, too, does the use of voice through exaggerated mimicry and aggressive rhetoric move neoliberal capitalism and speciesism toward a state of crisis. The dialectical discipline of disidentification through both the construction of ecoterrorism and the refusal to submit to that paradigm, illustrate the performative power at stake. Those who are targeted by direct actions are left feeling helpless and frustrated with their lack of agency within the globalized neoliberal corporate terrain. Onlookers are left counting the ways in which politicians, corporate figureheads, scientists, and medical practitioners are cogs within the machine in the vast terrain of globalized capitalism. Neoliberal capitalism becomes the joke; it becomes the laughable social construction that holds no salient relationship to the false promises the demonstrators are calling out. Science is seen as violence. Meat is seen as murder. Other-than-human milk becomes a manifestation of rape and infanticide. The spectacular performances of eco-activist direct action confront the state's interpellation and propose an alternative. It is this strategic reframing that situates the chants and proclamations delivered by eco-activists, the direct rescue, the public vigils, and so on, within a trajectory of effective political theatre. The bolt cutters are the stiletto heels, the balaclava, the corset; eco-activists are but merely spectacular revolutionaries in drag.

Notes

There is significant overlap in philosophy and tactic between the two movements, thus the following analysis will refer to them as one movement. The conflation has been made by many activists and scholars throughout the movement's history (Nocella and Best 2004; Loadenthal 2010). The term "eco-activists" is used throughout to refer to individuals that self-identify as anarchist, as well as against the violent ideological structure of speciesism.

George Lakoff synthesizes how "terrorism" and "evil" are articulated within the frames of metaphor (Lakoff 2001, 3). The deployment of terrorism rhetoric through the metaphor of ecoterrorism demonstrates the wide scope of repression targeting the AELM (Liddick 2006, 102). Critical anthropologists have focused on how these discourses of "terrorism" and "war" are used to silence dissent (Price 2004, 25). Patricia Dunmire and INCITE! Women of Color against Violence expanded on the dichotomization of individuals as "good/bad activist" through the state's use of metaphor in the construction of "victims/terrorists" (Dunmire 2011, 61; INCITE! Women of Color against Violence 2009).

The term speciesism, coined by Richard Ryder in 1973, is used to describe the systematic privileging of the constructed category of human over the constructed category of animal (Singer 1977, 7; Foreman 1993, 27; Rosebraugh 2004a, 120) (Foreman 1993, 27; Rosebraugh 2004b, 120). Both Rosebraugh and Pickering detailed their years in these public solidarity roles, and how they experienced political repression (Rosebraugh 2004a; Pickering 2007).

5 I solely engage Nader's concept of studying up while strongly distancing myself from her history of problematic interactions with critical anthropologists. Without giving credence to her dismissive treatment of queer anthropologists, I have fractured studying up and focus on that specific scholarly contribution.

6 Intersectional politics with the AELM has meant a serious reckoning with structural racism, sexism and misogyny, ableism, and transphobia. For example, Earth First! and several environmental direct action campaigns have been critiqued for not confronting instances of sexual violence and intimate partner violence (Pellow 2014).

7 Vivisection is a term used to describe experimentation on living beings.

8 Neoliberal capitalism facilitates the reconceptualization of sovereignty to include corporations as a global power with state protection (Harvey 2007; Kotz 2015). Contemporary legislation anthropomorphizes corporations and awards a protected status similar to those awarded minorities in Hate Crime Legislation (Lovitz 2010).

9 One of the earliest texts I read as my vegan politic developed was *The Sexual Politics of Meat* by Carol Adams (1990). I have a great deal of gratitude toward Adams, and the many ecofeminists that provided the language for me to unpack how violence against animals is deeply connected to violence against human animals, particularly women.

10 Communication scholars Leslie Baxter and Barbara Montgomery proposed the theory of relational dialectic to explain the presence of tension and contradiction within relationships between individuals (Baxter 1988; Baxter and Montgomery 1996; Baxter 2010). The theory was based on the work of Mikhail Bakhtin that focused on the ways in which humans experience overlapping and contradicting needs within relationships through the concept of dialogism (Bakhtin 1982; Bakhtin 1984; Bakhtin 1986). Bakhtin argued that the dialectic of human experience is a dualism with centripetal and centrifugal forces that create tensions between unity and divergence (Bakhtin 1982). This book expands upon the ways in which confrontational tactics queer traditional modes of protest and create solidarity amongst activists facing political repression. The text is particularly focused on how activists negotiate the tension between feeling empowered feeling repressed within an overarchingly suffocating state of constant mourning.

11 This political distinction of anarchist and anti-speciesist hones in on activists that are critiquing the state, authoritarianism, capitalism, speciesism, and, holistically, how these systems of domination perpetuate

interconnected (but distinct) systems of domination like white supremacy, the patriarchy, and heterosexism.

2 Both the ALF and ELF emerged in the UK, in the early 1970s and 1990s, respectively. As globalization and world trade amplified, so too did activism in the name of earth and animal liberation. Folks in a range of disciplines have painstakingly traced these roots over the last seven decades (Steve Best n.d.; Nocella and Best 2004; Steven Best and Nocella 2006; Foreman 1993; Rosebraugh 2004a; Mann 2009; Young and Coronado 2011; Young 2019).

3 The phrase "by any means necessary" is attributed to French philosopher Frantz Fanon in 1960, in reference to the notion of liberating the mind from oppression. The phrase was popularized by the French philosopher Jean-Paul Sartre and by civil rights leader Malcom X. Dr Jerry Vlasik was one of the first animal liberation activists to advocate liberation by any means necessary. The interview can be found online with the NAALPO.

4 The SHAC campaign, described in chapter 2, was founded in the UK in 1999 after a series of successful pressure campaigns targeting breeding facilities and leaked investigative footage taken inside Huntingdon Life Sciences laboratories. Animal liberation activist Kevin Jonas travelled to Britain and participated in the British SHAC campaign. In 2001, the SHAC USA campaign began to take shape following the financial backing of Stephens, Inc. based out of Arkansas of HLS (Marut 2009).

5 The campaign has experienced political repression in various ways over the years, ranging from increased surveillance, arrest of activists, and incarceration of activists. The campaign has also announced periods of dormancy, while activists prominent in the collective have engaged in solidarity work with other animal liberation collectives and anarchist legal defence collectives.

6 It is not uncommon for activists to have crossover between movements, for example, with ALA. The fluidity of the ALA collective specifically lends itself to a clandestine presence in WDC and contributes to the heavy police presence at ALA demonstrations.

7 Environmental anthropologists in particular have examined communities taking on governments and corporations that are privatizing resources, degrading ecosystems, and contributing to climate change (Haenn and Wilk 2005; Pine 2008).

8 Anthropologists have examined the ways in which neoliberal capitalism facilitates the masking of a central site of government to evade accountability for monitoring "the market," and the [neoliberal] performance of

democracy that facilitate corporations operating as the exception through "corporate sovereignty" (Graeber 2004a; 2009b; Ong 2006; Price 2011).

19 Elly Teman's ethnographic study that examined pregnancy and childbirth through the experiences of surrogates and intended mothers challenged the academic tendency to fracture empathy and compassion from anthropological research and infused this throughout her analysis of troublesome metaphors (Teman 2010, 31–9).

20 To be clear, I fully support anyone undergoing elective procedures, such as sterilization, if they choose to do so without coercion.

21 I am not asserting that I am actually one of the few women who has birthed children in the AELM. I include this other person's assertion because it illustrates perception versus reality about the erasure of reproductive labour.

22 Within the ideologies of heterosexism and capitalism, access to and engagement with the institution of marriage and human reproduction are sites of privilege. Rightfully so, activists in the AELM have advanced inter-sectional critiques of compulsory heterosexuality that are woven into anti-speciesist discourse. These critiques, however, can perpetuate individual-istic moral purity. Without mitigating the structural problems with marriage, or negating the environmental impacts of human reproduction, it is important to note that what gains someone access to privilege in one community is what can deny them access to privilege in another.

23 I have written extensively on the connections between gender, race, sexual-ity, and species through the lens of ecofeminism. The literature builds on the significant contributions from Carol Adams, Greta Gaard, Lori Gruen, Josephinne Donovan, and Marti Kheel. These women have served as both academic and personal influences on my scholarship and activism. I met each of these women at different points in my life and maintain a personal relationship with each of them, though Marti Kheel unfortunately passed away in 2013. I have been an invited keynote speaker at ecofeminist con-ferences, as well as a contributor in edited anthologies about the connec-tions between gender and species exploitation (Adams and Donovan 1995, 2007; Adams 2004; Kemmerer 2011; Gaard 1993; Gaard and Murphy 1998; Gaard, Estok, and Oppermann 2013; Kheel 2007; Grubbs 2011; Grubbs and Adams 2013).

24 Although Puar focuses on the construction of homonationalism through terrorist assemblages, Puar aptly highlights the flexible nature of these assemblages by the state to naturalize structural violence (Puar 2007).

25 Direct action is not defined solely by the physical act, but also the

ideological underpinnings and symbolic meaning the act represents. Thus it is not a label of tactic demarcation, but rather it is an inclusive framework to conceptualize activism (Graeber 2009b, 210; Thompson 2010, 57). This point is further examined in subsequent chapters.

6 The term "queer theory" has been credited to Teresa de Lauretis to serve as a conference title at the University of California, Santa Cruz in 1990. She had heard the term used by activists and knew it would be "deliberately disruptive" because of the provocative challenge the term made to lesbian and gay studies (Halperin 2003, 340). The term then catapulted Butler's and Sedgwick's published texts to the forefront of the growing field.

7 Although there is still much progress to be made enhancing intersectional politics that critique species in mainstream spaces, there are expanding conversations happening in gender and sexuality studies conferences, environmental studies areas, public anthropology, and queer linguistics, just to name a few.

8 I have expanded on this point in conference presentations and publications (Grubbs 2012c, 2012b, 2014; Grubbs and Loadenthal 2013).

9 The case is referred to throughout the manuscript as simply "J20," following a consistent coding schema used by anarchists to denote the month and year of the action. In this case, the arrests occurred on 20 January 2017.

CHAPTER ONE

1 This chapter focuses on the political economy of animal-and-ecology use industries within neoliberal capitalism in the US. Although the book is based on an ethnography that took place in North America, the backdrop and context teased out in this chapter is specific to the US.

2 This argument is an extension of the earlier discussion in chapter 1: introduction of subject formation and interpellation through Pêcheux's three modalities in which individuals respond to the "hailing" of ideology as the good subject, the bad subject, or through disidentification (Muñoz 1999, 11; Pêcheux 1982, 158).

3 For an in-depth analysis of felony convictions in the US for acts motivated by animal liberation, see Chapekis and Moore (2021).

4 For a nuanced and detailed discussion of the rhetorical construction of ecoterrorism within the context of eco-resistance citizenship, see Buell (2009, 157).

5 The naturalization and institutionalization of violence that marginalizes human and other-than-human animal bodies are interconnected and distinct. Intersectional feminists provide a detailed history and critique of the ways in which ideologies such as racism, xenophobia, sexism, ableism, transphobia, homophobia function (Adams 1990; 2011; Hill Collins 2005; Harper 2010; Ko 2019; Spiegel and Walker 1997; hooks 2000, 2014).

6 Anthropological and linguistic discourses on sovereignty have examined the relationship between capitalism, statecraft, power through false dichotomies of good/evil. Patricia Dunmire has critiqued the proliferation of Islamophobia through the constructed binaries used to demarcate "victims/terrorists" and "good/bad citizen." Chomsky examines the US manufacturing of xenophobia through hyperbolic language and patriotism rhetoric. Lakoff expands on the use of "terrorism" and "evil" as they have been articulated within the frames of metaphor (Chomsky 1991; 1999; 2004, 222; Dean 2009; Dunmire 2011; Hansen and Stepputat 2001; Ong 2006).

7 In early 2016, grassroots organizers mobilized in response to Energy Transfer Partners' approved construction of Dakota Access Pipeline. The pipeline posed serious environmental threats to the land, and disproportionately impacted sacred indigenous sites. In addition to ecological threats, the pipeline would disrupt ancient burial grounds and significant historical sites. Throughout 2016, thousands of people established the Standing Rock Sioux encampment to halt construction, and, more importantly, to illustrate the struggle for Indigenous sovereignty. Activists were brutally repressed by private security workers and police. As President Obama left office, the easement for the Corps of Engineers was denied, halting the expansion of the pipeline. Three days into President Trump's term, on 24 January 2017, he signed an executive order authorizing the construction and it was completed just three months later.

8 The neoliberal reshaping of global capitalism and the nepotistic overlap between government and corporate entities facilitates the decentralization of corporations, ambiguous loci of accountability, and the façade of individual agency (Leitner, Peck, and Sheppard 2008, 3).

9 The abundance of regulatory groups and committees has meant the obfuscation of actual regulation and accountability (Graeber 2009b, 81).

10 Schools, religion, family units, and arguably, the media, are larger ideological state apparatuses that use subtle and discrete ways to garner consent by making government policies seem in our best interest.

11 The AEPA established three tiers of prison sentencing penalties in addition to the financial penalties, "(1) for damage exceeding $10,000, one-year

imprisonment; (2) for personal injuries caused, up to ten years imprisonment; and (3) for death caused, entire life imprisonment" (Lovitz 2010, 50).
Many critical race scholars have articulated poignant critiques
of the racist function that the carceral system has within US society. ALEC
is one powerful example of how business-government overlap can dictate
policy and enforcement (Alexander 2012; Davis 1998; 2016).

CHAPTER TWO

Voltairine de Cleyre was a feminist thinker who articulated a particular
anarchist politic that inspired many. She disavowed oppressive social
structures like capitalism and religion and worked closely with prolific
anarchist thinkers at the turn of the century. Her poetry and essay have
inspired generations of anarchists and outlined a framework for direct
action that is still used today (Avrich 2018; de Cleyre 2009).
Safety precautions include clearing that a building is vacant before it is
targeted and accessing private property without physically harming
anyone. Animal raids are typically done in the evening, though there have
been some done during the daytime. Activists are careful with how they
handle the animals and ensuring they receive proper medical care (Steve
Best et al. 2007, 4).
The concept of SHACtivism, popularly used by scholars like David Naguib
Pellow, illustrates the global application of this particular form of activism
(Pellow 2014, 153).
The SHAC campaign would focus on a bank that lent money to HLS, but
also had thousands of clients around the world. By repeatedly targeting
individuals at that bank, it became too disruptive to continue working
with HLS. So the bank dropped HLS as a client. Then SHAC would move
on to the next financial institution, and so on (Collective n.d.).
The authors do a quantitative study of the economic impacts of various
campaigns and focus on SHAC in this section. The authors use a chart to
map the increased impact to HLS over time, illustrating the effectiveness of
the campaign (Shannon, Nocella, and Asimakopolous 2012, 109–13).
The use of the term *ecological* refers to living entities. This includes human
animals, other-than-human animals, biological ecosystems, natural
resources, and genetic engineering.
The attention to the detail is paramount. Activists engaging in direct
action within the AELM go to great lengths to avoid harming living beings
(Jensen 2012).

8 The ideological divisions between these social movements, though often-times described as being a part of an overarching advocacy movement are based on their stance on speciesism. The welfare and conservation movement accept the ideology of speciesism but argue humans can alleviate some of the "undue" suffering. The animal rights and ecological sustainability movement challenge speciesism under the constraints of a rhetoric of rights. Animals and ecological systems should be awarded rights and it is then human obligation to protect those rights. The animal and ecological liberation movement, however, challenges the notion of rights as relational privilege. These activists believe that liberation from exploitation is necessary for survival and challenge the speciesist notion that humans possess a unique ability to act rationally in the relationship of rights. Liberation is justified by any means necessary.

9 In the WDC area there is a visible activist who attends many demonstrations in various anti-oppression movements to capture video footage and publish. The activist has his own YouTube channel, and also submits video to DCindymedia.org. In other cities, videos were obtained through online sources.

10 For the purpose of this book, I distinguish between chants and proclamations. I use the term *chant* to describe the call-and-return slogans and collective sayings recited during the demonstrations. The term *proclamation*, in contrast, refers to lengthier speeches delivered by one individual person.

11 I chose not to wear a wedding band all the time because the material marker of heteronormative monogamy is not something I am particularly attached to. To the contrary, the material marker I do wear is not actually connected to marriage at all. I wear a simple, stoneless band that I purchased for myself a few years after getting married, and interchange which fingers I wear it on. I own a ring with heirloom diamonds that I rarely wear, and I address this in a subsequent chapter. The other reason I chose not to wear identifiable jewellery at public demonstrations connects to the disciplinary punishment and surveillance teased out in subsequent chapters. The more distinguishing your clothing, accessories, and physical appearance, the more you stand out in a crowd.

12 The brilliant work of Bruce Schneier articulates how security theatre is both performative and prescribed and distracts us from thinking about what would actually keep us safe and from whom (Schneier 2006).

13 Years later, Levi told me that one of their biggest achievements during this campaign was the anti-SLAPP legislation that they lobbied for, and the number of SLAPP suits that were thrown out because of it.

4 The history of applications like RedPhone and TextSecure are beyond the scope of this analysis, but worthy of their own attention and space.

5 These local divides resemble much larger trends where issues of intersectionality, tactics, and overarching movement strategies are contentious.

6 I took audio recordings from the demonstration, and also archived video footage posted from a demonstrator on YouTube.

CHAPTER THREE

1 The concept of the absent referent, articulated by Adams, illustrates how humans use language to fracture living animals from the commodities created with their bodies. Specifically, Adams extensive research on commercialism shows how terms like "nuggets" and "bacon" not only erase the species these products are derived from, but they completely erase the individual identity of each animal life taken to create the products. As an ecofeminist, Adams has brilliantly theorized on the interconnectedness of sexualization, racialization, animalization, and gender between species. Her work has inspired an entire generation of ecofeminists, myself included (Adams 1990, 2010, 2011; Donovan and Adams 2007; Grubbs and Adams 2013).

2 The post was found on Facebook, shortly after a demonstration had taken place in 2012.

3 Activists used the chant to make a humorous comparison between the owner of the zoo and the fictional character (and leader of the evil group of witches and wizards called Death Eaters) from J.K. Rowling's Harry Potter series. It is worth noting that by including this chant that activists used during a demonstration, it is not an endorsement of Rowling as an author or individual. On the contrary, their toxic transphobia has caused a great deal of pain and she should be de-platformed.

4 The events serve a social function to gather activists in an informal, recreational space that solidifies a sense of common identity. Projects like Punk Rock Karaoke Chicago and Punk Rock Karaoke Northeast raise funds for prisoner support networks, activist legal defence funds, and various political support avenues.

5 It is again of note that I am not using spectacle in the precise way Debord and *The Society of the Spectacle* outlined. This was touched on in the introduction chapter, and also elaborated on later in this chapter. I am using Duncombe's application of Debord to articulate the ways in which spectacle can be articulated for the positive.

6 In Italy in 2012, activists had lined the fences of Green Hill Dog Breeder
   to protest that the company breeds and sells dogs to be used in experimentation. After demonstrating outside the facility for some time, activists
   climbed the fence and began to pass beagle puppies across the fence into
   the arms of fellow activists. The rescue was hailed as a beautiful suspension of repression. Police did seize some of the dogs and activists when
   they went to leave, but far more of the dogs and activists made it out
   safely (Potter 2012b).

7 Muñoz's work was deeply informative in my own thinking about how
   drag can subvert, not only by destabilizing but also by performing a world
   reimagined.

8 The image and Instagram feedback, including the Twitter integration
   through hashtags, illustrates the overlapping ways these posts reach wide
   audiences.

9 The words were identified through preliminary research with the End
   Captivity Now campaign, Bridges Brigade, NAALPO, EF!, and Gathering
   for Total Liberation. Additional phrases that are not explicitly linked to a
   campaign include (but are not limited to) #animalliberation, #earthliber-
   ation, #govegan, #anarchist, and #greenanarchy.

10 Facebook has been called out for complying with subpoenas from the US
   government as part of criminal cases against activists. The security information on Facebook's webpage state their complicity with government
   subpoenas (Facebook n.d.).

11 Anarchist historian Mark Bray provides a succinct discussion of the direct
   action strategy of de-platforming. The notion of ¡No pasarán! in an
   anti-fascist context illustrates the material value in not giving specific
   people a platform or access to the masses with problematic politics. Bray
   discusses the strategy used historically to deny Nazis and fascists spaces to
   promulgate their message, but this concept is still an important organizing
   principle in other leftist spaces. Activist convergences and academic conferences globally have grappled with the dilemma of de-platforming, and
   it is beyond the scope or focus of this section to dive into that important
   issue within movement strategies (Bray 2017, 143–67).

12 There are many forms of protest utilized by direct action eco-activists.
   The method of concealing one's identity by wearing black clothing is an
   anarchist tactic referred to as black bloc. It is a form of collective camouflage: wear unidentifiable black clothing, cover your face and hair, and, if
   you carry a backpack, it should blend into the outfit and not stand out.
   Although at many of the home demonstrations activists were not in black
   bloc, they used a different form of camouflage. These protests took place

on crowded streets, and sometimes we dispersed quickly into the crowd afterward. This meant we dressed casually and needed to blend in with onlookers. However, at many of the other demonstrations, public protests, and gatherings I attended, I met activists that use black bloc. The strategy is not only in response to resisting the police state, but also as a way to challenge other social movements that use physical appearance as a vehicle of privilege. Many activists and scholars have written on this strategy, but I point to Bray again for a contemporary, concise discussion.

3 They are not called the "public relations representative," but they essentially serve this function. Additionally, many campaigns and collectives with the NLG have a legal observer present. The presence of a legal observer is predicated on the scope of the demonstration, and the availability of an observer in that area and time.

4 There is a lot of debate within the movement regarding protest permits. Many activists believe the process of obtaining a permit minimizes the impact and also reduces the ways in which they are confronting the establishment. During the Occupy encampments, many regional Occupy chapters refused to even file permits on the basis of pandering to the system.

5 Although this ethnographic description of events is focused on home demonstrations with ALA, the larger ethnographic data illustrated commonalities and overlap in the scripts used by eco-activists at other demonstrations. In this way, the example here illustrates a commonly used performance to create a specific spectacle.

6 There are many that have documented the horrors of vivisection on the bodies of Jews, African slaves and their descendants, religious and ethnic minorities, and those who are disabled (Spitz 2005; Steizinger 2018; Rurke 1987; Washington 2008).

7 One of the main individuals that interviewed me for this job was an executive at Novartis, a longstanding target of eco-activist direct action. Though I did keep all of my academic and activist presentations on my curriculum vitae (that clearly demonstrate political support of these activists) I chose to "hide" my social media accounts from my work community.

8 There are pockets of neighbourhoods with a concentration of activists in Cincinnati, such as Northside and Clifton, but these are insular. As someone who had just returned to the city after living somewhere else, I had yet to meet any activists who shared my politics. That is not to say they don't exist, but they are not easily penetrable by those "new" to the area. Six years later, I have yet to find a vibrant community of intersectional eco-activists who engage in direct action.

CHAPTER FOUR

1 State repression has taken various amalgamations over time and been overtly and covertly deployed against activists in a range of movements. The concept of "state repression" is a strategy to stifle and silence dissent through a series of coercive (oftentimes violent) tactics. These tactics range from infiltration and surveillance to assassination.

2 Social movement studies scholars Bowers et al. (2009) outline a binary framework to understand resistance and repression. According to this model, agitation exists when those outside of the decision-making establishment advocate for significant social change and encounter enough resistance that they have to move beyond the "normal" discursive means of persuasion. Control, simply put, is how the establishment responds to agitation and tries to suppress it. Their model provides an accessible vocabulary to conceptualize how power is exerted and negotiated.

3 Max Weber is most notably associated with the paradigm of a "monopoly of violence." Weber argued that the state has legal impunity to use violence, and an asymmetric access to power. Many scholars have applied this framework to study global and localized conflict, armed resistance, and structural violence (Baudrillard 2001; Loadenthal 2013b; Weber 1919; 1978).

4 Although Foucault argued the increased use of surveillance facilitated a veiled use of state violence through disciplinary punishment, the targeted legislation, terrorist enhancements, and excessive police force follow a monarchical construct of state power (Foucault 1977; 1980; 1991).

5 The next chapter examines the ways in which activists resist and rearticulate these measures through direct action.

6 The US judicial system is one of the most pervasive examples of disciplinary punishment. The rhetoric of a rehabilitative justice system is a farce. Michelle Alexander, Angela Davis, and many other brilliant scholars have detailed how the penal system and carceral state are steeped in a history of racism and xenophobia. The notion of punishing the body for violating a law, using the threat of incarceration, is not rehabilitative or restorative. The imprisoned body is forced to internalize the punishing capacity of the state, and once incarcerated, the body surrenders all biopolitical power. Despite the violence of this structure, the prison system allows the state to appear rehabilitative by providing an imagined pathway for redemption for those that work for it. Such appearances reinforce the spurious neoliberal logic of exceptionality.

It is of importance to note this section focuses on North America and the UK. It is outside the scope and aim of this study to include an overview of the intricacies of policing internationally.

There are many activists who make it an intentional practice to travel in clothing that clearly marks their politics and solidarity with political prisoners, to pack political propaganda, and to adopt an aggressive posture with TSA security.

Activist-scholarship has interrogated the role of technology in state violence against anti-war, anti-nuclear, and anti-capitalist movements (Scheper-Hughes and Bourgois 2003; Žižek 2008; Price 2004; 2011; Loadenthal 2011a). Contemporary discourses on activist repression in social movement literature, however, should pay particular attention to the ways in which the state targets anarchists and anti-fascists, and, specifically, the overlap between these communities and the AELM. There is also a resurgence of political repression that targeted the civil rights movement and is now focused on the M4BL.

The prosecution of each individual deserves its own attention and discussion. However, a more detailed analysis of these activists is beyond the scope here. There are many useful texts that do this important work, thanks to scholars like David Naguib Pellow and Dara Lovitz.

It is worth noting that in 2014, Nathan Block was publicly called out for becoming a fascist. On his Tumblr *Loyalty Is Mightier than Fire*, Block shared out references to Nazism and the postwar fascist movement. NYCAntifa was one of the collectives to call out this problematic shift in Block's ideological leanings.

The prison sentence and release date take into consideration a credited amount of "good time" that may mean a shorter amount of time served. This "good behaviour time" is awarded in the beginning, and any infractions or disciplinary actions can result in a reduction of that time. Thus, the more infractions someone has, the less likely it is that they will be released before their full sentence has been served.

McGowan's article detailed the ways he faced repression in the prison, and specifically the use of CMUs to punish people that are incarcerated for their political views (McGowan 2013).

Luers was originally sentenced to twenty years in prison, but after consistent pressure on the Oregon Court of Appeals to overturn his sentence, he was released after serving almost nine years.

The Civil Liberties Defense Center provides a succinct and clear analysis of the law (Paige 2014).

16 Eco-activists practice lateral organizing that does not centralize a member-ship base. The organizational structures of collectives are also horizontal, leaderless, and clandestine. Activists within the movement have challenged religious, educational, familial, and local institutions that promulgate speciesism, capitalism, neoliberalism, etc. These activists oftentimes disengage with the institutions and create alternative forms of community.

17 Letter writing sessions are one way for activists to show solidarity for people that are incarcerated. Depending on the collective organizing the session, there may be a list of political prisoners to write to, or a session can be organized around writing to one specific person.

18 In this analysis, TPP provides a succinct analysis of how the AEPA/AETA have been used. (Chapekis and Moore 2021, 17).

19 In additional to conferences and activist convergences, I wrote and contributed to pieces that articulated how the Green Scare was a mani-festation of monarchical power (Grubbs and Loadenthal 2011a; Grubbs 2014a; Loadenthal 2016).

20 The chants were described in sentencing documents produced by the US government.

21 This topic and specific case studies have been expanded upon in several formal paper presentations and activist workshops. These include: confer-ence presentation presented at the New York Anarchist Bookfair, April 2011; conference presentation presented at the Animal Liberation Forum, University of California Long Beach, April 2011; Public Anthropology Conference – (Re)Defining Power: Paradigms of Praxis, American University (Washington, DC), October 2011; and Graduate Student Sociological Association, George Mason University (Fairfax, VA), October 2011.

22 The individual cases are terrifying, and worthy of their own interrogation. For more information about these cases, see Loadenthal (2014; 2015a; 2015b) and Rob and Lewis (2014).

23 Brandon Darby, former anarchist organizer, spent years perpetrating acts of violence against women. Darby, alongside several well-respected activ-ists including former Black Panther Malik Rahim, helped found Common Ground, an anarchist-aligned network providing relief post–Hurricane Katrina in New Orleans. Darby was an FBI informant, and continuously disrupted the important relief work Common Ground was trying to do. For an extensive history of Darby's infiltration of this network, see Fithian (2010); Loadenthal (2015b); and Luft (2008).

24 There are different taxonomies and typologies that distinguish the categories of people that provide evidence to the police against activists.

You can find one example of such typology in Steve Hewitt's *Snitch! A History of the Modern Intelligence Informer* (Hewitt 2010, 19).

5 I would later read Adrian Parr's articulation of how sustainability had been hijacked, which succinctly articulated this cultural process (Parr 2009).

6 In 2014, Mason's support committee published a statement on www.supportmariemason.org announcing that "Marie" would be transitioning, under the restrictive, limited confines of living in prison. Moving forward, the article requests people use the name Marius Jacob Mason and male pronouns. The URL also changed to www.supportmariusmason.org (Support Marius Mason, "Free Marius" n.d.).

7 Ambrose completely disavows direct action and provides intimate details about conversations and actions that implicate Mason. The document, when referencing how Ambrose was influenced by Mason, uses phrases like "under her spell" and "under her tutelage" (Brady 2008).

8 As an informant with the FBI, Zoe Elizabeth Voss was given the pseudonym "Anna" and is only referred to as this in legal proceedings, media coverage, and all documents discussing the case. She is referred to as "Anna" throughout this chapter.

9 The case has been discussed in academic and journalist contexts (Aaronson and Galloway 2015; York 2015; Pilkington 2015; Collective n.d.; Todd, n.d.; Potter 2008b).

10 The BBC coverage of the encampment detailed the collaborative solidarity movement that emerged at Standing Rock Sioux Reservation (*BBC News* 2016).

11 The corporations invested in heavy public relations campaigns to deter the public from supporting NO DAPL. They issued press statements, and created a website, "daplpipelinefacts.com." (Energy Transfer 2020; n.d.)

12 The police dropped the third charge, discharge of a firearm during a felony crime of violence (Estes 2019, 64).

13 The *Intercept*'s detailed reporting on the case reveal that phone records were given to the ATF, local sheriff departments, and the USAO in Bismark.

14 Boykoff provides a detailed history and discussion about how activists have been repressed.

15 The same activist, Julie Henry, who provided details about how Coronado assaulted her was approached by an FBI agent who had previously worked as a counsellor with sex offenders. The FBI agent posed as a support person for Henry but was actually manipulating her trauma to garner evidence against Coronado for unrelated alleged crimes (Brown and Knefel 2018).

36 There are countless databases that AELM collectives run and contribute to that track informants and infiltrators. These databases are useful for activists trying to protect their communities against predatory individuals and state repression (North American Animal Liberation Press Office, "Snitches" n.d.; Lilia 2016; *Earth First! Newswire* n.d.).

37 I am not defending or justifying Powell's decision to take a plea in any way here. By taking a plea, Powell confirmed the state's theory of the case, putting his co-defendants in an even more vulnerable position.

CHAPTER FIVE

1 Foucault expands on the ways in which power and discourse are exposed and reinforced (1990).

2 The important, lengthy history of direct action in the Pacific Northwest has been extensively documented by activists, and through the digital archives of communiqués. For a more detailed history, see Loadenthal (2013a); Pickering (2007); Rosebraugh (2004); Scarce (2006).

3 The convergence organizers stressed solidarity with aboveground and underground activists, political prisoners, and international movements. The notion of "community" was used throughout to stress interconnectedness and solidarity. Community does not refer to geographic communities, but it loosely defines kinship networks of activists that share intersectional critiques of authoritarianism and speciesism.

4 My partner has an extensive knowledge of licence plate markers and vehicle designation used by the state in various degrees of law enforcement.

5 Although my partner was present and more than willing to help, I often was the default caregiver. The combination of breastfeeding on demand and emotional attachment resulted in a disproportionate amount of time that I would wear or carry both children while manoeuvring strange surroundings with a mobile toddler and infant.

6 One of the most notable writers to theorize anarcho-primitivism is John Zerzan.

7 In 2014, Greenpeace activists entered Proctor & Gamble (P&G) headquarters in Cincinnati, Ohio, to engage in direct action challenging the controversial sourcing of palm oil. Greenpeace had contacted P&G throughout the campaign, but the company refused to engage in the conversation. The protest garnered national attention and led to the announcement from P&G that the company would change its practices

over the course of several years. The activists faced a collective sentence of nine and a half years, and ultimately the felony charges were dropped.

8 Activists challenged ag-gag legislation that made it illegal to take footage inside factory farms in six states (Potter 2012; 2014).

9 Bond was sentenced to twelve years for committing three arsons (a sheepskin factory in Denver, Colorado, a leather factory in Salt Lake City, Utah, and a restaurant in Sandy, Utah).

0 Shortly after he was incarcerated, Walter assumed the name Abdul Haqq and announced that he had converted to Islam. In 2012, Bond announced that he no longer uses the name Abdul Haqq, and would like to go by Walter Bond. Five years later, in 2017, Bond issued a statement that he was no longer a devout Muslim, and had no religious affiliation.

1 In July 2020, I received an email from Bond's support website that he and Camille Marino had created a new website, http:// veganfinalsolution.com.

2 Bond's brother, Trapper Zuehlke, was contacted by the FBI and worked with the government in a sting operation. Bond pled guilty to all three charges and was also charged with one count of AETA. His total prison sentence is twelve years and three months, and he was released to a half-way house in 2020 (Bond 2011a).

3 I have preserved the author's text, including his use of capitalization.

4 A handful of the environmental activists arrested with Operation Backfire participated in the filming of a documentary titled *If a Tree Falls: A Story of the Earth Liberation Front*. The film portrayed several of the defendants questioning their specific actions and if they were effective.

5 Several of the online resources to track informants and infiltrators are mentioned in the previous chapter.

6 Marius Mason and Daniel McGowan were both held in CMU prisons, and their support networks spoke out at the time (Center for Constitutional Rights 2012; Support Marius Mason 2013).

References

Aaronson, Trevor, and Katie Galloway. 2015. "Manufacturing Terror: An FBI Informant Seduced Eric McDavid into a Bomb Plot. Then the Government Lied about It." *Intercept*, 19 November 2015. https://theintercept.com/2015/11/19/an-fbi-informant-seduced-eric-mcdavid-into-a-bomb-plot-then-the-government-lied-about-it/.

"About Earth First!" N.d. *Earth First! Journal*. https://earthfirstjournal.org/about/.

Abu-Lughod, Lila. 2008. *Writing Women's Worlds: Bedouin Stories*. Berkeley: University of California Press.

– 2013. *Do Muslim Women Need Saving?* Cambridge: Harvard University Press.

Adams, Carol J. 1990. *The Sexual Politics of Meat: A Feminist-Vegetarian Critical Theory*. New York: Continuum International Publishing Group.

– 2004. *Pornography of Meat*. New York: Continuum.

– 2010. *The Sexual Politics of Meat: A Feminist-Vegetarian Critical Theory, 20th Anniversary Edition*. New York: Continuum.

– 2011. *Sister Species: Women, Animals and Social Justice*. Edited by Lisa A. Kemmerer. Chicago: University of Illinois Press.

Adams, Carol J., and Josephine Donovan, eds. 1995. *Animals and Women: Feminist Theoretical Explorations*. Durham: Duke University Press Books.

Adamson, Walter L. 1983. *Hegemony and Revolution: Antonio Gramsci's Political and Cultural Theory*. Berkeley, CA: University of California Press.

Against Me! 2002. "Baby, I'm an Anarchist." *Reinventing Axl Rose*. Gainesville: No Idea Records.

Agamben, Giorgio. 2005. *State of Exception*. Translated by Kevin Attell. Chicago: University of Chicago Press.

– 1998. *Homo Sacer: Sovereign Power and Bare Life*. California: Stanford University Press.

Agency. 2017. "The J20 Case: What You Need to Know – It's Going Down." *It's Going Down*, 3 November 2017. https://itsgoingdown.org/ j20-case-need-know/.

Ahmed, Akbar S. 2003. *Islam under Siege: Living Dangerously in a Post-Honor World*. Cambridge, UK: Polity.

Ahmed, Sara. 2006. *Queer Phenomenology: Orientations, Objects, Others*. Durham: Duke University Press Books.

ALEC (American Legislative Exchange Council). N.d. "American Legislative Exchange Council – Limited Government · Free Markets · Federalism." http://www.alec.org/.

Alexander, Michelle. 2012. *The New Jim Crow: Mass Incarceration in the Age of Colorblindness*. New York: The New Press.

Althusser, Louis. 1970. *Lenin and Philosophy and Other Essays*. New York, NY: Monthly Review Press.

– 1971. "Ideology and Ideological State Apparatus (Notes toward an Investigation)." In *Lenin and Philosophy and Other Essays*, 127–86. New York City: Monthly Review Press.

– 2005a. *For Marx*. Translated by Ben Brewster. New York: Verso.

– 2005b. "On the Materialist Dialectic on the Unevenness of Origins." In *For Marx*, translated by Ben Brewster, 161–218. New York: Verso.

American Civil Liberties Union. N.d. "ACLU Letter to the House of Representatives Regarding the Animal Enterprise Terrorism Act." American CivilLibertiesUnion.https://www.aclu.org/national-security/aclu-letter-house-representatives-regarding-animal-enterprise-terrorism-act.

Amster, Randall, Abraham DeLeon, Luis Fernandez, Anthony Nocella, and Deric Shannon, eds. 2009. *Contemporary Anarchist Studies: An Introductory Anthology of Anarchy in the Academy*. New York: Routledge.

Anarchist News. 2019. "Eric King Facing 20 More Years." *Anarchist News*, 1 September 2019. https://anarchistnews.org/content/ eric-king-facing-20-more-years-prison.

Anderson, Kiera Loki. 2015. "Monkeywrenching the Misogynists in Our Movements: A Historical Exploration of Call Outs and Anti-Feminist Backlash in Cascadia." *Earth First! Journal*. https://itsgoingdown.org/ monkeywrenching-misogynists-movements-historical-exploration-call-outs-anti-feminist-backlash-cascadia/.

– 2016. "When We Are Silent We Are Still Afraid, We Speak Up to Survive: An Interview with Julie." *Earth First! Journal*. https://earthfirstjournal.org/ newswire/2016/06/24/when-we-are-silent-we-are-still-afraid-we-speak-up-to-survive-an-interview-with-julie/.

– 2018. "Addressing Sexual Violence and Misogyny within the Green Movement." *Truthout*. https://truthout.org/articles/addressing-sexual-violence-and-misogyny-within-the-green-movement/.

Animal Liberation Always. 2011. [URL redacted.]

Anonymous, A. 2013. *My Thirst.*

Anonymous, B. 2014. "Facebook Post: Seattle Airport Comment." Facebook.

Anonymous, C. 2013. "Facebook Post: Personal Attack through Fake Facebook Account." Facebook.

Anonymous, D. N.d. "Discussion of Hosting Problematic Activist."

Anonymous, E. 2013. "Instagram Post: Flyer outside of End Captivity Now." Instagram.

Anonymous, F. 2013. "Facebook Post: Response to Caged Entertainment." Facebook.

Anonymous, G. 2008. Sticker found inside *Elle.*

Anonymous, H. 2014. Earth First! Rendezvous Notes.

Anonymous, I. 2014. Gathering for Total Liberation Notes.

Anonymous, J. N.d. "The Final Nail #4." *The Final Nail*, 2013. https://final-nail.wordpress.com/.

Anonymous K. 2020. "Thousands of Captive Mink Liberated in Idaho, Utah. North American Animal Liberation Front Press Office. 30 September 2020. https://animalliberationpressoffice.org/NAALPO/2020/09/30/10854/.

Anonymous L. 2020. "Ten Hunting Towers Destroyed in Wisconsin." NAALPO. 24 September 2020. https://animalliberationpressoffice.org/NAALPO/2019/09/24/ten-hunting-towers-destroyed-in-wisconsin-usa/.

Anzaldúa, Gloria, Norma Cantú, and Aída Hurtado. 2012. *Borderlands / La Frontera: The New Mestiza.* Fourth edition. San Francisco: Aunt Lute Books.

Anzaldúa, Gloria, and Cherríe Moraga, eds. 1984. *This Bridge Called My Back: Writings by Radical Women of Color.* Second edition. New York: Kitchen Table/Women of Color Press.

Avrich, Paul. 2018. *An American Anarchist: The Life of Voltairine de Cleyre.* Chico, CA: AK Press.

Baker, Paul. 2008. "'Eligible' Bachelors and 'Frustrated' Spinsters: Corpus Linguistics, Gender and Language." In *Gender and Language Research Methodologies*, edited by Kate Harrington, Lia Litosseliti, Helen Sauntson, and Jane Sunderland, 73–84. New York: Palgrave Macmillan.

Bakhtin, Mikhail. 1982. *The Dialogic Imagination: Four Essays*, edited by Michael Holquist. Translated by Caryl Emerson. Second edition. Austin: University of Texas Press.

– 1984. *Problems of Dostoevsky's Poetics*. Minneapolis: University of Minnesota Press.

– 1986. *Speech Genres and Other Late Essays*. Edited by Caryl Emerson and Michael Holquist. Translated by Vern W. McGee. Austin: University of Texas Press.

Bakunin, Mikhail. 1970. *God and the State*. New York: Dover.

Bari, Judi. 1994. *Timber Wars by Judi Bari*. Monroe: Common Courage Press.

Barkan, Joshua. 2013. *Corporate Sovereignty*. Minnesota: University of Minnesota Press.

Baudrillard, Jean. 1994. *Simulacra and Simulation*. Translated by Sheila Faria Glaser. Ann Arbor: University of Michigan Press.

– 2001. "The Spirit of Terrorism." *Le Monde*, 2 November 2001.

Baxter, Leslie A. 1988. "A Dialectical Perspective on Communication Strategies in Relationship Development." In *Handbook of Personal Relationships*, edited by Steve Duck, 257–74. Wiley.

– 2010. *Voicing Relationships: A Dialogic Perspective*. Thousand Oaks: SAGE Publications.

Baxter, Leslie, and Barbara Montgomery. 1996. *Relating: Dialogues and Dialectics*. New York: Guilford Press.

BBC News. 2016. "Life in the North Dakota Protest Camps." https://www.bbc.com/news/world-us-canada-37249617.

Bertani, Francois, and Fontana Alessandro, eds. 2003. *Michel Foucault: Society Must Be Defended: Lectures at the College De France, 1975–76*. London: Picador.

Best, Steve. 2004. "Thinking Pluralistically: A Case for Direct Action." *Animal Liberation Front* (blog). http://www.animalliberationfront.com/Philosophy/A_Case_for_Direct_Action.htm.

Best, Steve, Anthony Nocella, Richard Kahn, Carol Gigliotti, and Lisa Kemmerer. 2007. "Introducing Critical Animal Studies." *Journal for Critical Animal Studies* 5, no. 1: 1–36.

Best, Steven, and Anthony Nocella, eds. 2006. *Igniting a Revolution: Voices in Defense of the Earth*. Chico, CA: AK Press.

Bey, Hakim. 2003. *TAZ: The Temporary Autonomous Zone, Ontological Anarchy, Poetic Terrorism*. New York: Autonomedia.

Bloc Party. "Dane Powell: J20 Prisoner Interview." *It's Going Down* (blog), 7 July 2017. https://itsgoingdown.org/dane-powell-j20-prisoner-interview/.

Bonanno, Alfredo M. 1987. *Let's Destroy Work, Let's Destroy the Economy*. Translated by Jean Weir. London: Elephant Editions (republished by the Anarchist Library).

– 1999. "Insurrectionalist Anarchism – Part One [Anarchismo insurrezion-alista]." Translated by Jean Weir. *I libri di Anarchismo (republished by The Anarchist Library)* Edizioni Anarchismo (10). http://theanarchistlibrary.org/library/alfredo-m-bonanno-insurrectionalist-anarchism-part-one.

Bond, Walter. 2011a. "Final Statement to the Court (Colorado)." *Support Walter Bond* (blog). http://supportwalter.org/SW/index.php/2011/02/11/final-statement-to-the-court-colorado/.

– 2011b. "Final Statement to the Court (Utah)." *Support Walter Bond* (blog). http://supportwalter.org/SW/index.php/2011/10/13/final-statement-to-the-court-utah/.

Border Officer. 2013. Border crossing in Toronto, Canada.

Bowers, John W., Donovan J. Ochs, Richard J. Jensen, and David P. Schulz. 2009. *The Rhetoric of Agitation and Control*. Third edition. Long Grove: Waveland Press.

Boykoff, Jules. 2007. *Beyond Bullets: The Suppression of Dissent in the United States*. Chico, CA: AK Press.

Brady, Michael Joseph. 2008. "Sentencing Memorandum for Frank Ambrose." Western District of Michigan.

Bray, Mark. 2017. *Antifa: The Anti-Fascist Handbook*. Brooklyn: Melville House.

Bridges Brigade. 2014a. "Facebook Post: Pathway to Liberation Digital Direct Action." Facebook.

– 2014b. "Facebook Post: Snitch Alert: Agranoff."

Brown, Alleen, and John Knefel. 2018. "The FBI Used the #METOO Movement to Pressure an Environmental Activist into Becoming an Informant." *Intercept*. https://theintercept.com/2018/09/01/metoo-fbi-informant-environmental-activism-rod-coronado/.

Bubel, Claudia. 2008. "Film Audiences as Overhearers." *Journal of Pragmatics* 40: 55–71.

Buell, Lawrence. 2009. "What Is Called Ecoterrorism." *Gramma: Journal of Theory and Criticism* 16: 153–66.

Burchell, Graham, Colin Gordon, and Peter Miller, eds. 1991. *The Foucault Effect*. Chicago: University of Chicago Press.

Burke, Kenneth. 1969a. *A Grammar of Motives*. Berkeley: University of California Press.

– 1969b. *A Rhetoric of Motives*. Berkeley: University of California Press.

Butler, Judith. 1990. *Gender Trouble: Feminism and the Subversion of Identity*. New York: Routledge.

– 1993. "Critically Queer." *GLQ: A Journal of Lesbian and Gay Studies* 1: 17–32.

– 2006. *Precarious Life: The Powers of Mourning and Violence*. Brooklyn: Verso.

– 2011. *Bodies That Matter: On the Discursive Limits of "Sex."* New York: Routledge.

Cargas, Harry James. 1981. *When God and Man Failed: Non-Jewish Views of the Holocaust*. New York: Macmillan.

Center for Constitutional Rights. 2012. "CMUs: The Federal Prison System's Experiment in Social Isolation." Center for Constitutional Rights. http://ccrjustice.org/cmu-factsheet.

Chapekis, Athena, and Sarah M. Moore. 2021. "'What's in a Name?': The Construction of Eco-Terrorism and Legal Repercussions of the AEPA/AETA." In *Prosecuting Political Violence: Collaborative Research and Method*, edited by Michael Loadenthal, 151–80. New York: Routledge.

Chomsky, Noam. 1991. *Deterring Democracy*. Brooklyn: Verso.

– 1999. *Fateful Triangle: The United States, Israel, and the Palestinians (Updated Edition)*. Revised edition. Cambridge, MA: South End Press.

– 2002. *American Power and the New Mandarins: Historical and Political Essays*. Second edition. New York: The New Press.

– 2004. "The New War against Terror: Responding to 9/11." In *Violence in War and Peace: An Anthology*, edited by Nancy Scheper-Hughes and Philippe I. Bourgois, 217–23. Malden: Blackwell Publishing.

– 2005. *Chomsky on Anarchism*, edited by Barry Pateman. Chico: AK Press.

– 2012. "Reflections on a Lifetime of Engagement with Zionism, the Palestine Question, and American Empire: An Interview with Noam Chomsky (Interview by Mouin Rabbani)." *Journal of Palestine Studies* 41, no. 3: 92.

Chomsky, Noam, Robert B. Silvers, Hannah Arendt, Susan Sontag, and Conor Cruise O'Brien. 1967. "The Legitimacy of Violence as a Political Act? – Noam Chomsky Debates with Hannah Arendt, Susan Sontag, et al." *Chomsky.info*. http://www.chomsky.info/debates/19671215.htm

Churchill, Ward, and Jim Vander Wall. 2002. *The COINTELPRO Papers*. Cambridge, MA: South End Press.

Churchill, Ward, and Jim Vander Wall. 1990. *Agents of Repression: The FBI's Secret Wars against the Black Panther Party and the American Indian Movement*. Boston: South End Press.

Civil Liberties Defense Center. 2015. "Federal Government Releases Environmental Activist Eric McDavid From Prison." http://cldc.org/2015/01/08/federal-government-releases-environmental-activist-eric-mcdavid-from-prison/.

– 2012. "ALEC: Corporate Interests Undermining Democracy in Our State Legislatures." Civil Liberties Defense Center. http://cldc.org/dissent-democracy/patriot-act-government-repression/fighting-corporate-control/.

Cleyre, Voltairine de. 2009. *Written-In-Red!: The Collected Writings of Voltairine de Cleyre*. Shirley Strutton Dalton and Lawerence Dalton, eds. Scotts Valley: CreateSpace Independent Publishing Platform.

Collective, CrimethInc. N.d. Ex-Workers. "CrimethInc: *Elle* Magazine: Retraction or Hoax?" https://crimethinc.com/2008/04/23/elle-magazine-retraction-or-hoax.

– N.d. "CrimethInc.: The SHAC Model: A Critical Assessment." https://crimethinc.com/2008/09/01/the-shac-model-a-critical-assessment.

Collins, Patricia Hill. 1991. *Black Feminist Thought: Knowledge, Consciousness, and the Politics of Empowerment*. New York: Routledge.

Conquergood, Dwight. 2002. "Interventions and Radical Research." *Drama Review* 46, no. 2: 145–56.

Cooper, Brittney C. 2017. *Beyond Respectability: The Intellectual Thought of Race Women*. Champaign: University of Illinois Press.

Coronado, Rod. 2014. "About Wolf Patrol." *Wolf Patrol*. https://wolfpatrol.org/about/.

Cowperthwaite, Gabriela. 2013. *Blackfish*. CNN Films.

Crenshaw, Kimberlé. 1989 "Demarginalizing the Intersection of Race and Sex: A Black Feminist Critique of Antidiscrimination Doctrine, Feminist Theory, and Antiracist Politics." *University of Chicago Legal Forum*: 139–67.

– 1991. "Mapping the Margins: Intersectionality, Identity Politics, and Violence against Women of Color." *Stanford Law Review* 43, no. 6: 241–79.

Curry, Marshall. *If a Tree Falls: A Story of the Earth Liberation Front*. Oscilloscope Pictures.

Davis, Angela Y. *Women, Race, & Class*. New York: Vintage, 1983.

– 1998. "Masked Racism: Reflections on the Prison Industrial Complex." *Colorlines*. 10 September 1998. https://www.colorlines.com/articles/masked-racism-reflections-prison-industrial-complex.

– 2013. *Angela Davis: An Autobiography*. New York: International Publishers Co.

– 2016. *Freedom Is a Constant Struggle: Ferguson, Palestine, and the Foundations of a Movement*. Edited by Frank Barat. Chicago: Haymarket Books.

Davis, John, ed. 1991. *Earth First! Reader: Ten Years of Radical Environmentalism*. Kaysville: Gibbs Smith.

Dean, Mitchell. 2009. *Governmentality: Power and Rule in Modern Society*. London: SAGE Publications.

Debord, Guy Ernest. 1967. *Society of the Spectacle*. Detroit: Black & Red.

– 1998. *Comments on the Society of the Spectacle*. Brooklyn: Verso.

Decena, Carlos Ulises. 2008. "Profiles, Compulsory Disclosure and Ethical Sexual Citizenship in the Contemporary USA." *Sexualities* 11, no. 4: 397–413.

Del Gandio, Jason. 2010. "Neoliberalism and the Academic Industrial Complex." *Truthout* (blog). http://truth-out.org/archive/component/k2/item/91200:neoliberalism-and-the-academicindustrial-complex.

Della Porta, Donatella. 1995. *Social Movements, Political Violence, and the State: A Comparative Analysis of Italy and Germany*. Cambridge: Cambridge University Press.

Della Porta, Donatella, and Olivier Fillieule. 2004. "Policing Social Protest." In *The Blackwell Companion to Social Movements*, edited by David A. Snow, Sarah Anne Soule, and Hanspeter Kriesi, 217–41. Malden: Blackwell Publishers.

Department of Homeland Security. 2012. "Prevent Terrorism and Enhance Security." US Department of Homeland Security. http://www.dhs.gov/prevent-terrorism-and-enhance-security.

Dicum, Gregory. 2006. "An Interview with Jailed "Eco-Terrorist" Jeffrey Luers." *Grist*. 4 May 2006. https://grist.org/article/dicum1/.

Donovan, Josephine, and Carol Adams, eds. 2007. *The Feminist Care Tradition in Animal Ethics*. New York: Columbia University Press.

Dunmire, Patricia L. 2011. *Projecting the Future through Political Discourse: The Case of the Bush Doctrine*. Philadelphia: John Benjamins Publishing Company.

Earth Liberation Front. "Beltane, 1997."

Earth First! Newswire. N.d. "Informant Tracking." *Earth First! Newswire* (blog). https://earthfirstjournal.org/newswire/informant-tracking/.

– 2014. "2014 Earth First! Rendezvous Call For Workshops and Donations." *Earth First! Newswire* (blog), 2 May 2014. http://earthfirstjournal.org/newswire/2014/05/02/2014-earth-first-rendezvous-call-for-workshops-and-donations/.

Energy Transfer. 2020. "Energy Transfer Statement on Dakota Access Pipeline," 6 July 2020. https://ir.energytransfer.com/news-releases/news-release-details/energy-transfer-statement-dakota-access-pipeline/.

– N.d. "Home: Dakota Access Pipeline Facts." Dakota Access Pipeline. https://daplpipelinefacts.com/.

Esposito, John L., and Ibrahim Kalin, eds. 2011. *Islamophobia: The Challenge of Pluralism in the 21st Century*. New York: Oxford University Press.

Estes, Nick. 2019. *Our History Is the Future: Standing Rock versus the Dakota Access Pipeline, and the Long Tradition of Indigenous Resistance*. Brooklyn: Verso.

Facebook. N.d. "Law Enforcement & Third-Party Matters." Facebook Help Center. https://www.facebook.com/help/473784375984502.

Fauconnier, Gilles, and Mark Turner. 2003. *The Way We Think: Conceptual Blending and the Mind's Hidden Complexities*. New York: Basic Books.

Federal Grand Jury Hearing of Justin Samuel. 2000. Madison, WI.

Fernandez, Belen. 2011. "Honduras' Very Own War on Terror." *Al Jazeera News*. http://www.aljazeera.com/indepth/opinion/2011/06/20116308238988474.html.

Fithian, Lisa. 2010. "FBI Informant Brandon Darby: Sexism, Egos, and Lies." *The Rag Blog*, 22 March 2010. http://theragblog.blogspot.com/2010/03/lisa-fithian-fbi-informant-brandon.html.

Foreman, Dave. 1993. *Confessions of an Eco-Warrior*. New York: Crown Trade Paperbacks.

Foreman, Dave, and Bill Haywood, eds. 2003. *Ecodefense: A Field Guide to Monkeywrenching*. Chico: Abbzug Press.

Foucault, Michel. 1977. *Discipline and Punish*. New York: Vintage Books.

– 1980. *Power/Knowledge: Selected Interviews & Other Writings 1972–1977 by Michel Foucault*. Edited by Colin Gordon. Translated by Colin Gor, Leo Marshall, John Mempham, and Kate Soper. New York: Pantheon Books.

– 1990. *The History of Sexuality, Vol. 1: An Introduction*. Reissue edition. New York: Vintage.

– 1991. "Governmentality." In *The Foucault Effect: Studies in Governmentality*, edited by Graham Burchell, Colin Gordon, and Peter Miller, 87–104. Chicago: University of Chicago Press.

– 2010. *The Birth of Biopolitics: Lectures at the Collège de France, 1978–1979*. New York: Picador.

Fulkerson, Lee. 2011. *Forks Over Knives*. Virgil Films and Entertainment. https://www.forksoverknives.com/the-film/.

Gaard, Greta, ed. 1993. *Ecofeminism*. Philadelphia: Temple University Press.

Gaard, Greta, Simon C. Estok, and Serpil Oppermann, eds. 2013. *International Perspectives in Feminist Ecocriticism*. New York: Routledge.

Gaard, Greta, and Patrick D. Murphy, eds. 1998. *Ecofeminist Literary Criticism: Theory, Interpretation, Pedagogy*. Urbana: University of Illinois Press.

Gathering for Total Liberation. N.d. "About." URL redacted.

Gellman, Barton. 2020. *Dark Mirror: Edward Snowden and the American Surveillance State*. New York: Penguin Press.

Gershkoff, Amy, and Shana Kushner. 2005. "Shaping Public Opinion: The 9/11-Iraq Connection in the Bush Administration's Rhetoric." *Perspectives on Politics* 3: 525–37.

Glaberman, Martin, ed. 2012. *Marxism for Our Times: C.L.R. James on Revolutionary Organization*. Jackson: University Press of Mississippi.

Goffman, Erving. 1959. *The Presentation of Self in Everyday Life*. New York: Doubleday.

Goldman, Emma. 1911. *Anarchism: What It Really Stands For*. New York: Mother Earth Publishing Association.

Gordon, Andrea. 2013. "Two Crowds Arrive for Opening Day: One Checking out the Tourist Attraction, and One Denouncing It." *Toronto Star*.

Graeber, David. 2004. *Fragments of an Anarchist Anthropology*. Chicago: Paradigm Publishers.

– 2009a. "Anarchism, Academia, and the Avant-Garde." In *Contemporary Anarchist Studies: An Introductory Anthology of Anarchy in the Academy*, edited by Randall Amster, Abraham DeLeon, Luis Fernandez, Anthony Nocella, and Deric Shannon, 103–12. New York: Routledge.

– 2009b. *Direct Action: An Ethnography*. Chico, CA: AK Press.

Gramsci, Antonio. 1971. *Selections from the Prison Notebooks*. Quintin Hoare and Geoffrey Nowell Smith, eds. Reprint edition. New York: International Publishers.

– 1994. *Antonio Gramsci: Pre-Prison Writings*. Cambridge: Cambridge University Press.

Grubbs, Jennifer. 2011. "The Black Sexual Politics of PETA." Keynote address. Wesleyan University.

– 2012a. "Inquiries and Intersections: Queer Theory and Anti-Speciesist Praxis." *Journal for Critical Animal* 10, no. 3: 2–4.

– 2012b. "Name, Shame, and Blame: Neoliberal Proclamations as Anarchist Veganism in Drag." Paper presented at Lavender Languages and Linguistics Conference, American University, Washington, DC.

– 2012c. "Queering the Spectacle of the Protest: Animal Liberation in Drag." Paper presented at All Power to the Imagination Conference, New College of Florida.

– 2013. "The Sexual Politics of Breastfeeding." *Defiant Daughters: 21 Women on Art, Activism, Animals, and the Sexual Politics of Meat*, edited by Kara Davis and Wendy Lee, 28–38. New York: Lantern Books.

– 2013a. Field Notes: Home Demonstrations with ALA.

– 2013b. Field Notes: End Captivity Now.

– 2013c. Anti-Captivity Interview with Activist.

– 2014a. "Stop Huntingdon Animal Cruelty: A Queer Critique of the AETA." *The Terrorization of Dissent: Corporate Repression, Legal Corruption, and the Animal Enterprise Terrorism Act*, edited by Jason Del Gandio and Anthony Nocella, 236–254. Brooklyn: Lantern Books.

– 2014b. Field notes in an ecological encampment.

– 2014c. Field Notes Britches Brigade demonstration.

Grubbs, Jennifer, and Michael Loadenthal. 2011a. "Sexuality, Surveillance, and Government Infiltrators: Fragmenting the Radical Left through the Terrorization of Animal Advocacy." Conference presentation presented at the Animal Liberation Forum, University of California Long Beach, CA, April.

– 2011b. "Eco-Terrorists Unite!: Reclaiming the Commons through Public Performance." Paper presented at the Graduate Student Sociological Association, George Mason University (Fairfax, VA).

– 2011c. "Green Anti-Capitalism & Animal Liberation: The Erosion of State Power through Direct Action." Paper presented at the Public Anthropology Conference – (Re)Defining Power: Paradigms of Praxis, American University, Washington, DC.

– 2013. "From the Classroom to the Slaughterhouse: Animal Liberation by Any Means Necessary." In *Defining Critical Animal Studies: An Intersectional Social Justice Approach for Liberation*, edited by Atsuko Matsuoka, Anthony Nocella, Kim Socha, and John Sorenson, 79–201. Counterpoints: Studies in the Postmodern Theory of Education. New York, NY: Peter Lang Publishing Inc.

Gupta, Akhil. 2012. *Red Tape: Bureaucracy, Structural Violence, and Poverty in India*. Durham: Duke University Press.

Gusterson, Hugh, and Catherine Besteman. 2009. "Neoliberalism, or the Bureaucratization of the World." In *The Insecure American: How We Got Here and What We Should Do about It*, edited by Hugh Gusterson and Catherine Besteman, 79–96. Berkeley: University of California Press.

Habermas, Jürgen. 1984. *The Theory of Communicative Action*. Translated by Thomas McCarthy. Boston: Beacon Press.

Halberstam, Jack, and Del LaGrace Volcano. 1999. *The Drag King Book*. London: Serpent's Tail.

Hall, Stuart. 2004. "Cultural Studies and the Centre: Some Problematics and Problems." In *Culture, Media, Language: Working Papers in Cultural Studies*, edited by Stuart Hall, Dorothy Hobson, Andrew Lowe, and Paul Willis, 1–34. New York: Routledge.

Halperin, David. 2003. "The Normalization of Queer Theory." *Journal of Homosexuality* 45, nos 2–4: 339–43.

Hansen, Thomas, and Finn Stepputat, eds. 2001. "Introduction: State of Imagination." In *States of Imagination: Ethnographic Explorations of the Postcolonial State*, 1–39. Durham: Duke University Press.

– 2006. "Sovereignty Revisited." *Annual Review of Anthropology* 35: 295–325.

Hardt, Michael, and Antonio Negri. 2001. *Empire*. Boston: Harvard University Press.

Harper, A. Breeze. 2010. *Sistah Vegan: Food, Identity, Health, and Society: Black Female Vegans Speak*. New York: Lantern Books.

Harper, Josh. 2012. "SHAC Revisited." *Talon Conspiracy*. http://
thetalonconspiracy.com/2012/07/shac-revisited/.

Harvey, David. 2004. "The 'New' Imperialism: Accumulation by
Dispossession." *Socialist Register* 40: 63–87. http://socialistregister.com/
index.php/srv/article/view/5811.

– 2005. *The New Imperialism*. New York: Oxford University Press.

– 2007. *A Brief History of Neoliberalism*. New York: Oxford University Press.

Herman, Edward S., and Noam Chomsky. 1988. *Manufacturing Consent: The
Political Economy of the Mass Media*. New York: Pantheon Books.

Hewitt, Steve. 2010. *Snitch! A History of the Modern Intelligence Informer*.
New York: Continuum Books.

Higginbotham, Evelyn Brooks. 1994. *Righteous Discontent: The Women's
Movement in the Black Baptist Church, 1880–1920*. Revised edition.
Cambridge: Harvard University Press.

Hill, Jane. 1995. "The Voices of Dan Gabriel: Responsibility and Self in a
Modern Mexicano Narrative." In *The Dialogic Emergence of Culture*,
edited by Dennis Tedlock and Bruce Mannheim, 96–147. Urbana: University
of Illinois Press.

– 2005. "Finding Culture in Narrative." In *Finding Culture in Talk: A
Collection of Methods*, edited by Naomi Quinn, 157–202. New York:
Palgrave Macmillan.

Hill Collins, Patricia. 2005. *Black Sexual Politics: African Americans, Gender,
and the New Racism*. New York: Routledge.

– 2006. *From Black Power to Hip Hop: Racism, Nationalism, and Feminism*.
Annotated edition. Philadelphia: Temple University Press.

– 2008. *Black Feminist Thought: Knowledge, Consciousness, and the Politics
of Empowerment*. New York: Routledge.

Hodges, Adam. 2011. *The "War on Terror" Narrative: Discourse and
Intertextuality in the Construction and Contestation of Sociopolitical
Reality*. New York: Oxford University Press.

Hoffman, Bruce. 2006. *Inside Terrorism*. New York: Columbia University
Press.

Hoft, Jim. 2015. "Activists Hold Conference in Support of 'Queer Animal
Liberation.'" *Progressives Today*. http://www.progressivestoday.com/
activists-hold-conference-in-support-of-queer-animal-liberation/.

hooks, bell. 2000. *Feminist Theory: From Margin to Center*. Second edition.
Cambridge, MA: South End Press.

– 2014. *Ain't I a Woman: Black Women and Feminism*. New York: Routledge.

Hunston, Susan. 2002. *Corpora in Applied Linguistics*. Cambridge University
Press.

Hunston, Susan, and Geoff Thompson, eds. 2001. *Evaluation in Text: Authorial Stance and the Construction of Discourse*. New York: Oxford University Press.

Immergut, Karin J., Kirk A. Engdall, Stephen F. Peifer, and John C. Ray. 2007. "Government's Sentencing Memorandum in the United States District Court for the District of Oregon [Case Numbers CR 06-60069-AA, CR 06-60070-AA, CR 06-60071-AA, CR 06-60078-AA, CR 06-60079-AA, CR 06-60080-AA, CR 06-60120-AA, 06-60122-AA, 06-60123-AA, 06-60124-AA, 06-60125-AA, 06-60126-AA]." United States District Court for the District of Oregon.

INCITE! Women of Color against Violence, ed. 2009. *The Revolution Will Not Be Funded: Beyond the Non-Profit Industrial Complex*. Cambridge: South End Press.

Ivie, Devon. 2018. "Dan Levy Explains Why Homophobia Will Never Infiltrate *Schitt's Creek*." *Vulture*. https://www.vulture.com/2018/11/dan-levy-explains-why-schitts-creek-has-no-homophobia.html.

Jackson, Richard, Marie Breen Smyth, Jeroen Gunning, and Lee Jarvis. 2011. *Terrorism: A Critical Introduction*. New York: Palgrave Macmillan.

Jensen, Tim. 2012. "The Rhetoric of Eco-Terrorism." *Harlot: A Revealing Look at the Arts of Persuasion* (blog), 11 March 2012. http://harlotoft-hearts.org/blog/2012/03/11/the-rhetoric-of-eco-terrorism/.

Jones, Pattrice. 2006. "Stomping with the Elephants: Feminist Principles for Radical Solidarity." In *Igniting a Revolution: Voices in Defense of the Earth*, edited by Steven Best and Anthony Nocella, 319-334. Chico, CA: AK Press.

Joseph, George. 2016. "30 Years of Oil and Gas Pipeline Spills, Mapped." *Bloomberg*, 30 November 2016. https://www.bloomberg.com/news/articles/2016-11-30/30-years-of-oil-and-gas-pipeline-spills-mapped.

Kemmerer, Lisa A., ed. 2011. *Sister Species: Women, Animals and Social Justice*. Urbana: University of Illinois Press.

Kheel, Marti. 2007. *Nature Ethics: An Ecofeminist Perspective*. Lanham: Rowman & Littlefield Publishers.

King, Elizabeth. 2018. "J20, One Year Later: What Happened to Defendants?" *Rolling Stone*. 20 January 2018. https://www.rollingstone.com/culture/culture-features/j20-one-year-later-what-its-like-to-face-decades-in-prison-for-protesting-117207/.

King, Eric. 2016. "Final Statement to the Court (Missouri)." *Unicorn Riot* (blog). https://unicornriot.ninja/2016/eric-king-given-10-yr-sentence-throwing-molotovs-empty-govt-building/.

Klein, Naomi. 2000. *No Logo*. New York: Macmillan.

– 2007. *The Shock Doctrine: The Rise of Disaster Capitalism*. New York: Picador.

Klepfer, Mike. 2013. "Interview with Former SHAC 7 Prisoners Jake Conroy and Josh Harper." *Earth First! Journal.* https://earthfirstjournal.org/newswire/2013/07/23/interview-with-former-shac-7-prisoners-jake-conroy-and-josh-harper/.

Knaiz, Laura. 1995. "Animal Liberation and the Law: Animals Board the Underground Railroad." *Buffalo Law Review* 43: 765–834.

Ko, Aph. 2019. *Racism as Zoological Witchcraft: A Guide to Getting Out.* New York: Lantern Books.

Kotz, David M. 2015. *The Rise and Fall of Neoliberal Capitalism.* Cambridge: Harvard University Press.

Kropotkin, Peter. 1897. *The State: Its Historic Role.* London: Freedom Press.

Kuipers, Dean. 2009. *Operation Bite Back: Rod Coronado's War to Save American Wilderness.* New York: Bloomsbury.

Labov, William. 1972. *Language in the Inner City: Studies in the Black English Vernacular.* Philadelphia: University of Pennsylvania Press.

Lakoff, George. 2001. *Metaphors of Terror.* Chicago: University of Chicago Press.

Leader, Stefan H., and Peter Probst. 2003. "The Earth Liberation Front and Environmental Terrorism." *Terrorism and Political Violence* 15, no. 4: 37–58.

Leap, William L. 1996. *Word's Out: Gay Men's English.* Minneapolis: University of Minnesota Press.

– 2011. "State Regulatory Power, Effects and Responses in Late Modernity: Neoliberalism and Necropolitics." Presented at the Current Issues: Reading and Resisting Neoliberalism, American University, Washington, DC.

– 2015. "Queer Linguistics as Critical Discourse Analysis." In *The Handbook of Discourse Analysis*, Second edition, edited by Deborah Tannen, Heidi Hamilton, and Deborah Schiffrin, 661–80. New York: John Wiley & Sons.

– 2020. *Language before Stonewall: Language, Sexuality, History.* New York: Palgrave Macmillan.

Leap, William L., and Tom Boellstorff. 2003. *Speaking in Queer Tongues: Globalization and Gay Language.* Champaign: University of Illinois Press.

Leap, William L., and Heiko Motschenbacher. 2012. "Launching a New Phase in Language and Sexuality Studies." *Journal of Language and Sexuality* 1, no. 1: 1–14.

Leitner, Helga, Jamie Peck, and Eric S. Sheppard. 2008. "Contesting Neoliberalism: Urban Frontiers by Helga Leitner; Jamie Peck; Eric S. Sheppard." *Economic Geography* 84, no. 3: 359–61.

Lennard, Natasha. 2018. "In the J20 Trials, the Feds Said They Went after 'Bad Protesters.' That Just Means Another Crackdown on Dissent." *Intercept*, 14

July 2018. https://theintercept.com/2018/07/14/inauguration-protest-prosecutions/.

– 2019. "How the Prosecution of Animal Rights Activists as Terrorists Foretold Today's Criminalization of Dissent." *Intercept*, 12 December 2019. https://theintercept.com/2019/12/12/animal-people-documentary-shac-protest-terrorism/.

Levi. "Facebook Post: End Captivity Now." Facebook. https://facebook.com.

Levinson, Stephen C. 1983. *Pragmatics*. Cambridge: Cambridge University Press.

Lewis, Tim, and Tim Ream. 1999. *Pickaxe: A Cascadia Free State Story*. CrimethInc.

Lewis, John E. 2004. "Animal Rights Extremism and Ecoterrorism." Federal Bureau of Investigation, 18 May 2004. http://www.fbi.gov/news/testimony/animal-rights-extremism-and-ecoterrorism.

Liddick, Donald R. 2006. *Eco-Terrorism: Radical Environmental and Animal Liberation Movements*. Westport: Praeger Publishers.

Lilia. 2016. "Informants and Information: Looking at the Green Scare and Surveillance with Lauren Regan." *It's Going Down*, 4 August 2016. https://itsgoingdown.org/informants-information-looking-green-scare-surveillance-lauren-regan/.

Linde, Charlotte. 1993. *Life Stories: The Creation of Coherence: The Creation of Coherence*. Oxford: Oxford University Press.

Loadenthal, Michael. 2010. "Nor Hostages, Assassinations, or Hijackings, but Sabotage, Vandalism & Fire: 'Eco-Terrorism' as Political Violence Challenging the State and Capital." MLitt dissertation, University of St Andrews.

– 2011a. "Asymmetric Labeling of Terrorist Violence as a Matter of Statecraft Propaganda: Or, Why the United States Does Not Feel the Need to Explain the Assassination of Osama Bin Laden." *Anarchist Developments in Cultural Studies* 1: 113–39.

– 2011b. "Operation Splash Back! Queering Animal Liberation through the Contributions of Neo-Insurrectionist Queers." *Journal of Critical Animal Studies: Special Edition: Intersecting Queer Theory and Critical Animal Studies* 9, no. 3: 85–112.

– 2013a. "The Earth Liberation Front: A Social Movement Analysis." *Radical Criminology* 2: 15–46.

– 2013b. "The Framing of (Counter) State Violence: Challenging the Rhetoric of Non-State Actors, Political Violence & 'Terrorism.'" *Affinities: A Journal of Radical Theory, Culture, Action* 6, no. 1: 1–15.

– 2014. "When Cops 'Go Native': Policing Revolution through Sexual Infiltration and Panopticonism." *Critical Studies on Terrorism* 7, no. 1: 24–42.

– 2015a. "6 Ways Cops Have Used Sex to Infiltrate and Disrupt Protest Groups." *Green Is the New Red.* 20 January 2015. http://www.greenisthenewred.com/blog/6-ways-cops-used-sex-infiltrate-disrupt-protest-groups/8146/.

– 2015b. "Sexuality, Assault, Police Infiltration and Foucault: Notes for Further Inquiry." In *New Developments in Anarchist Studies*, vol. 3, edited by pj lilley and Jeff Shantz, 63–87. Goleta: Punctum Books.

– 2016. "Activism, Terrorism, and Social Movements: The 'Green Scare' as Monarchical Power." *Conflicts and Change* 40: 189–226.

– 2017. *The Politics of Attack: Communiqués and Insurrectionary Violence.* Manchester: Manchester University Press.

– 2019. "Introduction: Studying Political Violence while Indicted – against Objectivity and Detachment." *Critical Studies on Terrorism*: 1–10.

Lovitz, Dara. 2010. *Muzzling a Movement: The Effects of Anti-Terrorism Law, Money, and Politics on Animal Activism.* New York: Lantern Books.

Luft, Rachel E. 2008. "Looking for Common Ground: Relief Work in Post-Katrina New Orleans as an American Parable of Race and Gender Violence." *NWSA Journal* 20, no. 3: 5–31.

Luxemburg, Rosa. 1900. *Reform or Revolution.* Internet Archive/Marxists.org. http://www.marxists.org/archive/luxemburg/1900/reform-revolution/.

Manes, Christopher. 1991. *Green Rage: Radical Environmentalism and the Unmaking of Civilization.* New York: Back Bay Books.

Mann, Keith. 2009. *From Dusk 'til Dawn: An Insider's View of the Growth of the Animal Liberation Movement.* London: Warcry Communications.

Marion Young, Iris. 1990. *Justice and the Politics of Difference.* Princeton: Princeton University Press.

Marut, Ret. 2009. "The SHAC Model." *CrimethInc. Far East Blog* (blog), 28 March 2009. http://www.crimethinc.com/texts/rollingthunder/shac.php.

Mason, Marius. 2009. Sentencing statement to the court. Western District of Michigan: Southern Division.

McCoy, Kimberley. 2007. "Subverting Justice: An Indictment of the Animal Enterprise Terrorism Act." *Animal Law* 14: 53–70.

McGowan, Daniel. 2020. In discussion with the author. 7 December 2020.

Miner, Horace. 1956. "Body Ritual among the Nacirema." *American Anthropologist* 58, no. 3. https://msu.edu/~jdowell/miner.html.

Morris, Courtney Desiree. 2010. "Why Misogynists Make Great Informants: How Gender Violence on the Left Enables State Violence in Radical Movement." *Make/Shift (Republished by INCITE!).* http://inciteblog.wordpress.com/2010/07/15/why-misogynists-make-great-informants-how-gender-violence-on-the-left-enables-state-violence-in-radical-movements/.

Morris, Rosalind. 1995. "All Made Up: Performance Theory and the New
    Anthropology of Sex and Gender." *Annual Review of Anthropology* 24:
    567–92.
Mortimer-Sandilands, Catriona, and Bruce Erickson. 2010. *Queer Ecologies:*
    Sex, Nature, Politics, Desire. Indiana: Indiana University Press.
Motschenbacher, Heiko. 2010. "The Discursive Interface of National,
    European and Sexual Identities: Preliminary Evidence from the Eurovision
    Song Contest." In *Intercultural Europe: Arenas of Difference,*
    Communication and Mediation, edited by Barbara Lewandowska, 85–103.
    Bilingual edition. Hannover: Ibidem Press.
Muñoz, Jose Esteban. 1999. *Disidentifications: Queers of Color and the*
    Performance of Politics. Minnesota: University of Minnesota Press.
– 2009. *Cruising Utopia: The Then and There of Queer Futurity.* New York:
    NYU Press.
Nader, Laura. 1972. "Up the Anthropologist – Perspectives Gained from
    Studying Up." In *Reinventing Anthropology*, edited by Dell H. Hymes,
    284–311. Ann Arbor: University of Michigan Press.
Naples, Nancy A. 2003. *Feminism and Method: Ethnography, Discourse*
    Analysis, and Activist Research. New York: Routledge.
Nibert, David, and Michael W. Fox. 2002. *Animal Rights/Human Rights:*
    Entanglements of Oppression and Liberation. Lanham, MD: Rowman &
    Littlefield Publishers.
Nicholson, Linda, ed. 1997. *The Second Wave: A Reader in Feminist Theory.*
    New York: Routledge.
Nocella, Anthony, and Steven Best, eds. 2004. *Terrorists or Freedom Fighters?*
    Reflections on the Liberation of Animals. New York: Lantern Books.
Spirit of Freedom. 2002. *Welcome to the Green Scare!* North American Earth
    Liberation Prisoner Support Network.
North American Animal Liberation Press Office. N.d. "FAQ's: North American
    Animal Liberation Press Office." https://animalliberationpressoffice.org/
    NAALPO/f-a-q-s/.
– N.d. "Snitches." https://animalliberationpressoffice.org/NAALPO/snitches/.
– 2014. "Washington State Mobile Slaughter Truck Sabotaged by ALF." 15
    July 2014. https://animalliberationpressoffice.org/NAALPO/2014/07/15/
    washington-state-mobile-slaughter-truck-sabotaged-by-alf/.
Nugent, David. 1997. *Modernity at the Edge of Empire: State, Individual, and*
    Nation in the Northern Peruvian Andes, 1885–1935. California: Stanford
    University Press.
NYC Antifa. 2014. "Former ELF/Green Scare Prisoner 'Exile' Now a Fascist."
    NYC Antifa (blog), 5 August 2014. https://nycantifa.wordpress.
    com/2014/08/05/exile-is-a-fascist/.

Ong, Aihwa. 2006. *Neoliberalism as Exception: Mutations in Citizenship and Sovereignty*. Durham: Duke University Press Books.

Orwell, George. 2013. *Politics and the English Language*. Penguin Modern Classics. London: Penguin Classics.

Paige. 2014. "Animal Enterprise Terrorism Act (AETA)." Civil Liberties Defense Center. 24 April 2014. https://cldc.org/animal-enterprise-terrorism-act-aeta/.

Parker, Andy. 2009. "Beyond AETA: How Corporate-Crafted Legislation Brands Activists as Terrorists." National Lawyers Guild. http://www.nlg.org/Beyond%20AETA%20White%20Paper.pdf.

Parmar, Priya, Anthony J. Nocella, and Scott Robertson, eds. 2014. *Rebel Music: Resistance through Hip Hop and Punk*. Charlotte: Information Age Publishing.

Parr, Adrian. 2009. *Hijacking Sustainability*. Cambridge: MIT Press.

– 2014. *The Wrath of Capital: Neoliberalism and Climate Change Politics*. New York: Columbia University Press.

– 2017. *Birth of a New Earth: The Radical Politics of Environmentalism*. New York: Columbia University Press.

Parrish, Will. 2017. "An Activist Stands Accused of Firing a Gun at Standing Rock. It Belonged to Her Lover – an FBI Informant." *Intercept*, 11 December 2017. https://theintercept.com/2017/12/11/standing-rock-dakota-access-pipeline-fbi-informant-red-fawn-fallis/.

Pathway to Liberation. N.d. "Who We Are, What We Do & Why." URL redacted.

Patterson, Charles. 2002. *Eternal Treblinka: Our Treatment of Animals and the Holocaust*. New York: Lantern Books.

Pêcheux, Michel. 1982. *Language, Semantics, and Ideology*. New York: Palgrave Macmillan.

Pellow, David Naguib. 2014. *Total Liberation: The Power and Promise of Animal Rights and the Radical Earth Movement*. Minneapolis: University of Minnesota Press.

– N.d. "My Student Is a Sociologist, Not a Terrorist." *Green Is the New Red*. http://www.greenisthenewred.com/blog/student-scott-demuth-sociologist-not-terrorist/2423/.

Pickering, Leslie James. 2007. *The Earth Liberation Front 1997–2002*. Second edition. Portland: Arissa Media Group.

Pilkington, Ed. 2015. "Role of FBI Informant in Eco-Terrorism Case Probed after Documents Hint at Entrapment." *Guardian*, 13 January 2015. http://www.theguardian.com/us-news/2015/jan/13/fbi-informant-anna-eric-mcdavid-eco-terrorism.

Potter, Will. 2008a. "Green Scare, The." *Vermont Law Review* 33: 671.

– 2008b. "Like OMG! *Elle* Glams Up the Green Scare … And Issues a Retraction?" *Green Is the New Red*, 8 May 2008. http://www.greenisthenewred.com/blog/elle_anna/421/.

– 2009. "Making an Animal Rights 'Terrorist.'" *Bite Back Magazine.*

– 2011. *Green Is the New Red: An Insider's Account of a Social Movement under Siege.* San Francisco: City Lights Publishers.

– 2012a. "Utah 'Ag Gag' Bill Passes House – Urgent Action Needed." *Green Is theNewRed*.http://www.greenisthenewred.com/blog/utah-photograph-video-factory-farm-passes-hb187/5757/.

– 2012b. "Incredible Photos from Daylight Raid at Green Hill Dog Breeder in Italy." http://www.greenisthenewred.com/blog/italy-dog-breeder-rescue-photos/5974/.

– 2014. "Hold Factory Farms to Account, with Drones." *Green Is the New Red.* http://www.greenisthenewred.com/blog/journalism-drones/8097/.

– N.d. "Analysis of Animal Enterprise Terrorism Act." *Green Is the New Red.* http://www.greenisthenewred.com/blog/aeta-analysis-109th/.

– N.d. "FBI Harasses Sociology Professor Who Has Spoken against Labeling His Student a Terrorist." *Green Is the New Red.* https://www.greenisthenewred.com/blog/david-pellow-visited-by-fbi/2848/.

Pollard, Alexandra. 2020. "Farewell *Schitt's Creek*, the Hit Sitcom with a Heart of Gold." *Independent.* https://www.independent.co.uk/arts-entertainment/tv/features/schitts-creek-season-6-finale-netflix-uk-dan-levy-annie-murphy-a9512601.html.

Price, David H. 2004. *Threatening Anthropology: McCarthyism and the FBI's Surveillance of Activist Anthropologists.* Durham: Duke University Press Books.

– 2011. *Weaponizing Anthropology: Social Science in Service of the Militarized State.* Reprint edition. Chico, CA: AK Press.

Proudhon, Pierre-Joseph. 1840. *What Is Property?* Edited by Donald R. Kelley and Bonnie G. Smith. Cambridge: Cambridge University Press.

Puar, Jasbir. 2007. *Terrorist Assemblages: Homonationalism in Queer Times.* Durham: Duke University Press.

"Queering Animal Liberation." N.d. VINE Sanctuary. http://vine.bravebirds.org/connections/queering-animal-liberation/.

Quigley, Bill, and Rachel Meeropol. 2010. "The Case of the AETA Four." CounterPunch.Org, 16 July 2010. https://www.counterpunch.org/2010/07/16/the-case-of-the-aeta-four/.

Rob, Evans, and Paul Lewis. 2014. *Undercover: The True Story of Britain's Secret Police.* London: Guardian Farber Publishing.

Rosebraugh, Craig. 2004a. *Burning Rage of a Dying Planet: Speaking for the Earth Liberation Front.* New York: Lantern Books.

– 2004b. *The Logic of Political Violence: Lessons in Reform and Revolution.* Portland: Arissa Media Group.

Rurke, Nicolaas A. 1987. *Vivisection in the Historical Perspective.* New York: Routledge.

Salter, Colin. 2011. "Activism as Terrorism: The Green Scare, Radical Environmentalism and Governmentality." In "Ten Years after 9/11: An Anarchist Evaluation," special issue, *Anarchist Developments in Cultural Studies*, no. 1: 211–38.

Salter, Mark B. 2012. "Introduction." In *Research Methods in Critical Security Studies: An Introduction*, edited by Mark B. Salter and Can E. Mutlu, 1–14. First edition. New York: Routledge.

Scarce, Rik. 2006. *Eco-Warriors: Understanding the Radical Environmental Movement.* Walnut Creek: Left Coast Press.

– N.d. "Rik Scarce Faculty Bio." https://www.skidmore.edu/sociology/faculty/scarce.php.

Schatz, Amy. 2013. *An Apology to Elephants.* HBO. https://www.hbo.com/documentaries/an-apology-to-elephants.

Scheper-Hughes, Nancy. 1993. *Death without Weeping: The Violence of Everyday Life in Brazil.* Berkeley: University of California Press.

– 1995. "The Primacy of the Ethical: Propositions for a Militant Anthropology." *Current Anthropology* 36, no. 3: 409–40.

Scheper-Hughes, Nancy, and Philippe Bourgois. 2003. *Violence in War and Peace: An Anthology.* Hoboken: Wikey-Blackwell Publishing.

Schneier, Bruce. 2006. *Beyond Fear: Thinking Sensibly about Security in an Uncertain World.* Göttingen: Copernicus Books.

Schorn, Daniel. 2005. "Burning Rage: Reports on Extremists Now Deemed Biggest Domestic Terror Threat." CBS, 10 November 2005. http://www.cbsnews.com/news/burning-rage/.

SHAC (Stop Huntingdon Animal Cruelty). 2012. "SHAC Victories." http://www.shac.net/SHAC/victories.html.

Shannon, Deric, Anthony J. Nocella, and John Asimakopolous, eds. 2012. *The Accumulation of Freedom: Writings on Anarchist Economics.* Chico, CA: AK Press.

Shepard, Benjamin. 2011. *Queer Political Performance and Protest: Play, Pleasure and Social Movement.* New York: Routledge.

– 2013. *Play, Creativity, and Social Movements: If I Can't Dance, It's Not My Revolution.* New York: Routledge.

Shepard, Benjamin, L.M. Bogad, and Stephen Duncombe. 2008. "Performing vs. the Insurmountable: Theatrics, Activism, and Social Movements." *Liminalities: A Journal of Performance Studies* 4, no. 3: 30.

Shepard, Benjamin, and Ronald Hayduk, eds. 2002. *From ACT UP to the WTO: Urban Protest and Community Building in the Era of Globalization.* New York: Verso.

Shiva, Vandana. 2005. *Globalization's New Wars – Seed, Water & Life Forms.* New Delhi: Kali/Women Unlimited.

Simpson, Leanne Betasamosake. 2017. *As We Have Always Done: Indigenous Freedom through Radical Resistance.* University of Minnesota Press.

Singer, Peter. 1977. *Animal Liberation.* New York: Avon Books.

Skocpol, Theda. 2002. "'Will 9/11 and the War on Terror Revitalize American Civic Democracy?'" *PS: Political Science & Politics* 35, no. 3: 537–40.

Snowden, Edward. 2020. *Permanent Record.* New York: Picador.

Sorenson, John. 2016. "Ecoterrorism and Expansionary Counterterrorism." In *Routledge Handbook of Critical Terrorism Studies,* edited by Richard Jackson, 553–79. New York: Routledge.

The Sparrow Project. 2015. "Journalist Barrett Brown Sentenced to 63 Months in Prison on Charges Stemming from Proximity to Sources in Anonymous, Releases Post-Sentence Statement." *The Sparrow Project* (blog), 22 January 2015. http://www.sparrowmedia.net/2015/01/barrett-brown-sentenced-to-5-years-issues-official-statement/.

Spiegel, Marjorie, and Alice Walker. 1997. *The Dreaded Comparison: Human and Animal Slavery.* Third edition. New York: Mirror Books/IDEA.

Spitz, Vivien. 2005. *Doctors from Hell: The Horrific Account of Nazi Experiments on Humans.* Illustrated edition. Boulder: Sentient Publications.

"Statement from Kevin." 2016. *SUPPORT KEVIN & TYLER* (blog), 21 September 2016. http://supportkevinandtyler.com/statement-from-kevin/.

Steizinger, Johannes. 2018. "The Significance of Dehumanization: Nazi Ideology and Its Psychological Consequences." *Politics, Religion & Ideology*: 1–19.

Stover, Richard. N.d. "America's Dangerous Pipelines." Center for Biological Diversity. https://www.biologicaldiversity.org/campaigns/americas_dangerous_pipelines/.

Stryker, Kitty. 2015. "Who's Afraid of Call-out Culture? Jerks Mostly." *Kitty Stryker.* http://198.20.234.8/~herekittykitty/2015/03/05/whos-afraid-of-call-out-culture-jerks-mostly/2015.

Sub.Media. N.d. "Trouble #16: Conspiracy To Riot." https://sub.media/video/trouble-16-conspiracy-to-riot/.

Sugarman, Emily. 2017. "All You Need to Know about the Nearly 200 People Facing 60 Years in Jail for Protesting Trump." *Independent,* 16 November 2017.http://www.independent.co.uk/news/world/americas/j20-trump-protests-trials-jail-threat-inauguration-demonstrations-explained-a8057521.html.

Support Eric King. N.d. "About Eric." https:supportericking.org/about-eric-2/.

Support Marius Mason. N.d. "About Marius Mason." *Free Marius Mason* (blog). http://supportmariusmason.org/about/.

– N.d. "Free Marius Jacob Mason." *Free Marius Mason* (blog). http://support-mariusmason.org/2014/07/07/free-marius-jacob-mason/.

– 2013. "Eco-Prisoners Continue Exposing BOP's Shady 'Communications Management.'" *Support Marius Mason* (blog). https://supportmariusmason. org/2013/03/08/eco-prisoners-continue-exposing-bops-shady-communications-management/.

Taylor, Diana. 2003. *The Archive and the Repertoire: Performing Cultural Memory in the Americas*. Second edition. Durham: Duke University Press Books.

Teman, Elly. 2010. *Birthing a Mother: The Surrogate Body and the Pregnant Self*. Berkeley: University of California Press.

Thompson, A.K. 2010. *Black Bloc, White Riot: Antiglobalization and the Genealogy of Dissent*. Chico, CA: AK Press.

Todd, Andrea. N.d. "The Believers." *Elle Magazine*.

Traver, Ted. 2013. "End Captivity Now Demonstration – May 2013 'Know Your Rights.'" YouTube, 20 May 2013. https://www.youtube.com/watch?v=PK2JnlLE2eE.

US Attorney's Office. 2011. "Walter Bond Sentenced to Federal Prison for the Arson at the Sheepskin Factory in Glendale." FBI. 11 February 2011. http://www.fbi.gov/denver/press-releases/2011/dno21111.htm.

US EPA, OLEM. 2017. "CERCLA and EPCRA Reporting Requirements for Air Releases of Hazardous Substances from Animal Waste at Farms." Overviews and Factsheets. US EPA. 5 September 2017. https://www.epa. gov/epcra/cercla-and-epcra-reporting-requirements-air-releases-hazardous-substances-animal-waste-farms.

"USDA ERS – Agriculture Improvement Act of 2018: Highlights and Implications." N.d. https://www.ers.usda.gov/agriculture-improvement-act-of-2018-highlights-and-implications/.

Virilio, Paul. 2012. *The Administration of Fear*. Los Angeles: Semiotext(e).

Voss, Barbara. 2000. "Feminisms, Queer Theories, and the Archaeological Study of Past Sexualities." *World Archeology*, 32, no. 2: 180–92.

Walter Bond Prison Support Network. n.d. "Support Walter." *Supportwalter. Org* (blog). http://supportwalter.org/SW/index.php/walter/.

Washington, Harriet A. 2008. *Medical Apartheid: The Dark History of Medical Experimentation on Black Americans from Colonial Times to the Present*. New York: Knopf Doubleday Publishing Group.

Weber, Max. 1919. "Politik als Beruf (Politics as a Vocation)." Lecture presented at the Free Students Union, Munich University. http://www.ne.jp/asahi/moriyuki/abukuma/weber/lecture/politics_vocation.html.

– 1978. *Economy and Society: An Outline of Interpretive Sociology*, edited by Guenther Roth and Claus Wittich. Fourth edition. Oakland: University of California Press.

Wheeler, Andrew. N.d. *Amendment to Emergency Release Notification Regulations on Reporting Exemption for Air Emissions from Animal Waste at Farms; Emergency Planning and Community Right to Know Act.*

Wiesel, Elie. 1982. *Night.* Second edition. New York: Bantam Books.

– 1986. "The Nobel Peace Prize Acceptance Speech." Speech presented at the Nobel Prize Acceptance, Oslo City, Norway, 10 December 1986. http://www.nobelprize.org/nobel_prizes/peace/laureates/1986/wiesel-acceptance.html.

Williams, Patrick, and Laura Chrisman, eds. 1994. *Colonial Discourse and Post-Colonial Theory: A Reader.* New York: Columbia University Press.

World Health Organization. N.d. "Coronavirus Disease (COVID-19)." https://www.who.int/emergencies/diseases/novel-coronavirus-2019.

Wright, Melissa W. 2006. *Disposable Women and Other Myths of Global Capitalism.* New edition. New York: Routledge.

Young, Peter. 2019. *Liberate: Animal Liberation Above The Law, Stories And Lessons On The Animal Liberation Front, Animal Rights Activism, & The Animal Liberation Underground.* London: Warcry Communications.

Young, Peter, and Rod Coronado, eds. 2011. *Underground: The Animal Liberation Front in the 1990s, Collected Issues of the A.L.F.* London: Warcry Publications.

Zerzan, John. 2005. *Against Civilization: Readings and Reflections*, edited by Kevin Tucker. Port Townsent: Feral House.

– 2006. *Elements of Refusal.* Berkeley: University of California Press.

Žižek, Slavoj. 2008. *Violence: Six Sideways Reflections.* New York: Macmillan.

– 2009. *The Sublime Object of Ideology.* Second edition. New York: Verso.

– 2012. "Occupy Wall Street: What Is to Be Done Next?" *Guardian*, 24 April 2012. http://www.theguardian.com/commentisfree/cifamerica/2012/apr/24/occupy-wall-street-what-is-to-be-done-next.

Zuboff, Shoshana. 2020. *The Age of Surveillance Capitalism: The Fight for a Human Future at the New Frontier of Power.* New York: Public Affairs.

Index